What If I'm an Atheist?

A TEEN'S GUIDE TO EXPLORING A LIFE WITHOUT RELIGION

What If I'm an Atheist?

David Seidman

SIMON PULSE

New York London Toronto Sydney New Delhi

An imprint of Simon & Schuster
Children's Publishing Division
1230 Avenue of the Americas
New York, NY 10020

Managing editor: Lindsay S. Brown
Editors: Nicole Geiger, Sheila Ashdown
Copyeditor: Kristin Thiel
Proofreader: Jen Weaver-Neist
Interior and cover design: Sara E. Blum
The text of this book was set in Adobe Caslon Pro and ITC Franklin Gothic STD.

SIMON PULSE is a trademark of Simon & Schuster, Inc., and related logo is a registered trademark of Simon & Schuster, Inc.

For information about special discounts for bulk purchases, please contact Simon & Schuster Special Sales at 1-866-506-1949 or business@simonandschuster.com.

The Simon & Schuster Speakers Bureau can bring authors to your live event. For more information or to book an event, contact the Simon & Schuster Speakers Bureau at 1-866-248-3049 or visit our website at www.simonspeakers.com.

Manufactured in the United States of America

10 9 8 7 6 5 4 3 2 1

Library of Congress Cataloging-in-Publication Data

Seidman, David.
    What if i'm an atheist? : a teen's guide to exploring a life without religion / David Seidman
    pages   cm
    Includes bibliographical references.
    1. Atheism—Juvenile literature.   I. Title. II. Title: What if I am an atheist?
BL2747.3.S3765 2015
211'.8—dc23

                                                                                        2014026837

ISBN 978-1-58270-407-4 (hc)
ISBN 978-1-58270-406-7 (pbk)
ISBN 978-1-4442-7524-3 (eBook)

To Lea—my own personal goddess

Contents

Introduction _____ viii

Part I: What's an Atheist?

1. Who Are Atheists (and Agnostics and Other Unbelievers)? _____ 1

2. Is Atheism a Religion? _____ 15

3. Don't You Need God for a Moral Life? _____ 23

4. Are There Atheist-Friendly Religions? _____ 37

Part II: Life as an Atheist

5. How Do You Become an Atheist? _____ 49

6. How Will Becoming an Atheist Change You? _____ 61

7. What If You Were Raised an Atheist? _____ 67

8. Should You Tell? _____ 77

9. How Do You Tell Your Parents? _____ 83

10. How Will Your Parents React? _____ 91

11. How Will Your Friends React? _____ 103

12. How Do Unbelievers Handle Hostile Teachers,
    Principals, and Classmates? _____ 115

13. Can You Celebrate Christmas? And Other
    Holiday FAQs _____ 127

Part III: Arguing Atheism

14. How Can You Handle Arguments against
    Your Being an Atheist? _____ 137

15. How Can You Handle Arguments against
    Atheism in General? _____ 145

16. How Can You Handle Arguments for Religion? _____ 155

17. How Can You Make Arguments for Atheism? _____ 163

Part IV: The Rest of Your Life

18. What If You Turn from Atheist to Believer? _____ 175

19. What's Your Future Going to Look Like? _____ 185

Acknowledgments _____ 191

Appendix: More Information about Unbelief _____ 193

Notes _____ 205

Glossary _____ 243

Introduction

What If I'm an Atheist? is for anyone, teenage or otherwise, who wants to know about being an atheist or agnostic. It's got insights and anecdotes from the mouths (and keyboards) of young unbelievers themselves—plus journalists, psychologists, and others who have looked into this sometimes-secret world. I wrote it because there are plenty of books for and about teenagers of various religions but few that deal with the young and the godless.

A Note to Theists
(That Means "People Who Believe in God")

This book doesn't hate religion or God, and it won't try to turn you into an atheist.

The book *does* quote some people who don't like religion. It also quotes people—atheists, agnostics, and others—who respect theists and enjoy celebrating holidays based in religion, such as Christmas. The book may help you understand a friend, classmate, relative, or celebrity who doesn't believe in God.

A Note to Atheists, Agnostics,
and Other Unbelievers

Ever heard of service journalism? It means "news you can use" and usually applies to magazine stories with titles like "Where to Find Chicago's

Ten Best Chinese Restaurants" or "How Not to Get Ripped Off When Buying a Hybrid Truck."

But there's a higher kind of service journalism, which offers information that can help to change a life—or save it. For unbelievers, this book offers that kind of journalism. How can you tell your parents that you're an atheist? What can you do if your school imposes prayer or other religious rituals on you? How can you refute the lies that people tell about unbelievers? This book offers answers.

A Note on Sources

This book contains quotes from people who were willing to share their stories and feelings about their beliefs. Some are drawn from interviews that I conducted; others came from newspaper and magazine articles, blogs, online forum postings, and other publicly available sources. In these instances, I've included the name, age, and/or location that the source included at the time of his or her writing or posting.

This book often covers unbelievers' relations with Christians and Christianity; that's because the book primarily covers the English-speaking world—the United States, Canada, Australia, and the United Kingdom—where most people come from a Christian background. I've also included stories of unbelievers' relationships with other faiths, though.

My thanks to everyone who offered the personal—sometimes painfully personal—confessions that grace this book.

Finally . . .

If you have questions or comments about the book, please visit the book's website, whatifimanatheist.com. I look forward to hearing from you.

Welcome to *What If I'm an Atheist?*

I.

WHAT'S AN ATHEIST?

1

Who Are Atheists (and Agnostics and Other Unbelievers)?

The term that best describes me now is secular humanist.

CHARLES SCHULZ, CREATOR OF *PEANUTS*[1]

Atheists may not be who you think they are.

To begin with, *atheist* is a pretty narrow term. It doesn't include the whole spread of people who don't worship a god. Agnostics, freethinkers, humanists, rationalists, objectivists—there are lots of names.

What's an Atheist?

The most common name for an **unbeliever**—and a controversial name it is—is **atheist**. An atheist doesn't believe that God exists. Thus, God didn't create the universe, write the Bible, or care what you did on your date last Saturday.

Some people who believe in God can find atheism and atheists a threat.

In a 2007 poll of more than a thousand Americans, more than half of them wouldn't elect an atheist president even if he or she were qualified for the job.[2] A 2010 poll added that more than half of all Americans would be uncomfortable with an atheist on the Supreme Court.[3]

In 2010 Pope Benedict XVI associated godlessness with the Nazis. "Britain and her leaders stood against a Nazi tyranny that wished to eradicate God from society," he announced on a visit to England. "As we reflect on the sobering lessons of the atheist extremism of the twentieth century, let us never forget how the exclusion of God, religion, and virtue from public life leads ultimately to a truncated vision of man."[4]

The Boy Scouts don't let atheists become scouts or scoutmasters.[5] In a number of Islamic countries, atheists face discrimination up to and including execution.[6] A poll by the University of Minnesota found atheists to be "America's most distrusted minority," less trustworthy than Muslims, immigrants, or gay people. "Atheists are also the minority group most Americans are least willing to allow their children to marry."[7]

So yes, atheism can be dangerous—to atheists as well as to theists. (*Theist*, by the way, means "believer in God.")

Atheists come in a lot of varieties, but they often break down into two categories: **negative atheists** (also known as weak atheists or soft atheists) and **positive atheists** (also called strong atheists or hard atheists). These are pretty new terms, and exactly what they mean is still being nailed down, but here are a couple of examples.

▶ Negative/weak/soft atheists say that there is *no* proof that *any* god exists. Positive/strong/hard atheists say that there *is* proof that *no* god exists.

▶ Negative/weak/soft atheists tolerate religion and believers. Positive/strong/hard atheists, according to journalist Gary Wolf, "condemn not just belief in God but respect for belief in God." In their view, Wolf has said, "Religion is not only wrong, it's evil."[8]

There are millions of atheists, as you'll learn later in this chapter. They're all over the world. And a lot of them are teenagers.

The Ones Who Don't Know

The second-most-famous segment of unbelievers is agnostics. "An agnostic is a doubter," said Clarence Darrow, possibly the most famous trial lawyer of the past hundred years—and an agnostic. "The word is generally applied to those who doubt the verity of accepted religious creeds."[9]

Agnostic literally means "without knowing," and it's the viewpoint for people who aren't certain what's out there. Agnostics range from people who have no opinion at all to people who are pretty sure of their views but don't want to shut other possibilities out. "I like being agnostic," said an ex-Baptist on the site Teenage Writers who called herself CassieCasey. "I think it gives me the freedom to be a little bit more open-minded about other religions."[10]

"As an agnostic, I may not be religious, but I am still spiritual," said Gaarden (a screen name), a seventeen-year-old agnostic from Arizona. He started out Christian ("baptized when I was ten, without really knowing anything about Christianity") but switched to atheism until "I really began to *fear* the possibility of empty nothingness and oblivion after death." To find answers, he read up on different religions. He ended up respecting them but questioning their views on salvation and morality; he realized, "I am an *agnostic* at heart."[11]

So Many Different Flavors

If you've got a version of unbelief, you can probably find a name for it.

Freethinker sounds quaint, and it should. It's one of the oldest names for an unbeliever, dating to 1692.[12] "'Free thought' means coming to your own conclusion about religion and without the influences of religious dogma or doctrine," according to Blair Scott, who was a director of the unbelievers group American Atheists at the time of this comment.[13]

Rationalists trust logic and reason. Science-fiction writer Isaac Asimov said that he'd rather call himself a rationalist than an atheist because "'Atheist,' meaning 'no God,' is negative and defeatist. It says what you don't believe and puts you in an eternal position of defense. 'Rationalism,' on the other hand, states what you DO believe: That is, that which can be understood in the light of reason."[14]

Humanists focus on people rather than on God. Instead of taking guidance from a spirit in the sky, they emphasize humanity's "ability and responsibility to lead ethical lives of personal fulfillment that aspire to the greater good of humanity."[15] So says the American Humanist Association—but theirs isn't the only definition. Some people apply *humanism* to any attitude that cares about people, which means that it's possible to be a religious humanist. In fact, a tradition of Christian humanism dates back to the Renaissance.

Some nonreligious humanists call themselves *secular humanists*, a term that's suffered attacks from some Christian conservatives. "Most of today's evils can be traced to secular humanism," say evangelical ministers Tim LaHaye and David Noebel in their book *Mind Siege*. "Secular humanism . . . is driven by a flaming hatred for Jesus Christ that seeks to eradicate the Christian worldview."[16]

Objectivists follow the philosophy of Russian American novelist Ayn Rand, who promoted selfishness and wrote, "I raise this god over the earth . . . . This god, this one word: 'I.'"[17]

Materialists believe that the only reality is the world of physical matter and that supernatural forces play no part. **Naturalists** are a lot like materialists but focus on any laws, processes, and phenomena that science can explain.

A new label—one that's sparked some arguments—is *brights*. Mynga Futrell and Paul Geisert, a husband-and-wife team of atheist activists, came up with the word as a cheerful-sounding alternative to *godless* and other names. But calling unbelievers *brights* hints that believers are dim and dull, an attitude that's insulting and possibly self-destructive. "The 'bright' kids aren't always the ones with the most friends," said atheist author Chris Mooney.[18]

My Unbelief Is Better than Your Unbelief

Isn't [an agnostic] just an atheist without balls?
Stephen Colbert, comedian [19]

Despite their different labels, most unbelievers get along with each other. But arguments do happen. Take these comments from atheists about agnostics:

"[Agnosticism is] just watered down, hiding in the closet, rather cut off your own tongue than admit it atheism."[20]

"Agnostics are wimps! . . . It requires guts to let go of the nice comforting idea [of] a god who has a grand scheme for us and a plan for the universe. Agnostics are people who know they *ought* to take the step but don't want to commit themselves. Sounds like cowardice to me."[21]

"Agnostics are saying that they don't know and not only that, nobody knows or can know. So they are being just as arrogant as they say that fundamentalists and atheists are."[22]

And take these words from agnostics about atheists:

"The atheists of the world want to take control of all the philosophical stances outside theism . . . as though they have the divine right to do so."[23]

"The triumphalism that too often seems to be part and parcel of atheism entails a poverty of spirit that is detrimental to our humanity."[24]

"Agnostics are ethically superior to atheists."[25]

Others try to split the difference between atheist and agnostic by calling themselves atheistic agnostics or agnostic atheists.

Meanwhile, some positive/strong/hard atheists consider negative/weak/soft atheists to be nothing more than agnostics, while some negative/weak/soft atheists see the positive/strong/hard ones as inflexible and arrogant.

Who Needs Labels?

"Do I call myself an atheist or [an] agnostic?" asked an unbeliever on the internet forum *Newgrounds* who called himself ouchichi. He chose neither word, "because they have become religious labels themselves, almost as if atheism is a religion, or agnosticism. Anyone [who] wants to label me because of the way I think can go fuck themselves."[26]

Unbelievers like ouchichi don't want any labels. Quite a few atheists pride themselves on having independent minds. Tagging their viewpoints with a specific name feels almost like signing them up for a church denomination. As a seventeen-year-old unbeliever named Matt said, "I don't really wanna call myself anything or give myself a label. I just wanna live my life."[27]

SEVEN CELEBRITY UNBELIEVERS

The world knows about the clothes celebrities wear, the people they date, and the reasons why they get arrested. But celebrity disbelief in God? That's not something that you hear about much. Fortunately, some stars have come forward about being atheists or agnostics.

1. Angelina Jolie

When the *Onion A.V. Club* online magazine asked Jolie if there's a god, she answered, "For the people who believe in it, I hope so. There doesn't need to be a God for me."[28] The man in her life, Brad Pitt, is an unbeliever as well. In 2009 he told the German magazine *Bild*, "I'm probably 20 percent atheist and 80 percent agnostic."[29]

2. CM Punk

This World Wrestling Entertainment star is not just atheistic but combative about it. When a journalist told him, "Stop being a dogmatic atheist. It's overdone and annoying," the wrestler answered, "Stop believing in a man in the sky. It's illogical."[30]

3. Daniel Radcliffe

The guy you love as Harry Potter is an unbeliever. "I'm an atheist, but I'm very relaxed about it," he's said. "I don't preach my atheism, but I have a huge amount of respect for people like [atheist author] Richard Dawkins who do."[31] What's more, he's called himself "a militant atheist when religion starts impacting on legislation."[32]

4. George Clooney

"I don't believe in heaven and hell," Clooney said. "I don't know if I believe in God."[33] He doesn't object to religion, though. In an interview on CNN, he said, "Whatever anybody believes, as long as it doesn't hurt anyone else, it's fair enough and works. And I think it's real and matters. I don't happen to have those beliefs as much. I don't believe in those things."[34]

5. Mark Zuckerberg

Facebook's founder was born Jewish, but the young billionaire has listed himself as an atheist on his Facebook page.[35] He doesn't talk much about his beliefs (or lack thereof), though.

6. Tyler, the Creator (posting as wolfhaley)

"I hate religion; to me, it keeps people in a box and won't allow them to do what the f*** they want," the Odd Future rapper has written. When a fan challenged him about loving Jesus, he answered, "[Jesus] is not real. Why the f*** would I love someone that I haven't met?"[36]

7. Zac Efron

The *High School Musical* star has said, "I was raised agnostic, so we never practiced religion."[37] Although his ancestry is Jewish, he told the Jewish newspaper *Forward* that he remains agnostic.[38]

Who Are They and How Many?

Whether they're atheists, agnostics, or anything else, unbelievers are a minority group—but a big one. Fifteen to twenty percent of all adult Americans have no religion.[39] That's more than thirty-six million people.[40] In the United States, nonreligious Americans outnumber Methodists; they outnumber Lutherans; they outnumber Presbyterians. Among American religious groups, only Baptists and Roman Catholics have more adherents.[41] But not everyone who has no religion calls himself or herself an atheist. Self-declared atheists account for less than 3 percent of the American population. Agnostics are under four percent.[42] Do those numbers sound tiny? Consider:

▶ The United States has more agnostics than Episcopalians, Anglicans, Mormons, or Jews.[43]

▶ There are more US atheists than people in Philadelphia, Dallas, Detroit,[44] Idaho,[45] Maine,[46] or Hawaii.[47]

▶ Combined, atheists and agnostics account for at least 3.5 million Americans[48]—and that's the lowest reputable estimate. The actual figure may be millions higher.

What's more, the number of unreligious Americans has nearly doubled since the end of the 1980s. At the same time, most religions have held steady or lost members.[49]

And the unbelievers are young. The adults likeliest to have no religion are the youngest adults. While nontheists account for 10 to 15 percent of all American adults, they're 22 to 25 percent of American adults under age thirty.[50] At least 5 percent of Americans age thirteen through seventeen are atheists. As many as 18 percent are agnostics. And the numbers seem to be rising.[51]

The Ten Most Atheistic States

Here are the states with the highest percentage of nonreligious people in their populations.

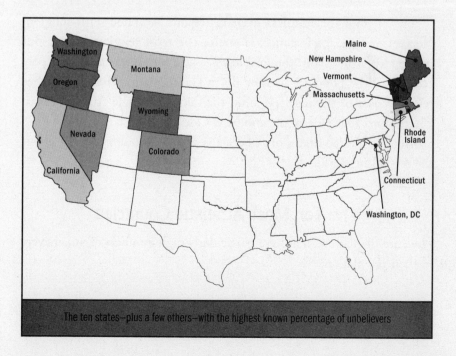

The ten states—plus a few others—with the highest known percentage of unbelievers

---

1. Vermont: More than one in four Vermonters (and possibly more than one in three) has no religion.

2. New Hampshire: Almost as high a proportion of the faithless as Vermont.

3. Maine: Nearly as big a percentage as New Hampshire.

4–8. Then comes a five-way tie: **Massachusetts**, **Oregon**, **Rhode Island**, **Washington**, and **Wyoming**. More than a fifth of the population in each state doesn't belong to any faith.

9–10. And finally, a two-way tie: **Colorado** and **Nevada**. A slightly lower percentage of unbelievers than the previous five states.

Bubbling up under the top ten: **California**, **Connecticut**, **Montana**, and **Washington, DC**.

Frank Newport, "Mississippi Maintains Hold as Most Religious U.S. State," Gallup Poll, February 13, 2013, http://www.gallup.com/poll/160415/mississippi-maintains-hold -religious-state.aspx; Barry A. Kosmin and Ariela Keysar, with Ryan Cragun and Juhem Navarro-Rivera, *American Nones: The Profile of the No Religion Population* (Hartford, CT: Trinity College, 2009), 9–10, http://commons.trincoll.edu/aris/files/2011/08/ NONES_08.pdf; The Pew, *U.S. Religious Landscape Survey* (Washington, DC: Pew Forum on Religion & Public Life, 2008), 90, http://religions.pewforum.org/pdf/report-religious-landscape-study-full.pdf.

You can find the faithless even in regions saturated with religion. North Carolina, for instance, is one of the most religious states. But in the city of Durham, the faithless account for almost as high a percentage of the populace as they do in California or Montana. Other relative oases of the faithless amid the faithful include Austin, Texas; Charleston, South Carolina; and New Orleans, Louisiana.[52]

Still, the United States of America is only one country. What about the rest of the world?

The Ten Most Atheistic Countries

Here are the nations that have particularly high numbers of unbelievers in their population.

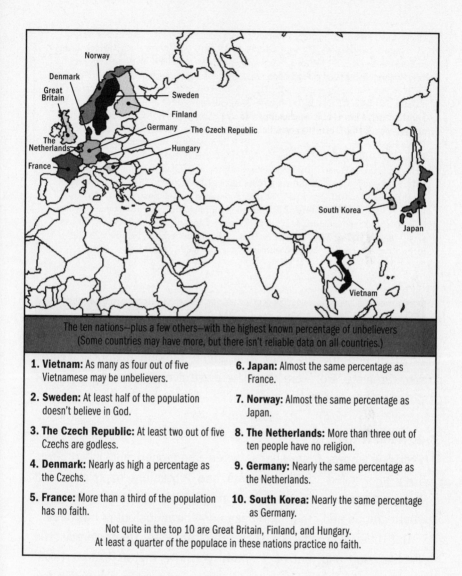

The ten nations—plus a few others—with the highest known percentage of unbelievers
(Some countries may have more, but there isn't reliable data on all countries.)

1. **Vietnam:** As many as four out of five Vietnamese may be unbelievers.

2. **Sweden:** At least half of the population doesn't believe in God.

3. **The Czech Republic:** At least two out of five Czechs are godless.

4. **Denmark:** Nearly as high a percentage as the Czechs.

5. **France:** More than a third of the population has no faith.

6. **Japan:** Almost the same percentage as France.

7. **Norway:** Almost the same percentage as Japan.

8. **The Netherlands:** More than three out of ten people have no religion.

9. **Germany:** Nearly the same percentage as the Netherlands.

10. **South Korea:** Nearly the same percentage as Germany.

Not quite in the top 10 are Great Britain, Finland, and Hungary.
At least a quarter of the populace in these nations practice no faith.

Nancy Wong and Vivienne Timmins, "Religious Views and Beliefs Vary Greatly by Country, According to the Latest *Financial Times*/Harris Poll," Harris Interactive website, December 20, 2006, accessed 2011, http://www.harrisinteractive.com/NEWS/allnewsbydate.asp?NewsID=1130 (page discontinued); Phil Zuckerman, "Atheism: Contemporary Rates and Patterns," in *Cambridge Companion to Atheism*, ed. Michael Martin (New York: Cambridge University Press, 2007), 15–17, http://www.pitzer.edu/academics/faculty/zuckerman/Ath-Chap-under-7000.pdf; Richard Lynn, John

Harvey, and Helmuth Nyborg, "Average Intelligence Predicts Atheism Rates Across 137 Nations," *Intelligence*, 37, no. 1 (2009): 11–15, http://davesource.com/Fringe/Fringe/ Religion/Average-intelligence-predicts-atheism-rates-across-137-nations-Lynn-et-al. pdf; Rushna Shahid and Sinead Mooney, *Global Index of Religion and Atheism* (Zurich, Switzerland: Gallup International, 2012), 10, http://redcresearch.ie/wp-content/ uploads/2012/08/RED-C-press-release-Religion-and- Atheism-25-7-12.pdf; Tom W. Smith, *Beliefs about God across Time and Countries* (Chicago: NORC at the University of Chicago, 2012), 7, http://www.norc.org/PDFs/Beliefs_about_God_Report.pdf; *The World Factbook*, s.v. "religions," accessed 2013, https://www.cia.gov/library/publications/ the-world-factbook/fields/2122.html; "Most Agnostic Nations," Association of Religion Data Archives, 2010, http://www.thearda.com/QL2010/QuickList_213.asp; "Most Atheist Nations," Association of Religion Data Archives, 2010, http://www. thearda.com/QL2010/QuickList_39.asp; "Population by Religion, Sex, and Urban/ Rural Residence," UNdata website, accessed November 2013, http://data.un.org/Data. aspx?d=POP&f=tableCode%3a28; ICM Research Limited, "What the World Thinks of God," in "UK among Most Secular Nations," BBC News website, February 26, 2004, http://news.bbc.co.uk/2/hi/programmes/wtwtgod/3518375.stm.

ATHEIST OR NOT?

Atheists and theists claim that some famous historical figures were atheists. But were they? Here are five people who often get described as atheist.

1. Adolf Hitler

Everyone knows that Hitler's forces imprisoned and killed Jews. They also jailed Catholic priests and Protestant ministers, shut down religious newspapers and magazines, and pushed religious youth groups and other faith-based organizations out of business.

But Hitler also outlawed societies of atheists. He declared, "The people need and require . . . faith. We have therefore undertaken the fight against the atheistic movement, and not merely with a few theoretical declarations: we have stamped it out."[53]

Hitler also had a spiritual side. "Providence," he said, "called upon me and vouchsafed it to me, once an unknown soldier of the Great War [World War I], to rise to be the leader of my people, so dear to me. Providence showed me the way to free our people from the depths of its misery without bloodshed and to lead it upward once again."[54] Whether or not Hitler believed in God, he thought that God believed in him.

2. Abraham Lincoln

Lincoln was raised in a hard-line Baptist faith, but he rejected it; and he never formally joined a church. "Mr. Lincoln had no hope and no faith, in the usual acceptance of those words," his wife said.[55]

But presiding over the Civil War seemed to bend Lincoln toward God. In his second inaugural address, Lincoln quoted the biblical books of Matthew and Psalms, and included lines like, "Fervently do we pray that this mighty scourge of war may speedily pass away. Yet, if God wills that it continue . . . so still it must be said, 'the judgments of the Lord are true and righteous altogether.'"[56]

3. Albert Einstein

Einstein was Jewish, but his view of God came from the philosopher Baruch Spinoza. Spinoza (1632–1677) was a Dutch Jew excommunicated from Judaism, presumably for his view that God had no mind or personality. To Spinoza (and Einstein), God was the substance of the universe.[57]

"Science," Einstein said, "can only be created by those who are thoroughly imbued with the aspiration toward truth and understanding. This source of feeling, however, springs from the sphere of religion. To this there also belongs the faith in the possibility that the regulations valid for the world of existence are rational—that is, comprehensible to reason. I cannot conceive of a genuine scientist without that profound faith. The situation may be expressed by an image: science without religion is lame, religion without science is blind."[58]

4. Mark Twain

Twain disliked religion and the God that the preachers of his time praised, particularly toward the end of his life. As he said:

"Faith is believing what you know ain't so."[59]

"To trust the God of the Bible is to trust an irascible, vindictive, fierce, and ever fickle and changeful master."[60]

"I cannot see how a man of any large degree of humorous perception can ever be religious—unless he purposely shut the eyes of his mind and keep them shut by force."[61]

5. Thomas Edison

Edison denied being an atheist: "I am not, never have been, never said I was," he told the *New York Times* in November 1910. He believed in what he called a Supreme Intelligence.[62]

But at the same time, he said, "I have grave doubts whether the good folk of this earth are going to be aroused from their graves to go to some beautiful, shining place up aloft. Don't see it, can't understand it, and neither can these ministers of fashionable churches."[63] Two months earlier, he had told the *Times*, "Nature made us—nature did it all—not the gods of the religions."[64]

What's It All Mean?

So now you know what an atheist is and who atheists are. But the unbelieving life is more complicated than a flat list of facts and explanations. (Keep going; you'll see.)

2

Is Atheism a Religion?

A slightly last-ditch argument that's becoming fashionable now among Christians is to say that people like [atheists] Richard Dawkins and myself are fundamentalists; that we're believers, if you like; almost that we're a church. Absolutely not so.

CHRISTOPHER HITCHENS, AUTHOR[1]

James Kaufman was a prisoner in Wisconsin's Waupun Correctional Institution. On September 3, 2002, Kaufman sent prison chaplain Jamyi Witch a "Request for New Religious Practice" form to ask "that a group be formed for atheists within the institution, for the purpose of study and education," on the grounds that "atheists are entitled to the same freedoms . . . as those inmates who profess a religion."[2]

Witch turned Kaufman down. Kaufman took his request to Warden Gary McCaughtry, who also turned him down.

Kaufman sued them for violating his right to religious freedom. And he won. On August 19, 2005, the Seventh Circuit of the United States

Court of Appeals declared, in Judge Diane Wood's words, "Atheism is Kaufman's religion."[3]

Was the court right?

The Religion Checklist

"If religion is, as many define it, a belief system to explain our existence on earth, how we should conduct ourselves while on earth, and where we go when we die, then atheism is, by definition, a religion."[4]

That's not from a hardcore theist trying to annoy atheists by telling them that they're actually religious. It's from Janna Seliger, an atheist writer.

She's not alone. "A person's religion is the sum total of his beliefs about God and the supernatural.... ATHEISM IS THE RELIGION WHICH SAYS THERE IS NO GOD," wrote Reverend Bill McGinnis, who runs an online ministry.[5] Another minister, Brandon Cox of Grace Hills Church in Bentonville, Arkansas, has offered more detail: "No gods, no devils, no angels, no heaven, no hell. Those are statements about what someone believes does *not* exist. Then, there is only the natural world. That's a statement of what one *does* believe. So the message competes with other religious messages and affirms an alternative system of beliefs." He concluded, "Sounds like a religion."[6]

Many unbelievers don't buy it.

"No matter how you define religion," said a writer on the blog *Debunking Christianity*, "it must include supernatural forces or beings, and atheists deny them."[7] The importance of the supernatural—or the lack of it—is key, according to Jeff Randall, a member of the skeptic and freethinker group Center for Inquiry–DC: "If you remove the supernatural aspect of [a] religion, [then] ANY club or ground would be a religion, [including the] religion of Democrats or Republican[s]."[8] D. Cancilla, who blogs at *I Am an Atheist*, agreed: "Atheism is the lack of belief in a deity and nothing more. If it is a set of beliefs, it is an empty set."[9]

Or as anthropologist David Eller said in his book *Atheism Advanced: Further Thoughts of a Freethinker*: "If atheism is a religion, then not collecting stamps is a hobby."[10]

The Faith Factor

People who say that atheism is a religion often say that atheists reach their unreligious beliefs the same way as many theists get to their religious beliefs: by faith. "You cannot prove that there is no God—you have to believe it," said Laura Lond, an ex-atheist turned Christian novelist and essayist.[11]

Wrong, say a lot of unbelievers. "To say that atheism requires faith is as dim-witted as saying that disbelief in pixies or leprechauns takes faith," argued British atheist Geoff Mather.[12] Humanist philosopher Julian Baggini has pointed out that atheists disbelieve because they have no faith—that is, no faith that God exists. "Atheists do not need faith to be atheists."[13]

But Ray Comfort, a prominent minister, has said that atheists *have* to have faith. "In the face of an incredibly intricate and ordered Nature, [atheists] believe that there is no evidence of intelligent design. That takes amazing faith."[14] And conservative Christian political columnist Cal Thomas has said, "It takes more faith not to believe in God than to believe in Him."[15]

There are various answers to the opinion that you need faith to believe that the universe developed without God. Chapter 16 will cover them in detail.

But "atheism requires faith" (let's call it ARF) isn't just an opinion; it is, often, a slander against atheists.

Many an ARFer "claims that atheists are claiming to know with faith-based, dogmatic, absolute certainty that God does not exist," said Staks Rosch, host of an atheist blog called *Dangerous Talk*. In other words, ARFers say that all atheists are positive/strong/hard atheists. "This is really just a false caricature or 'straw man' of what most atheists think."[16]

Besides, according to the website Atheists Frequently Asked Questions, most atheists usually don't take any claims on faith—even their own. "They consider faith to mean gullibility. They highly regard intellectual honesty, and prefer to wait until an assertion [like the existence of God] has been sufficiently demonstrated as true before accepting it."[17]

Preachers, Teachers, and Beseechers

Maybe atheism isn't a religion—but does it *act* like one? Ask Kevin Childs, lead pastor of The Rock, a Christian community in South Carolina. He summed up an opinion common among people who say that atheism's a religion: atheist leaders are the same as religious leaders. Let's take his points one by one.

"[Atheists] have their own messiah: He is, of course, Charles Darwin."[18]

Darwin—nineteenth-century biologist Charles Darwin—wrote *The Descent of Man* and *On the Origin of Species* to present the facts behind his theory of evolution. Darwin's discoveries revolutionized biology and other fields. To many unbelievers, Darwin was a liberator as George Washington and Nelson Mandela were in other realms.

But atheists don't venerate Darwin as Muslims revere Muhammad or Christians praise Jesus. They don't model their lives on Darwin's or call on him in times of trouble. A blogger named Vjack, of *Atheist Revolution*, spoke for millions of unbelievers when he said, "Darwin was certainly worthy of respect, admiration, and praise for his many contributions. But worship? I think not."[19]

Back to Kevin Childs's points that atheism is a religion: "[Atheists] have their own prophets: Nietzsche, Russell, Feuerbach, Lenin, Marx."[20]

The Nietzsche, Russell, Feuerbach, Lenin, and Marx that Reverend Childs mentioned are philosophers Friedrich Nietzsche, Bertrand Russell, and Ludwig Feuerbach; Russian dictator Vladimir Lenin; and theorist of communism Karl Marx. Most atheists don't think of them as prophets.

Lenin and Marx actually disgust many atheists—particularly people in countries like Russia, who have suffered under Leninist or Marxist dictatorships, and people in countries like the United States, who have opposed Leninist and Marxist regimes.

Nietzsche and Russell do have readers and fans among both atheists and theists; but their readers and fans are just readers and fans, not disciples who take their words as sacred.

As for Feuerbach, these days, most people—including atheists—don't even know who he is. (He proposed the idea that instead of God making humans in his own image, humans made God in theirs.)

Childs's third point: "[Atheists] have their own preachers and evangelists. And boy, are they 'evangelistic.' Dawkins, Dennett, Harris, and Hitchens are NOT out to ask that atheism be given respect. They are seeking converts. They are preaching a 'gospel' calling for the end of theism."[21]

Modern atheist writers Richard Dawkins, Daniel Dennett, Sam Harris, and Christopher Hitchens are antireligion. But they evangelize for their position, as Childs has claimed, and they have a following: their books are popular among unbelievers.

But trying to convert people to your ideas doesn't make your ideas a religion, even if your ideas are all about God. Religious evangelists say, *Listen to me, and you'll join the world of ideas that are important and true. You'll learn why the universe exists, how to live in it properly, and why sucky things happen to nice people while great stuff happens to scumwads.*

Atheist evangelists say, *Listen to me, and you'll join the world of ideas that are important and true.* That's as far as they go. Unlike religious leaders, most spokespeople for atheism usually don't

▶ build churches;

▶ gather congregations for weekly rituals;

▶ lay out rules on how to live;

▶ predict something mystical, like a heavenly afterlife or a miracle-working messiah;

▶ recommend a book as the solution to humanity's troubles;

▶ order people to tithe, fast, or go on pilgrimages; or

▶ tell people what to feel, whether it's guilt for committing sins, love and mercy for all humankind, or violent hatred for nonbelievers.

In any case, evangelizing for a viewpoint doesn't make that viewpoint a religion, because some religions don't evangelize. Judaism's a religion, but Jews generally don't send out missionaries, launch revival meetings, or preach on television that everyone should worship their way. Neither do Hindus, Wiccans, Quakers, or Buddhists.

AN ATHEIST BIBLE?

Related to the idea that Darwin's a messiah is the idea that his books are an atheist's version of holy scriptures. The religious website Revelation.co says, "Atheists have an unofficial Bible (called the *Origin of Species*)."[22]

Interesting charge. So let's look at *Origin*. Here's the start of chapter 1:

When we look to the individuals of the same variety or subvariety of our older cultivated plants and animals, one of the first points which strikes us is that they generally differ much more from each other than do the individuals of any one species or variety in a state of nature. When we reflect on the vast diversity of the plants and animals which have been cultivated, and which have varied during all ages under the most different climates and treatment, I think we are driven to conclude that this greater variability is simply due to our domestic productions having been raised under conditions of life not so uniform as, and somewhat different from, those to which the parent species have been exposed under nature.[23]

A rollercoaster of thrills, isn't it? Definitely one that billions of people would line up to read over and over, right?

Hardly.

Origin doesn't have the rich emotion, passionate struggles, and cosmic drama of most holy books. Most unbelievers have never read it, and they don't offer it the obedient reverence that Jews give to the Torah, Christians to the New Testament, and Muslims to the Koran. "[Darwin's] writings are not worshipped, nor even accepted uncritically," said John C. Snider, who cohosts the atheist podcast *American Freethought*. "Indeed, many of his theories and observations have been discarded and altered over the years."[24]

Do Atheists Worship Anything?

Some believers think that atheists worship themselves. The idea is that if people follow their own will instead of God's will, then they're putting faith in themselves as believers put faith in God. In living by their own minds and hearts rather than by the rules of God, atheists put themselves in God's place.

That path of logic makes sense if you believe that God reigns over people. But if you don't, those ideas are nonsense. If people don't believe that God exists, then they don't believe that they're putting themselves in God's place.

Occasionally, you'll hear claims that atheists worship science. And frankly, it's not hard to find atheists, agnostics, and others who trust science as the best tool that humanity has used in climbing from primitive superstitions to trustworthy truths. But saying that unbelievers worship this tool is saying that they treat it as a god to be obeyed and even prayed to. No one—not even the most atheistic scientist—treats science that way.

Yet another misconception is that atheists worship Satan. But if atheists don't believe in God, why would they believe in the devil, let alone worship him?

A subtler version of "atheists worship Satan" says that if you refuse to believe in God, then you're serving God's enemy—and serving Satan is a way to worship him. That idea can make sense if you believe that God and Satan exist. If you don't, the idea of helping one entity who doesn't exist as he battles another nonexistent entity is like asking who'd win a fistfight between Santa Claus and the Easter Bunny: silly and pointless. (My money's on Santa, though.)

Atheist Spirituality

If atheists and agnostics don't believe in God, do they have any spirituality at all? Some do. A minority even create their own rituals and churches. (Keep reading. You'll see.)

3

Don't You Need God for a Moral Life?

We know that men and women can be good without faith.
We know that.

PRESIDENT GEORGE W. BUSH[1]

In the Bible, Saint Paul said, "When Gentiles, who do not have the law [of God], by nature do the things of the [religious] law, they are a law unto themselves, [and] show the work of the law written in their hearts."[2] A variety of religious leaders agree. "Belief in God is not a requirement for ethical behavior," according to minister Matt Slick of the Christian Apologetics and Research Ministry.[3]

But a University of Minnesota study has said that more than a third of Americans associate atheists "with illegality, such as drug use and prostitution" or see atheists as "the ostentatiously wealthy who make a lifestyle out of consumption, or the cultural elites who think they know better than everyone else."[4] And according to a recent study by the Pew Research Global Attitudes Project (which presents "numbers, facts, and trends shaping your world"), more than half of all Americans say that to be moral, you have to believe in God.[5]

Are they right?

Does Morality Come from Religion?

Even a hardcore atheist has to admit: a lot of modern morality came from religion. Religious leaders have developed a mountain of the world's moral rules, including rules that atheists follow.

Still, you don't have to be Jewish to obey Moses's demand that "justice, justice shall you pursue" (Deuteronomy 17:20). You don't have to be Christian to respect Jesus's calls for peace and mercy in the Sermon on the Mount. And you don't have to be Muslim to practice *zakat* (tithing for charity).

What's more, religions have also imposed rules that both atheists and theists find disgusting—particularly rules from the Bible. Atheist author Sam Harris called the Bible's commands "odious and incompatible with a civil society," because "human sacrifice, genocide, slaveholding, and misogyny are consistently celebrated" in the book.[6]

Other unbelievers go along with atheist blogger Daniel Florien, who's said that the Bible "has good moral teachings and it has bad ones—just like most holy books."[7]

The Morals of Atheism, the Morals of Atheists

> Organized religion is great for defining what is good, but the rest of the stuff that goes along with it (myths, money, hypocrisy) is totally unneeded. We as humans have all that we need in front of us to define and execute what is morally proper.
>
> *Byron, college-age atheist, Georgia*[8]

What does atheism say about morality?

Nothing. Since unbelief isn't a religion but a lack of religion, it doesn't impose moral commandments.

But atheistic *people* have opinions on morality. For instance, many unbelievers find it immoral to impose restrictions (particularly religious restrictions) on thought, speech, and behavior. An atheist college student named Olivia, who writes for the site *Teen Skepchick*, has criticized religious people who display "an intolerance, a disrespect for other people's free choices, a self-importance and high moral certainty."[9]

So that's what many unbelievers oppose. What do they support?

"Almost all atheists stand for the values of reason and freethought," said Richard Carrier, author of *Sense and Goodness without God*. "There is the belief that inquiry and doubt are essential checks against deception, self-deception, and error. There is the belief that logic and proper empirical method is the only way the whole world can arrive at an agreement on the truth about anything."[10]

While many believers focus on God's desires, unbelievers tend to care most about their fellow humans. "Atheism shifts the basis of morality from faith in God to obligations of social living," said Gora, an atheist philosopher from India. "As we are all humans, belonging to the same species, we should live equal. Any attempt to transgress the obligation should be checked and punished here and now by fellow humans."[11] In the words of a teenage unbeliever from Illinois who uses the screen name CruxClaire, "Every atheist I know, myself included, believes all humans have potential, dignity, and worth."[12]

Viewpoints like these lead many unbelievers to value helping people. "An atheist believes that a hospital should be built instead of a church. An atheist believes that a deed must be done instead of a prayer said," said Madalyn Murray O'Hair, an atheist activist who sued to get prayer out of American public schools. "An atheist believes that heaven is something for which we should work now—here on earth, for all men together to enjoy."[13]

In addition, many unbelievers respect a guideline that runs throughout multiple cultures and religions. According to Richard Carrier,

"Every atheist I have known has always fallen back upon the one concept echoed worldwide, and taught by religious and secular leaders throughout all time: the famous 'Golden Rule.'"[14] (In case you've forgotten, the Golden Rule is "Do unto others as you would have them do unto you," or some variant thereof.)

Ten Atheist Commandments

When it comes to the most famous moral instructions—the Ten Commandments—most unbelievers respect the ones against stealing, killing, and lying. But they're not so wild for the laws about whom to worship. Some of the godless have even come up with their own sets of ten. No two lists are identical, but quite a few have similar ideas.

I. Don't hurt people.

Richard Dawkins, a leading modern atheist, has cited a ten-pack of commandments that includes "In all things, strive to cause no harm."[15] If you must hurt someone, make sure that you're right; as atheist author Bertrand Russell has advised, "When you think it is your duty to inflict pain, scrutinize your reasons closely."[16]

II. Certain types of harm are especially important to avoid.

For instance:

a. Don't kill people unless you have to. "Thou shalt not unsheathe the sword except in self-defense," wrote Robert Ingersoll, the nineteenth century's most famous American unbeliever. He added, "Thou shalt not wage wars of extermination."[17]

b. Don't treat people as if they were things. "Thou shalt not enslave thy fellow men," Ingersoll said.[18] In the early twenty-first century, Christopher Hitchens (author of *God Is Not Great: How Religion Spoils Everything*) said much the same thing: "*Do not* ever use people as private property."[19]

c. Don't hurt kids at all. "Hide your face and weep if you dare to harm a child," Hitchens demanded.[20]

III. Be good to people.

For some atheists, it's not enough just to avoid harming people. "Help the needy," said A. C. Grayling, author of a secular Bible called *The Good Book*.[21] Russell said, "When you have power, use it to build up people, not to constrict them."[22] And in general, says Dawkins's favored list, "Treat your fellow human beings, your fellow living things, and the world in general with love, honesty, faithfulness, and respect."[23]

IV. Think for yourself.

"Have no respect for the authority of others, for there are always contrary authorities to be found," Russell said. He added, "Do not fear to be eccentric in opinion, for every opinion now accepted was once eccentric."[24] Dawkins's recommended commandments include "Form independent opinions on the basis of your own reason and experience" and "Test all things; always check your ideas against the facts, and be ready to discard even a cherished belief if it does not conform to them."[25]

V. Let other people think for themselves.

"Never try to discourage thinking for you are sure to succeed," and "Do not use power to suppress opinions you think pernicious," said Russell.[26] Atheist comedian George Carlin had his own, very specific version: "Thou shalt keep thy religion to thyself!!!"[27]

VI. Don't lie.

Sam Harris, author of the atheist book *Letter to a Christian Nation*, gave a specific example: "Don't pretend to know things you don't know."[28] Russell forbade lying even to yourself, but he permitted lying to other people if they act like tyrants.[29]

VII. Keep your promises, especially when it comes to sex.

This one may seem like an extension of *Don't lie*, but many atheists who write lists of commandments have found it important enough to break it out on its own. Magician Penn Jillette, author of the antireligion book *God, No!*, decreed, "If you can't be sexually exclusive to your spouse, don't make that deal."[30] Or as Carlin said, "Thou shalt always be honest and faithful, especially to the provider of thy nookie."[31]

VIII. Oppose evil.

Hitchens favored denouncing all religious crusaders "for what they are: psychopathic criminals." He added, "Despise those who use violence or the threat of it in sexual relations."[32] Nevertheless, says Dawkins's list, "Always be ready to forgive wrongdoing freely admitted and honestly regretted."[33]

IX. Avoid envy.

"Do not feel envious of the happiness of those who live in a fool's paradise, for only a fool will think that it is happiness," according to Russell.[34] Jillette added, "Don't waste too much time wishing, hoping, and being envious; it'll make you bugnutty."[35]

X. Recognize that you are only a part of the universe—a small part.

"Do not think of yourself as a wholly self-contained unit," Russell said.[36] Hitchens went further: "Be aware that you, too, are an animal and dependent on the web of nature, and think and act accordingly."[37]

Is Unbelief More Moral than Belief?

Some atheists say that not believing in God makes them better than people who believe. After all, they say, unbelievers do good because they want to, while believers do good because they're scared. "Those who claim that religion is the only source of morality are indirectly saying that without the fear of going to hell, they would have no motivation to follow the morals," said a young Vermont unbeliever who has used the screen name RustinN.[38]

Others say that the morality of theists is the morality of people who obey without thinking—and unthinking obedience is immoral. "For those of us who are unbelievers, evil can best be described as the abandonment of our minds to the minds of others," according to Al Stefanelli, the former state director in Georgia for the group American Atheists. "To us, it is a travesty to blindly accept any doctrine on faith. We believe that the ability and willingness to stand alone, when necessary, and tell the majority that they are wrong is the pinnacle of virtue."[39]

But are unbelievers truly virtuous?

Do the Godless Give?

"My school is trying to run a charity drive to build a fence for a farm in Africa with a goal of $600," an atheist teenager named Daniel wrote on his Facebook page, the Catholic School Atheist. "I don't want to donate to them because personally I think the school will spend the money on trying to convert people instead of actually helping others.

"Instead I want to prove the Christians around me are wrong when they say atheists don't support charity. I want to double what my school makes on their fundraiser and donate it all to Responsible Charity. They are a secular charity that helps women and children in India, and are trying to build a school in Calcutta . . . . So far we have raised $12,000—enough to build the school!"[40]

Most people would say that Daniel's doing something moral. Unfortunately, he may be an exception. Charities tied to religion receive more donations than nonreligious charities.[41] And people who go to religious services and consider themselves highly religious do more giving, volunteer work, and other forms of help than unbelievers.[42]

The godless aren't completely selfish, though. They tend to be more generous than theists when giving to nature-related causes, such as animal welfare, wildlife, and the environment.[43] Atheist charities such as the Foundation Beyond Belief and SHARE (Skeptics and Humanists Aid and Relief Effort) have raised thousands of dollars for victims of earthquakes in Haiti[44] and typhoons in the Philippines.[45]

Overall, though, unbelievers have a long way to go before they match the religious in charity.

Unbelievers and Crime

Another test of atheist morality—or immorality—is to see if there's a connection between unbelievers and the rate of activities so evil that society throws people in jail for them.

Here are the American states that have the lowest rates of violent crime, are the most peaceful, and have the fewest people in hate groups like the Ku Klux Klan or the neo-Nazis. States with a high percentage of unbelievers are in **bold**.

MORALITY IN THE UNITED STATES

	LOWEST-CRIME STATES*	MOST PEACEFUL STATES†	STATES LOW ON HATE GROUPS‡
1	**Maine**	**Maine**	Alaska
2	**Vermont**	**Vermont**	Hawaii
3	**New Hampshire**	**New Hampshire**	New Mexico
4	Virginia	Minnesota	**Maine**
5	**Wyoming**	Utah	New York
6	Utah	North Dakota	**Connecticut**
7	Idaho	**Washington**	Minnesota
8	Kentucky	Hawaii	North Dakota
9	Minnesota	**Rhode Island**	Wisconsin
10	Hawaii	Iowa	Illinois

Sources:

* "Crime in the United States by State, 2012," Federal Bureau of Investigation, accessed January 2, 2014, http://www.fbi.gov/about-us/cjis/ucr/crime-in-the-u.s/2012/crime-in -the-u.s.-2012/tables/5tabledatadecpdf/table_5_crime_in_the_united_states_by_ state_2012.xls.

† Institute for Economics & Peace, 2012 *United States Peace Index* (New York: Institute for Economics and Peace, 2012), 16, http://www.visionofhumanity.org/sites/default/ files/2012-United-States-Peace-Index-Report_1.pdf

‡ R. Georges Delamontagne, "Religiosity and Hate Groups: An Exploratory and Descriptive Correlational Study," *Journal of Religion & Society* 12 (2010), 3–4, http:// moses.creighton.edu/jrs/2010/2010-10.pdf.

Some states that have a lot of unbelievers rank low in crime, low in hate, high in peacefulness, or some combination of the three. In other words, a high proportion of unbelievers doesn't necessarily lead to violence, bigotry, hate crimes, or other forms of immorality.

The Morality of Godless Nations

The Institute for Economics and Peace, which measured American states for peacefulness, has measured the rest of the world too—162 countries in all. Here are the top twenty-five most peaceable countries. The ones that have a high percentage of unbelievers are in **bold**.[46]

WORLD PEACEFULNESS

1	Iceland	8	Canada
2	**Denmark**	9	**Sweden**
3	New Zealand	10	Belgium
4	Austria	11	**Norway**
5	Switzerland	12	Ireland
6	**Japan**	13	Slovenia
7	**Finland**	14	**Czech Republic**

15	**Germany**	21	Mauritius
16/17	Australia/Singapore (tie)	22	**Netherlands**
18	Portugal	23	**Hungary**
19	Qatar	24	Uruguay
20	Bhutan	25	Poland

But what about the most immoral act of all? You know the one: murder. The United Nations ranks murder rates by country. The worldwide average is 6.9 murders for every hundred thousand people per year.[47] Here is the UN's list of the countries with the lowest murder rates. Unbeliever-heavy countries are in—well, **you know**.[48]

WORLD MURDER RATES
(PER 100,000 PEOPLE)

Monaco, Palau	0.0
Hong Kong	0.2
Iceland, Singapore	0.3
French Polynesia, **Japan**	0.4
Brunei	0.5
Austria, Bahrain, Guam, **Norway**	0.6
Macao, Oman, Slovenia, Switzerland	0.7
Germany, Spain, United Arab Emirates	0.8
Denmark, Italy, Micronesia, New Zealand, Qatar, Vanuatu	0.9
Australia, Bhutan, China, Malta, Saudi Arabia, **Sweden**, Tonga	1.0
France, **Netherlands**, Poland, Samoa, Tunisia	1.1

Egypt, Ireland, Portugal, Serbia, **United Kingdom**	1.2
Andorra, **Hungary**	1.3
Armenia, Croatia, Morocco	1.4
Algeria, Bosnia-Herzegovina, Greece, Slovakia, Somalia	1.5
Canada, Maldives, **Vietnam**	1.6
Belgium, Cyprus, **Czech Republic**	1.7
Jordan	1.8
Macedonia, São Tomé and Príncipe	1.9

It seems clear that life without religion doesn't automatically lead people to commit immoral acts.

SOME HIGHLY MORAL UNBELIEVERS

To prove that unbelief is immoral, some theists have pointed out that mass murderers such as Josef Stalin, Pol Pot, and Mao Zedong were atheists. But other unbelievers have done things that are almost saintly.

Henry Stephens Salt (1851–1939), Humanitarian

Salt, an atheist, led crusades for nature conservation, peace between nations, and improvements in schools and prisons.[49] He wrote the first book proposing animal rights,[50] and Mahatma Gandhi praised his high moral code.[51]

"Religion," Salt wrote, "has never befriended the cause of humaneness. Its monstrous doctrine of eternal punishment and the torture of the damned underlies much of the barbarity with which man has treated man."[52]

Fridtjof Nansen (1861–1930), Diplomat

Fridtjof Nansen was an agnostic and an international hero[53]—"The religion of one age," he wrote in 1907, "is, as a rule, the literary entertainment of the next."[54]

When his native Norway demanded independence from Sweden, he prevented a civil war by helping to negotiate a peaceful split. During World War I, when supplies were scarce and shipping was dangerous, he secured food for his hungry countrymen. After the war, he helped refugees and prisoners of war get home safely. And he won the Nobel Peace Prize.[55]

Andrei Sakharov (1921–1989), Physicist

Lifelong atheist Andrei Sakharov signed the 1973 "Humanist Manifesto II," which included the line "As nontheists, we begin with humans, not God."[56] But that was only one of the ways in which he championed his beliefs.

The Soviet Union had awarded Sakharov its highest honors for developing the country's nuclear weapons. But when he spoke out against those weapons and in favor of giving the Soviet people more freedom, the government arrested him and held him prisoner for six years. For his efforts on behalf of freedom and peace, he won the Nobel Peace Prize.[57]

Here are more unbelievers who have performed in conspicuously moral ways:

Clarence Darrow, lawyer (1857–1938): Defended disadvantaged people and unpopular causes

Linus Pauling, biochemist (1901–1994): Received the Nobel Peace Prize for antiwar activism

Warren Buffet, businessman (1930–present): One of the world's biggest charitable donors

Bob Geldof, musician (1951–present): Raised millions of dollars for famine victims in Africa

---

Are Atheists Moral?

Obviously, religion isn't the only source of morality. Atheists can and do act morally—even if they're not always as generous in some ways (e.g., charity) as their theist neighbors.

4

Are There Atheist-Friendly Religions?

Do not go by anything that you have acquired by repeated hearing, tradition, rumors, holy scripture, or surmise, or because it has been pondered over; or by the thought, "The monk who taught it to us is our teacher." When you yourselves know, "These things are good, these things are blameless, these things are praised by the wise, these things when undertaken and observed lead to benefit and happiness," enter and abide in them.

BUDDHA, RELIGIOUS LEADER[1]

Even a hard-shell atheist has to admit it: religion has things that people like. Worldwide, people bow and pray, and not just because (as some atheists claim) they're all unthinkingly kowtowing to the bullying force of leaden tradition. They get something good out of it.

So do some atheists and agnostics. They take on parts of religion without ever believing in God.

Atheist Spirituality

Zach, from Michigan, is only twelve. Still, he has a clear view of his spirituality.

"I'm an atheist, but I'm spiritual. I don't believe in a god of any supernatural form, but the fact that everything in nature shares a connection makes me feel like I have a place on earth."[2]

Zach isn't the only atheist to profess mystical feelings. "You can have your spirituality [if you're godless]," atheist author Sam Harris has said. "You can go into a cave and practice meditation, and transform yourself . . . . You can [even] feel yourself to be one with the universe."[3]

Quite a few of the godless do it Zach's way: through nature. Charles Darwin, a hero to many unbelievers, presented his own version: "It is interesting to contemplate an entangled bank clothed with many plants of many kinds, with birds singing on the bushes, with various insects flitting about, and with worms crawling through the damp earth, and to reflect that these elaborately constructed forms, so different from each other and dependent on each other in so complex a manner, have all been produced by laws acting around us." Darwin concluded, "There is grandeur in this view of life."[4]

But this kind of spirituality doesn't mean a belief in spirits. "Faced with the night sky, Darwin's entangled bank, or the newborn baby, the secularist's feelings of awe or wonder are directed where they should be: at the sky, the bank, or the baby," said British philosopher Simon Blackburn. "His attention does not stray to thinking about his own soul or the purposes of providence."[5] Or about God.

Going to Church

"I surveyed nearly 1,700 natural and social scientists at elite American universities," Rice University sociologist Elaine Ecklund wrote in 2011. "I found that nearly one in five (17 percent) of those who are atheists and parents are part of a religious congregation and have attended a religious service more than once in the past year."[6]

Ecklund said that the scientist unbeliever

▶ wanted a sense of community;

▶ had spouses who wanted them to attend church; or

▶ wanted to show their kids all sorts of knowledge, including religion.[7]

It's not just scientists who see benefits in belief. In a 2012 poll of Americans, most respondents said that religion is losing its influence—and at least one in ten American atheists and agnostics said that this decline is bad.[8]

So if you're an unbeliever who likes the benefits of church, you're not alone. But what church should you attend?

Atheist Christians

Can an atheist be a Christian?

The answer depends on what you mean. Take Craig Groeschel, author of *The Christian Atheist: Believing in God but Living as if He Doesn't Exist*. He said that as a teenager, "I believed in God, but I still cheated in school, drank the cheapest beer available, lied about what I did with my girlfriends, and hoped to find the occasional misplaced *Playboy*."[9] He said that he was a Christian atheist because he believed as a Christian but lived as he thought an atheist would.

That's not what most atheists are likely to think when they say "Christian atheist." Lots of atheists would never cheat in school, lie about girlfriends or boyfriends, or drink cheap beer.

To most atheists, a Christian atheist is more like Thorkild Grosboll, who in 2003 sparked a national scandal in his native Denmark when he declared, "I do not believe in a physical God, in the afterlife, in the res-urrection, in the Virgin Mary." Problem was, Grosboll was a Lutheran minister. He added, "I believe that Jesus was a nice guy who figured out what man wanted. He embodied what he believed was needed to upgrade the human being."[10]

Christian atheists don't believe in God, but they try to live by Christian values: the charity, mercy, and love that Jesus preached.

Not everyone buys the concept, of course. "You can't follow Jesus without religion," said a blogger who calls herself Godless Girl. "The only reason you even *know* about Jesus is because his followers created his legend within the framework of religion."[11]

Other atheists are more tolerant of the Christian style. According to *Teen Skepchick* blogger Olivia, "There are, in fact, some Christian atheists, who pray and partake of the Christian community but do not believe in God. I think there is something beautiful in this idea. God may be a symbol for all the goodness and truth we see in the world. Atheism is certainly compatible with those ideas."[12]

Atheist Jews

I'm attracted to the culture [of] Judaism, and maybe not entirely
devoted [to] the aspect of believing in a God that does things for me
(i.e., I'm not one of those kids that prays to God before a big test).

hillel2000 (screen name), age 15, California[13]

Nearly a quarter (23 percent) of American Jews say that they don't believe in God. Even more (38 percent) say that while they do believe, they're not absolutely certain.[14]

These Jews sometimes call themselves "cultural Jews." They rarely enter a synagogue, but they feel a kinship with other Jews. They respect Jewish history and ethics, enjoy old-fashioned Jewish food, and partici-pate in some Jewish holidays.

There are even synagogues for atheist Jews. The Society for Humanistic Judaism, which says that it "mobilizes people to celebrate Jewish identity and culture consistent with a humanistic philosophy of life,"[15] lists almost thirty congregations in the United States.[16]

"Any conception of God I might have held is probably more akin to a healthy spiritual awe for both science/nature and humanity," said Jonathan Zimmerman, a New Yorker in his twenties. "So there I am: a Jew by identity and practice, an atheist by logic and belief."[17]

The Unitarian Universe

I just never understood what spirituality was, if it did not involve a god, a church, or a religion. (Things I do not believe in, if that was not clear.) Due to a confusing and often painful series of events in my life, I recently started attending a Unitarian Universalist church—and I suddenly get it.

Vreify (screen name), early twenties [18]

UNITARIAN
UNIVERSALIST
ASSOCIATION

A religion that includes people who profess no religion? Unitarian Universalism sounds doomed to trip over its own feet.

But no: there are more than a thousand UU congregations.[19]

The UU faith started in 1793, when some New England religious leaders decreed Universalism—a faith in "the Saviour God, which hath appeared and bringeth Salvation unto all men,"[20] as opposed to a god who condemned sinners and unbelievers to hell. The Unitarian side came in 1825, when Christian churches that decreed a single, united version of God (instead of the traditional three-way, or trinitarian, setup of father, son, and holy spirit) declared themselves the American Unitarian Association. In 1961 the two groups merged into today's UUs.

The UUs welcome atheists and agnostics. "Although both groups are often defined by what they do *not* believe," says the UU website, "agnostics and atheists can be at home in Unitarian Universalism because of what we *do* believe." For instance: "The future . . . is in our hands, not those of an angry God . . . life's blessings are available to everyone, not just those who can recite a certain catechism . . . [and] those blessings are made manifest to us not just in the 'miraculous' or extraordinary but in the simple pleasures of the everyday."[21]

For teenagers, UU congregations often have a youth ministry that does the usual church-youth stuff: discussions, volunteering, worship services, and so on.

Some unbelievers don't feel comfortable among UUs. "Atheists and secular humanists are neither Unitarians (believing in one supernatural god) nor Universalists (believing in supernatural salvation for all)," said August Berkshire, a spokesperson for the godless group Minnesota Atheists.[22]

But your taste may vary. After Sierra, a godless sixteen-year-old from Wisconsin, tried a UU service, she wrote an open letter to her fellow unbelievers: "Believe me, atheists, Unitarians are good people."[23]

The Buddhist Way

I have met a lot of Buddhists who believe in God.
I have met a lot of Buddhists who don't believe in God . . . .
And a lot of Buddhists just don't know.
Kusala Bhikshu, Buddhist monk[24]

"If there is one religion which at least receives significant sympathy from irreligious atheists, and may even be accepted to varying degrees by a large number of atheists, it would have to be Buddhism," said Austin Cline, About.com's expert on atheism and agnosticism. "Buddhism is regarded by many atheists as at least being less superstitious and irrational than most other religions, and perhaps to a certain degree, being reasonable enough to adopt."[25]

Buddhism's main ideas are the Four Noble Truths:

▶ Life is suffering.

▶ The cause of suffering is our desires.

▶ We can end our suffering by overcoming these desires.

▶ There is an eightfold path of ways to live that can help us overcome our desires.

Buddhism doesn't have an eternal, omnipotent, universe-creating god, although some versions of the faith include supernatural beings. It concentrates more on humanity's desires than on God's demands. But atheist journalist John Horgan has written, "Buddhism is not much more rational than the Catholicism I lapsed from in my youth." Among other problems, he doesn't like "its implication that detachment from ordinary life is the surest road to salvation."[26]

So should atheists adopt Buddhism? One answer may lie in the words of Ken, a blogger who writes as the Arizona Atheist: "Basically, I view Buddhism as another false belief system," he says, "but at the same time, it does have some beneficial teachings."[27]

THE GOD OF THE NOODLES

In 2005 a three-member panel of the Kansas Board of Education voted that the state's schools must criticize the theory of evolution. The vote nearly told the schools to teach intelligent design, a theory based on the Bible.[28]

The news sparked protests from scientists and others who supported evolution. One of them was twenty-five-year-old Bobby Henderson, who had graduated with a degree in physics from Oregon State University. He wrote a letter to the school board and posted it on the internet.

Within two months, his website had received millions of hits and spilled into the offline world. Henderson had created a new "religion": the Church of the Flying Spaghetti Monster, also called "Pastafarianism."[29]

"I and many others around the world are of the strong belief that the universe was created by a Flying Spaghetti Monster," Henderson wrote. "It is for this reason that I'm writing you today, to formally request that this alternative theory be taught in your schools."

Henderson admitted that science contradicted his theory just as it undercut the claims of intelligent design—for instance, the claim that the world is only a few thousand years old. But he had an answer: "Every time [a scientist] makes a measurement, the Flying Spaghetti Monster is there changing the results with His Noodly Appendage."

Henderson insisted on the way to teach his creed. "It is disrespectful to teach our beliefs without wearing His chosen outfit, which of course, is full pirate regalia." Henderson even included a sketch of his deity: a creature with antennae and tentacles made of noodles extending from a body made of more noodles, plus two meatballs.[30]

Henderson's joke didn't change the Kansas board's decision, but it became a favorite among unbelievers:

In 2007, North Buncombe High School in Weaverville, North Carolina, suspended student Bryan Killian for coming to school bearing the Pastafarian pirate accessories of eye patch and inflatable cutlass.[31]

In 2008, artist Ariel Safdie erected a sculpture of the Flying Spaghetti Monster on the county courthouse lawn in Crossville, Tennessee. The sculpture stood more than six feet tall, and its base included the blessing "May You Be Touched By Its Noodley Appendage."[32]

In 2011, Austrian businessman Niko Alm won the right to have his driver's license picture feature him wearing a spaghetti strainer, which he claimed was Pastafarian religious headgear.[33]

Now let us close this sermon on the Flying Spaghetti Monster with a hearty "Amen."

Or, as Pastafarians say, "Ramen."

Atheist Churches

If Buddhism and Unitarian Universalism are too religious for you, you can find atheist congregations that offer many of the activities of theist churches without any of the gods. Here are some examples:

The Ethical Humanist Society of Chicago doesn't sound like the name of a church, but this "democratic fellowship and spiritual home for those who seek a rational, compassionate philosophy of life without regard to belief or nonbelief in a supreme being"[34] includes Sunday-morning gatherings and conducts weddings, memorial services, and baby namings.

The New York Society of Ethical Culture offers a full range of ceremonies plus a book group, exercise classes, lunchtime discussions, and other activities. For young members, it offers the Teen Ethical Leadership Program.[35]

The North Texas Church of Freethought, near Dallas, says that its Sunday services "are the largest regular gathering of Freethinkers in the Southwest." For kids and teenagers, the church offers classes in the intellectual heritage of freethinking.[36]

In Sacramento, California, the First Atheist Church of True Science (FACTS) recommends spiritual rituals such as gazing up at the new moon to reflect on the majesty of the universe. FACTS encourages members to dress in "church garb" (joyous but inexpensive costumes and headgear) and enjoy the FACTS libation—a "freethink drink" made of milk, bananas, ice cream, and broken pastries. There's even a FACTS hymn, which praises questioning and skepticism.[37]

The United States doesn't have a lock on secular churches. In Calgary, Alberta (Canada), the Calgary Secular Church offers monthly meetings for unbelievers "to share stories; to enjoy beautiful music; to have their children get excellent ethical and rational instruction; to be enlightened; and most importantly, to know they are not alone!"[38]

And London, England, has the Sunday Assembly. Founded by comedians Sanderson Jones and Pippa Evans, the Assembly's services include songs, readings, and guest speakers.[39] The church's first service, on January 6, 2013, drew atheists and journalists from both England and America.

Your Own Way

What if you want to make your own religious path?

As you know by now, unbelief sets down no laws about creating beliefs, inventing rituals, or simply being spiritual. But be careful not to spook your parents and other people who could restrict your freedom. If you feel that the best way to feed your soul is to climb up on the roof and shriek obscenities, give the plan a second thought.

What if you get carried away with inspiration and actually create your own religion?

You can expect atheists not to believe a word of it.

II.

LIFE AS AN ATHEIST

5

How Do You Become
an Atheist?

As teens, we shouldn't have the responsibility to have the whole religion question figured out. The important thing is that we at least spend time thinking about it, taking into account all sides of the argument.

CALEB, AGNOSTIC HIGH SCHOOL SENIOR, OREGON[1]

Teenage life is so carefree that becoming an atheist, agnostic, or other unbeliever is simplest during the teen years. If your parents practice a religion and want you to follow it, the transition to unbelief is especially easy.

Yeah, right.

Turning away from faith (also called *deconversion*) means grappling with hard, uncomfortable ideas. But the result is often a happy surprise.

Some teenage atheists suffer a single, painful event that pushes them to look beyond religion. Others are like nevadagrl435, a former Southern Baptist who looked back and said, "In my case it was a bunch of little things that led to me walking away."[2]

Can It Start at Birth?

Some young unbelievers reject religion immediately. As Hannah, a twenty-five-year-old unbeliever from Washington, DC, said, "I never 'became' an atheist. I had doubts since I was very young."[3] And a younger unbeliever was even more certain: "I knew church sucked since I was a kid. I knew it [to] be BS when religion school started. I was agnostic by [the] time I was 14, atheist by 18."[4]

"I always questioned God's existence," said a northern California college student who uses the screen name Forwhatiamworth. "When I was, like, eight years old my Bible study teacher told us that the beauty of the Lord was that a murderer could be saved by God and go to heaven. I was WHAT!!!????' Maybe I might get some crap for this, but if you are a serial rapist/murderer, you will not go to 'heaven.'"[5]

Tom, a teenage unbeliever in New Jersey, has probably the most straightforward summary of the shortcut to disbelief: "Religion just never made sense to me. It's that simple."[6]

Guilt and Shame

Most teenagers aren't so quick to embrace godlessness. They walk a long road to get there, and the process sometimes starts with shame and guilt. "I just remember thinking things [during church services] such as 'This is stupid, I don't want to be here,' and then immediately feeling guilty and repenting: 'God can hear my thoughts, so I shouldn't think that,'" said Elizabeth, age nineteen. "I realized I wasn't even safe within my own head. That realization really spurred me to examine my beliefs."[7]

One particularly strong strain of guilt comes when teenagers run into a religion's rules about love. "I was seventeen," said a young unbeliever who calls himself LS. "I had met one of the most amazing women it has ever been my privilege to know . . . . [But] I was becoming increasingly concerned with the fact that she was Mormon, whilst I was Catholic."

He tried to reason away his heartbreak: "Due to religion, we cannot marry . . . . God cannot care about our love, yet allow it to be destroyed in his name. [Therefore,] there is no God." LS admitted, "There are a number of logical leaps there which make me wonder if I was just looking for an excuse to dump the abusive religion I'd been raised with. But whatever flaws the argument may have, it freed me."[8]

Where there's love, there's usually sex, and that's another source of guilt. "Sophomore year [of college], I began to seriously struggle with my faith," said a young New York atheist with the screen name greylight. "It is when I first became sexually active. Not even with anyone, just began to masturbate. I felt like a sexual deviant. It was horrible how much shame this caused me. I would pray and ask for forgiveness and the strength to have self-control but inevitably end up doing it again. More doubts began, and the more I would pray for solace and guidance, [the more] I wouldn't receive anything."[9] These struggles were her first steps toward rejecting religion.

Boredom

Another common spur toward godlessness is plain, flat boredom. Meatball, from Manitoba, Canada, said, "I can remember being given a Bible by the Gideons at school (probably grade 1) and going home a bit confused. It claimed if I read a passage a day, I could go to heaven. I actually started reading it but stopped because it was boring as shit. I eventually settled into [an] agnostic mindset."[10]

Another source of boredom—and frustration—is church. "I used to cry and cry when I was forced to go to church and Sunday school, especially when I'd rather be out riding my bike," said twenty-three-year-old fleur.[11] Mark, from England, has similar memories: "My mother used to take my brother and I to church every Saturday evening. [We] were too young to have any moral objection to it, but we objected out of the sheer tedium of the mass . . . . By the time I reached fifteen, I was simply refusing to go."[12]

Thinking Hard about Religion

Quitting religion isn't just the result of suffering emotions like shame and boredom; it often comes from deep thought. University of Connecticut sociology professor Bradley Wright has surveyed Christians who left the faith and found that two-thirds of them cited "intellectual and theological concerns."[13] And according to Heather Downs of the University of Northern Colorado, who has studied college students who became atheists and agnostics, "Students consider the change carefully, and it is a significant part of their identity development and educational process."[14]

Said Michael, a fourteen-year-old unbeliever: "I was raised Catholic, and until about a week ago, I was a firm believer. But last week I began to think. And the more I thought, the more it didn't make sense. I'm pretty confident at this point that I don't believe in God, and I'm pretty sure that I'm an atheist."[15]

This process isn't limited to Christians. "I was a true believer in Islam until a few years back. That's when my critical thinking faculties started kicking in," said a young unbeliever who uses the screen name Rainer206. "What my parents taught me began to fall under close scrutiny, and after much thought and deliberation, I am at a point where I can make a proud declaration of disbelief in Islam."[16]

Bad News in the Bible

A young unbeliever named Troy said, "As I grew up and began acting on my curiosity to understand the world and the community where I live, I started to read the Bible and about the history of religion(s) in depth. I also noticed how religion controls and influences societies. I must say I was pretty disturbed and angry by what I saw."[17]

When Troy read the Bible, he was doing what plenty of other young doubters have done. As nevadagrl435 has said, "I sat at home and read my Bible. After reading it I found the thing to be full of it, and even worse, that not a single Christian I had ever met even lived according to the Bible. I called [my] church and formally had my membership removed."[18]

What bothers young doubters about the Bible? Steven, age fifteen, who blogs under the name Atothetheist, posted that when he read the book, "I read about many horrible things, from slavery, child abuse, genocide, etc., to take no thought for the morrow [Matthew 6:34]. It made me think in a . . . newer direction. By the time I was done with it, I was an atheist."[19]

These young unbelievers might agree with scientist and novelist Isaac Asimov: "Properly read, the Bible is the most potent force for atheism ever conceived."[20]

Inflexible Rules

I was an ardent little crusader for my Christ, believing everything the good Lord, the Bible, and every preacher with Jesus Christ on his lips said to me. But for some reason, I decided that I'd had enough, and began to wonder if what I believed was true.

Tom, 15-year-old atheist[21]

Another problem for young believers: Theists who impose harsh religious doctrine. "At the age of fourteen," said Joel, a nineteen-year-old from Maryland, "I started to attend church with the adults, and I started to listen to what the pastor said and did—and it shocked me . . . . God told him that unless the people repent, and the ministry is strengthened (with money), that an attack will hit America in three weeks exactly. And I was flabbergasted; if this is how one is supposed to worship a god, I wanted no part of it."[22]

Sometimes the doctrine comes as a personal attack. "[I was] sent to a private Christian school for eight years," said John, a twenty-one-year-old from Australia. "On repeated occasions at the school, I had my iPod confiscated and searched. Then I would be pulled into an office with the head of the school and be told that I will be going to hell because of the music I listen to."[23] This event helped John reject religion.

Cruelty and Suffering

Quite a few teenage unbelievers make their first break with religion over human suffering. As a young atheist who uses the screen name tranquildream said, "How ****ed up the world is made an impact on me not believing that there was some god watching over everything."[24]

"The inequality in the world was the first sign that turned me away from God," said a young unbeliever named Scarlett. "The Bible claims that 'we are all equal in the eyes of God.' So, if we're all equal, [why are we] not born equal? Why are some born just to suffer and others born to live well?"[25]

Sometimes, the boot that kicks a young believer toward unbelief is close and personal. Said Sabrina, another young unbeliever, "The defining moment was [when] my aunt and uncle passed away, leaving their young children truly traumatized and lonely without their parents. It's just so heartbreaking to see my cousins constantly mourn them. I completely lost faith then and there."[26]

Just as God permits suffering here and now, some religions say that he decrees even more of it after death. That doctrine troubles quite a few teenagers. "I could never imagine people going to a hell for all eternity for being either gay or 'sinning,'" said a fifteen-year-old atheist who uses the screen name Glass Child. "It makes me laugh because pretty much everything is sinning to begin with. I changed to atheist when I was thirteen, and it relaxed a lot of the ongoing mental torture I was dealing with. Ended up probably being one of the best decisions of my life."[27]

As Glass Child said, some faiths would ship lesbian, gay, bisexual, and transgender (LGBT) people to hell. Some young unbelievers have considerable sympathy for LGBTs, even when they themselves don't identify that way, possibly because they have similar problems: religions criticize them, and "coming out" to parents and friends can be agony. According to a young unbeliever from the site LiveJournal's *Atheist Teens' Journal* forum: "The main reason that I decided to become atheist (hadn't really thought about it before this incident) is that one of my close friends turned out to be a lesbian and explained how her Christian father hated her because of this, and I realized that I just couldn't be [in] a religion that was so biased and unaccepting."[28]

When God Ignores You

I thought if I prayed enough, had enough faith, that I could convince God to save [my atheist boyfriend] from an eternity of torture . . . . I felt like God was telling me I had to break up with him because he wasn't a believer. I couldn't do it—I was far too in love with him . . . . After looking at both sides evenly, I started to really begin to question if God was seriously real.

Sunflower (screen name), age 21, Australia[29]

Almost half of the ex-Christians that Bradley Wright surveyed at the University of Connecticut "expressed sentiments that in some way God had failed them . . . . God's perceived failure took various forms, most of which fall under the general heading of 'unanswered prayers.'"[30] For instance: "When I was fourteen, in 2009, my granny died suddenly. I prayed all day, hoping that 'god' would save her. But that didn't happen," said Austin, an unbeliever writing on the Atheist Nexus website. "I started searching online for the truth about 'God' and came across a few things that challenged my religious beliefs; so I become an agnostic."[31]

Sometimes, all that a young believer wants is God's presence. Kate, age eighteen and raised a Reformed Baptist, said that by thirteen, "I just didn't feel any sort of divine presence in my life, and realized I never had. My default reaction was to assume that something was wrong with me . . . that maybe I hadn't been predestined. Convinced I was going to hell, I prayed for God to just make me a Christian. I told him my heart was open and the holy spirit could waltz right in anytime. It was only when nothing happened that I began to wonder if there was actually anyone up there."[32]

When Theists Dislike Your Thoughts

When a young believer starts doubting God and religion, he or she may try to talk over the doubts with a religious leader or some other authority. That's often when more troubles begin. Professor Wright said that in his study of ex-Christians, nearly all of them mentioned "frustration with how their fellow Christians reacted to their doubts [about God]."[33]

"In my years of college, I was still in a small Christian group," said greylight, the New Yorker who found guilt (and godlessness) via masturbation. "I remember talking to the head person of the group and telling her my doubts about Christianity. I remember her looking at me with judging eyes."[34]

"I studied philosophy and eventually majored in it," said Paul, another ex-believer. "My youth pastor explicitly told me that I was wrong to study philosophy because the Bible gives the answers, not philosophy."[35]

Darius, a young Texan, said, "I tend to play devil's advocate, and there were many times when I would pose or argue a non-Christian viewpoint with [theist] friends, and the most intelligent answer was always 'only God knows' or 'we just have to have faith.' My mind had so many unanswered questions, and I couldn't understand how everyone could just brush them aside so easily."[36]

Trying On Other Ways

While my peers were succumbing to the brainwashing, turning
into carbon copies of their fundamentalist parents and each other,
I was reading, writing, developing the critical thinking skills

that I would later apply to religion.

Kate, age 18[37]

Once a believer starts doubting his or her beliefs, he or she will often look for new beliefs. "A thirst for knowledge and explanations was an important force in the deconversion experience," said Heather Downs in her study of former theists. "[They] spoke about needing Truth, using Reason as their emphasis, and relying on texts, great thinkers, and academic disciplines."[38]

Michele, a twenty-year-old Ohio unbeliever, is a typical example: "In intermediate and high school, I read about different faiths to see if there might be something more appealing away from dogma and anthropomorphic gods, particularly neopaganism and Eastern traditions. Nothing took. The more you know, the less it seems like one could be right when all sound wrong."[39]

AUTHORS AND AUTHORITIES

Voltaire and Thomas Paine became my mentors through
my teen years. I admired their courage, their nonconformity,
and their dedication to dispelling superstition.

Kate, age 18[40]

Some teenagers come to godlessness via arguments by atheist writers. One young ex-fundamentalist, weareg0d, has said, "It all started when I was in the school library with my friend. He pointed out a book to me and said that I should read it. The book was called *The God Delusion*, by Richard Dawkins. Knowing all too well that my parents would be outraged if they saw this book in our house, I buried it in the backyard. I would wake up at the crack of dawn every morning and read it until my parents woke up." He continued the process with other books on atheism. After a few weeks, "I began to regard the Bible as a work of fiction."[41]

Other young unbelievers take a path more modern than books. "When I was fifteen," said Scarlett, "I watched a documentary by Dawkins. In it he claims that when one person suffers from a delusion it's madness, but when many suffer from a delusion, it's a religion. This was the turning point [for me]—it made so much sense I couldn't deny it."[42]

The words of unbelievers such as Dawkins don't usually shatter the faith of people who are firmly devout. But if a believer is already questioning God's existence, atheist authors can transform vague doubts into firm convictions.

The Influence of Science

Most polls show that about 90 percent of the general public believes in a personal God; yet 93 percent of the members of the National Academy of Sciences do not. This suggests that there are few modes of thinking less congenial to religious faith than science is.

Sam Harris, atheist author[43]

Whether or not Harris is right, science has helped to turn many young believers into unbelievers. "I started reading about biology, anthropology, physics, and geography," said Troy, the young unbeliever who studied the Bible and the history of religion. "Suddenly, everything I wanted to know about human life, every other life form on the planet, and the planet itself made sense, and unlike my experience with religion, every question I had was tied to an answer—and then to further questions. I enjoyed the clarity and wonder of science so much that I saw no point [in] having a religion."[44]

One science that turns a lot of teenagers is evolutionary biology. Young ex-theist Atheist Anon said, "I remembered from Sunday school that God created the universe and that evolution was therefore false, so I was skeptical to the point of ignorance in biology classes that taught the subject. [A] close friend of mine, a born-and-raised atheist, got under my skin by explaining the basic tenets of the science that I so devoutly denied, and I was shaken by how much more sense it made than what I was raised on."[45]

Kay, an atheist college student in Illinois, said that when she studied evolution, "I started considering why we behave the ways that we do, and why we have certain physical capabilities but lack others. And on top of that, the utter imprecision that our bodies work with—we are such imperfect beings that it was difficult to believe that we were designed [by a god]."[46]

How Long Does It Take?

Some unbelievers go through a lot of the experiences in this chapter; some go through only one or two. But most of the time, turning from belief to unbelief is a long, slow process. A study of college students who changed from believers to unbelievers "reported their deconversion experiences lasting from eight months to six years, with an average time of three and a half years."[47]

And once you come to the end of that period—well, that's when some really hard work begins.

6

How Will Becoming an Atheist Change You?

Were I to declare myself an atheist, what would this mean?
Would my life have to change? Would it become my moral obligation
to be uncompromising toward fence-sitting friends? That person at
dinner, pissing people off with his arrogance, his disrespect,
his intellectual scorn—would that be me?

GARY WOLF, JOURNALIST[1]

So you've quit theism. Now what?

There's a good chance that you'll feel happy. Researcher Heather Downs has said that the college-age ex-theists she's interviewed "speak about being happier now without Christianity and 'never going back.'"[2]

"While my family, friends, and teachers look upon my choice [to be an unbeliever] as questionable," said Thomas, a high school student in Alberta, Canada, "I have never in my life felt better about myself."[3]

Feeling Grief for Belief

I became an agnostic today . . . . I actually can't believe I did. I honestly feel like I've lost my mind . . . maybe because I'm intimidated by this unexpected worldview change . . . . I never thought I would come to this point in my life.

Peregrinus (screen name), age 17, California[+]

And now, the bad news. Before you get to the happiness that often comes with giving up religion, you may have to pass through a lot of pain.

Becoming godless can hurt like losing someone you love. "I remember crying on multiple occasions because I literally felt nothing for this faith I had for the majority of my life. I felt like I was mourning something," said greylight, the young unbeliever from New York mentioned in the last chapter.[5] And Downs said that most of the ex-theists in her survey of college-age deconverts have suffered "sadness, depression, confusion, stress, and physical angst."[6]

Just as someone who loses a loved one will yearn for that person to come back, someone who loses God may want him back too. "I *wanted* God to exist, very badly," said Charizard, a young unbeliever from Michigan. "I would beg and plead 'God, if you exist—please tell me! Show me! Give me *anything*.' I wanted that moral authority to exist, to bring some kind of order to the chaos of existence."[7]

Chaos can be confusing. "I couldn't trust myself or anything, because what I had believed was true with all my heart turned out to be one big illusion," said greylight.[8] Downs quoted one unbeliever: "'I didn't know what to believe anymore.'"[9]

Even if you can leave your old beliefs behind easily, you may still have trouble digesting your new beliefs. "Accepting that the universe doesn't care about you and that humanity is a dust speck is tough," said

David, a twenty-year-old in Massachusetts, about his deconversion at age fourteen.[10]

A Bitter Breakup

Like losing a loved one, losing a belief can be infuriating as well as saddening. University of Connecticut sociology professor Bradley Wright's study of deconversion stories said, "These accounts speak of a broken relationship with God as one might talk about a marital divorce. They are emotional, bitter at times."[11]

Many ex-theists seem angrier at religion than at God. "Spending most of my life with blinders on in the church has really left me with a feeling of being robbed," said a young atheist who calls himself J.[12]

For many former theists, the anger eventually evaporates, although the memories don't. "[At] the age of fifteen, I managed to detach from [my church] and first I was full of hatred, but after some time, I kinda managed to find my own way and my own [beliefs]," said a German unbeliever in his early twenties who calls himself freud. "But the dogmas which they imprinted into my mind and the traumatic experiences will probably never fade."[13]

A Lonely Life

Yet another problem is loneliness. *Boston Globe* journalist Eric Gorski has reported, "Young people who leave organized religion miss something: a sense of community."[14]

A fifteen-year-old going by spikedhair95 would probably agree: "Man, there's just so much frustration with my new life [as an atheist]. Especially when you live in a town full of idiots. Every time I tell someone I'm an atheist at school, they give me a dirty look or act so shocked."[15]

If you feel lonely or alienated too, check this book's appendix and its resources for finding other unbelievers.

MAINTAINING THE OLD WAYS

Changing your viewpoint on God and religion doesn't automatically change your habits. "Several months after my deconversion," said a young unbeliever who uses the screen name Adept, "I'd kneel down and pray before getting into bed, only realizing what I had done about twenty minutes later."[16] A music-loving unbeliever from Tennessee, like WOAH its Mia!, said that she still loves Christian rock. "I can go and rock out, even raise my hands during the 'worship' part. . . . I felt united with my fellow young adults just rocking out and appreciating the music."[17]

Keeping up theist-style activities may seem hypocritical, but it can ease a painful transition into a new way of life by letting you hold on to experiences that you've always liked from your theist days. It's like bringing a comforting childhood teddy bear with you when you leave home for college. As a college-age Texas atheist with the screen name longhorn_fraz said, "Why can't I celebrate Christian holidays, occasionally go to church, and respect a few Christian religious conventions, not because I actually believe in any of it but because it is part of who I am."[18]

And, of course, you can revisit your old ways for other purposes. A young unbeliever with a screen name of ChadOnSunday has even gone to church: "I actually enjoyed church more as an atheist. When you're a theist, church is long and boring and serious. When you're an atheist, it's like free standup comedy."[19]

Freedom of the Mind

The best part of being an atheist is the freedom. As a Christian, I was always worried about my deeds, asking, "Is this going to land me in

hell?" As an atheist, I don't have to worry about that. I just do what
my own moral compass tells me to do, and that's good enough.

Dylan, age 18, Arkansas[20]

The most common reactions to deconverting are relief and a feeling of liberation.

"Previously, my way of controlling [my feelings about God] had been to pray all the time, which put the responsibility on me. But after I just began to let it go and stopped always praying," said Sunflower, the twenty-one-year-old Australian quoted in the last chapter, "I didn't have to feel responsible anymore. There was no hell, no God. Everything was so much simpler."[21]

Fez, a nineteen-year-old Washingtonian, felt the change in his body. "I remember the day I finally told myself 'I'm atheist.' It was like a huge weight was lifted off my shoulders."[22]

John, age twenty-one and from Australia, found a whole list of new pleasures. "[I like] not having to worry about 'being born with sin' and all the repercussions that go with leading a normal human life. Not having to feel guilty for being happy in life. Not having to worry about pleasing someone else."[23]

Some joys of freedom are more down-to-earth. Said Alex, a seventeen-year-old from Georgia: "Well, I get to sleep in now on Sundays."[24]

Life without an Afterlife

Many ex-believers find that they're particularly happy about something that sounds unhappy: death without an afterlife.

Mark, the English unbeliever first quoted in the previous chapter, said that "the notion that my life is so fragile and it could all end in a heartbeat" has given him "renewed vigor in my life, a greater focus on my life's goals and the relationships I strike up with people."[25] John, the twenty-one-year-old Aussie, agreed: "I'm not living this life preparing for the next, wasting it all away. I live life to the max because you only get one chance, then it's over."[26]

Finding Meaning in a Godless Life

"Although Christianity is supposed to provide all this meaning for your life and all this fulfillment, I was finding more fulfillment and more meaning in other things. Basically I was realizing that there were a lot more answers in this other [unreligious] framework that I was building for myself."[27] That's from an unbeliever in Heather Downs' survey of college-age deconverts. Other young ex-theists feel the same way: "I like the feeling of being responsible for your actions," said Matthew, a twenty-year-old from Australia. "[Since] you cannot blame Satan or a divine plan . . . being an atheist really forces you to think about life more existentially. You ask questions like 'What meaning can I make my life have?' 'What is the good thing to do?'"[28]

Some young ex-theists find a kind of meaning that you could call spiritual. "After I deconverted," said a young Arkansan who goes by the screen name The Sanhedrin, "I found a new respect for life and humanity like I had never had before, and it felt good."[29] Vanessa, a college student in New York, said, "I feel like a more ethical, rational, tolerant, and loving person now that I no longer believe in God."[30] (You can find more on this subject in chapter 15.)

Will You Be Happy?

Like any big change, deconverting brings a messy mix of feelings. Quitting religion has delighted and liberated plenty of teenagers and other people, but you can't depend on it to free you from your worries as automatically as aspirin frees you from a headache.

So what will happen to you? Aidan, a girl who's said that becoming an atheist profoundly affected her spirit, has thought deeply about the power of going godless: "It's never determined my happiness," she said. "But it widened the scope of my mind."[31]

7

What If You Were Raised an Atheist?

My parents are both nonreligious and only make veiled references to God along the lines of "I thank God every day that we have such a wonderful daughter." I'm not tooting my own horn, my father has actually made such a statement. Of course, I'm quick to quip up and remind him that there is no God.

AIDAN, AGE 18, CANADA[1]

Some atheist teenagers never quit religion; they never had one to quit at all. Their parents have allowed them—or encouraged them—to grow up as atheists or agnostics.

Unbelievers are a minority, and people who were raised as unbelievers are a minority within a minority. *The American Religious Identification Survey* says that nearly three-quarters (73 percent) of all adult nontheists had parents who believed in at least one religion. Only one in six (17 percent) of the godless had nontheistic parents.[2]

What's it like to grow up in this rare environment?

What Do They Unbelieve?

My parents never told me "there is no God" and stuff like that.
They let me make my own choice.

Vitharr (screen name), a young unbeliever[3]

Just as there are different kinds of unbelievers (atheists, agnostics, humanists, you know the list), there are a variety of unbeliever parents and families.

Gralian, from the United Kingdom, said that his mom and dad were flatly antifaith. "Any possible belief or hope I may have had in a god as a small child was emphatically crushed by my parents. [There was] my father who only thinks with pure logic stating that such a concept is ridiculous and my mother simply not caring for religion, period."[4]

By contrast, the parents of twenty-one-year-old Mary, from Ontario, Canada, kept up a veneer of religion. "Nominally, we're all Buddhist, but this doesn't come up until a funeral or something. Since I also grew up in a more rural community, we didn't attend temple either, so most of the at-home 'religious' activities were treated as traditional 'respect for your ancestors' activities. For example, we have a small shrine, for luck. Underneath that shrine, we keep photos of my deceased grandparents, and on traditional days or the anniversary of their deaths, we burn incense for them, but for us it is all about remembrance rather than anything else."[5]

Eliane, another young unbeliever, had a different experience. "I was raised atheist and I still am . . . . though my parents believe that [spirituality] is important and that there are things that can't be explain[ed] just by science. But I don't consider them agnostic since they never really talked about a 'god' but more about a way to live your life with spirituality."[6]

Often, godless parents simply ignore religion. "My parents, both atheists, . . . never outwardly rejected religion, nor did they present me and my brother with various options to choose from," said Stephanie, an unbeliever from New York. "Religion was just absent from my child-hood altogether."[7]

Faithless Families, Part I:
The Atheist Andersons vs. the Religious Rapper

When your parents are as godless as you, they might be ready to fight for your faithlessness.

On September 1, 2011, New Heights Middle School, near the rural town of Jefferson, South Carolina, staged a religious revival in the gym. Rapper B-SHOC (real name Bryan Edmonds), whose songs include "The Jesus in Me" and "Crazy Bout God," filled the room with fog, lights, and hard beats. Youth minister Christian Chapman urged the kids: "A relationship with Jesus is what you need more than anything else." And a Christian group called Bridging the Gap Ministries asked students to fill out a form saying that they had accepted Jesus as their savior. At the end of the day, B-SHOC said that "324 kids at this school have made a decision for Jesus Christ."[8]

Eighth grader Jordan Anderson wasn't one of them. An atheist, he didn't want to go to the assembly. But, he said, "If I didn't go, I would have to go to the in-school suspension room. It seemed like I was being punished just because I did not want [to] attend a religious event. So, I went to the rally."[9]

Jordan's parents were as godless as their son. They went to the American Civil Liberties Union (ACLU), which defends freedom of (and from) religion. On December 5, the ACLU sued the school district for "violations of civil rights under the First and Fourteenth Amendments to the United States Constitution."[10]

And they were able to get the school to back down. The school district and the ACLU settled the case out of court. In the settlement, the district agreed to stop religious activities.[11]

But Jordan's troubles didn't end. He's said that students have teased, bullied, and threatened him and that his teachers punished him for behavior that they ignored in other students. And his father, who owned a landscape-design company, stopped getting customers and couldn't even get a job working for other firms. "I've been told straight up it's because of my religious views," he said.[12]

"Being branded as outcasts and unwelcome in your community . . . is a steep price to pay in the name of religious freedom," said Heather Weaver, an ACLU lawyer specializing in religion. "Jordan and his family deserve better."[13]

Learning about Religion

"I was exposed at a very young age to church. We never actually attended a Sunday service, but I went to a Bible day camp," said Reilly, the thirteen-year-old son of a blogger who runs *Blessed Atheist*, an online Bible-study group for unbelievers. "Now one thing I must get straight is that my parents are just as atheistic as I am. However, I didn't find that out until I was seven. I think that they wanted to let me make my own choice and expose me to everything."[14]

If unbelieving parents don't expose their kids to religion, other relatives may take up the job. "My mother's parents are Baptist, and I recall that they sent my sister and me a children's Bible that I read cover to cover when I was about six," said Jeannette, from Tennessee. "To me, it was just another story book."[15]

What happens if exposure to religion leads the offspring of atheists to go religious? The parents don't like it, but they usually don't show as much panic and fury as some hardcore religious parents who discover that their kid has gone godless. "Before I turned thirteen, I was convinced I wanted to be a Christian and begged my mother to buy me a gold cross to represent my new-found faith," said eighteen-year-old Aidan. "Then, when those beliefs faded, my parents understood I was just trying to find truth in a world filled with questions."[16]

Faithless Families, Part II:
Slam-Dunking the Lord's Prayer

Hardesty, Oklahoma, is a tiny town (population about 220)[17] with a tiny high school. The entire student body, ninth through twelfth grades, numbers under forty.[18] But as the school system's website says, "The school is the life of the Town of Hardesty. It is the town center. It is the focus of the people."[19]

Nicole Smalkowski was one of Hardesty High's best athletes. In November 2004, Nicole and the other members of the Hardesty girls basketball team had just finished the season's first game when, according to Nicole, the coach gathered her and the other girls to recite the Lord's Prayer. Nicole, an atheist, refused.

Soon thereafter, Nicole said, the coach kicked her off the team.[20] What's more, "[My schoolmates] would call me 'devil worshipper.' I'd walk down the halls, people would laugh at me." Even teachers harassed her, she's said.[21]

Fortunately, Nicole had defenders: her parents. Unbelievers themselves, they teamed up with the faithless group American Atheists to sue the Hardesty school system.

Eventually, Nicole and her family settled out of court with the Hardesty schools.[22] The terms of the settlement are secret. But one thing is obvious: Nicole was not someone to mess with, either on a basketball court or in a court of law.

Life in the Minority

It's not easy being one of the few teenagers growing up without religion—particularly among classmates. "I had never met anyone who approached religion like my family did," said a young Michigan unbeliever who uses the screen name fibonaccimathgenius. "When my peers would talk about [a] church group or similar activities, I would just quietly blend in with the nearest wall and try to look like I had some inkling of what they were talking about."[23]

"When I was a kid, even though there was absolutely no religion in my house, I was constantly bombarded with it [elsewhere]," said Christine, age twenty-three, from Ontario. "I remember once having an assembly [at school] where they were trying to give us the New Testament. Even then I didn't want it. I remember being the only one in my class that said no, and the people around me were surprised."[24]

Some theist kids can't understand that a classmate has no faith. "In grade school, I would see the Catholic girls and boys talking about their CCD classes (Catholic education before confirmation / first communion)," said Noah, age fifteen, from New Jersey. "Inevitably, one of them would turn to me and say, 'What church do you go to?' My response, a seemingly innocent 'I don't go to one,' brought about a wide array of responses. Everything from the expected eyebrow raise or confused look to a more aggressive 'but you have to go to church,' or the more childish response: 'So are you Jewish?' As a child, this confused me more than anything. I wasn't Jewish and I wasn't Catholic (the only religious demographics that existed in my area), so what was I?"[25]

Being the focus of curiosity can be distressing, but it's easier to handle than another common reaction: hostility.

"Somehow, students discovered my beliefs or lack thereof, and treat me like a freak," said Megan, who's only twelve. "I have lost popularity, and feel that students pick on me in other ways because of the topic. It has caused depression."[26] And a young unbeliever named Karen has said, "It took me until I was an adult to develop the language skills required to defend myself from the attacks of the faithful (everything from 'how could you not love Jesus?' to 'you and your family are all going to hell')."[27]

How you handle being in the minority depends largely on your attitude. "I never found a good way of coping with the fact that my friends and neighbors all believed something different than I did," Karen confessed. "The best I managed was a sort of 'I know that Santa's not real, but I don't want to spoil it for the other dumb kids who haven't figured it out yet' sort of smugness."[28]

Fortunately, some nontheists have it easier than Karen. According to Christopher, an eighteen-year-old from Georgia, "There were very few times when I knew that I was in a minority. Several of my friends attended church, but they did not actively talk of it or of Jesus."[29] And Reilly, the thirteen-year-old son of a proud atheist blogger, said, "All of my friends know that I am an atheist. It would seem like this would be something you would tread lightly on, but no, it's actually a bit of a joke to us. We point out ironic moments, like when we play Clue and I get stuck as the Reverend."[30]

THE ALWAYS ATHEIST AND THE EX-THEISTS

Even among the godless, I feel out of touch.

Stephanie, a New York atheist[31]

Stephanie was talking about being raised atheist when most unbelievers seem to have started out with religion and then endured the sometimes painful process of rejecting it:

"I find little identity in the conventional Atheist community in its current form because most of them are people who were raised Christian and then proceeded to have a moment of personal awakening, and then became Atheist," said a Michigan unbeliever with the screen name nakile. "These individuals almost always explicitly hate the religion from which they came, which in the US tends to be Christianity. [But] I just don't share the feeling. For the longest time, I refused to even call myself an Atheist as to not be associated with them."[32]

People raised without religion may not feel so alienated for long, though. As the number of unbelievers grows, the number of those who grow up atheist may grow too.

Faithless Families, Part III: Speaking Out against Silence

Dawn Sherman and her father, Rob, are atheists. In the fall of 2007, Dawn was a fourteen-year-old high school freshman in the Chicago suburb of Buffalo Grove. On October 11, the Illinois General Assembly passed Public Act 095-0680, which required every public school class to "observe a brief period of silence with the participation of all the pupils therein assembled at the opening of every school day."[33] Although the law added, "This period shall not be conducted as a religious exercise," it also said, "[This period] shall be an opportunity for silent prayer or for silent reflection on the anticipated activities of the day."[34]

Dawn and Rob didn't like the law. On October 26, they sued Illinois's governor and the school district for injecting religion into public schools. "People shouldn't be stopping my education for prayer that they could be doing any time in the eighteen hours they have the rest of the day," Dawn declared.[35]

The reaction got nasty. State representative Monique Davis yelled at Rob, "It's dangerous for our children to even know that your philosophy exists! . . . You have no right to be here! We believe in something. You believe in destroying!"[36]

The Shermans' won their case in the lower court, but it was reversed on appeal. Finally, they petitioned to be heard by the the United States Supreme Court. But in October 2011, the Court decided that it wouldn't consider the case.[37]

The Supreme Court's refusal meant that Illinois could (and would) keep imposing a moment of silence.[38]

By that time, though, Dawn had graduated. She would never again have to stand for a moment of silence in a public school.

Born Free

Even though people can react badly to someone from an unbeliever family, most teenagers who've grown up that way seem to feel that their families have done right by them. The stories of teenagers who have been godless from birth don't boil with the "my parents drive me nuts" attitude that sometimes erupts among unbelievers whose parents pulled them into religion.

And that may be the best legacy of being raised without religion.

8

Should You Tell?

My family says that God is real, but I do not. I want to be able to tell
my family who I really am, but I am afraid of them doing put-downs
on me and rejecting me based on what I believe. I want them
to understand and be able to accept what I believe.

ISIAH, AGE 13[1]

Deciding whether or not to tell people—particularly if they're religious—can be like SCUBA diving toward an unknown shoreline. Will the people there welcome you or attack? If you're predicting an attack, can you expect to get through it safely, or would you rather hide out year after year, working every minute to ensure that no one detects you?

Why You Should Speak Out

My mom is [one of] those type of hypocrite "religious" persons, but I
respect her . . . . I want to tell her that I'm atheist, out of respect.

Because the more I fake the prayers and stuff, I feel guilty—because
I feel like I'm being a hypocrite and disrespecting her religion.

Sgokills (screen name), age 15[2]

A lot of young unbelievers feel like Sgokills. They all want to speak out, and each has his or her own reasons.

Take a fifteen-year-old unbeliever from Ireland who calls himself RHRN. "I . . . hate having to go through the motions when my family goes to mass and having to say prayers to a god I don't believe in, and accept sacraments in a religion I don't really follow."[3]

Other teenagers face the agony of staying quiet when they want to speak up. Said Darius, a Texan in his early twenties, "Living in the era of Facebook, it can be a bit unnerving to see so many religious comments posted and not feel the desire to have my viewpoint represented as well."[4]

And sometimes the reasons for speaking out have nothing to do with such lofty issues as honesty and forthrightness. "I'm tired of not being able to be out late because I have CHURCH! in the morning," griped Nathan, a nineteen-year-old unbeliever, "and missing out with friends because I have to go make 'friends' (it really just involves me sitting in the back, away from everybody, thinking about what I'm going to do when I finally get out) with the church teenagers."[5]

Freeing yourself from these pressures can be wonderful. The blogger Teen Atheist was originally scared to come out of the closet. "Let me tell you, though, it's *very* liberating to be open about your beliefs."[6]

Why You Shouldn't Speak Out

Day after day you sit in class, and your secret sleeps silently
below the surface. You hear classmates discussing their lifestyles
comfortably; their way is the societal norm. You can't help but feel
like an outsider, and you doubt the time will ever be right to speak

your mind. You fear that your parents will weep in shame, your pastor will rally the congregation against you, and, above all, you fear your friends will alienate you.

Childrenof Sodom (screen name), high school student [7]

Let's go back to Nathan, the guy who wanted to stay out late rather than go to church. Why didn't he just tell his parents that he was quitting religion? "I would love to not get beaten within an inch of my life, kicked out, or disowned," he said.[8]

The fear of bad parental reaction is a key reason to consider not telling the world that you're an unbeliever. "Of all the classes of problems in the letters I get for 'Ask Richard'," said Richard Wade, an advice columnist for young unbelievers, "by far the most common is high school or college students having to keep their atheism a secret from their parents, or suffering awful consequences because they have told them."[9]

A common consequence is emotional pain. "My mom loves me with all of her heart whether I am Atheist, [Agnostic], Muslim, or Jewish," wrote Kawaiigurl1234. She's thought about revealing her atheism to her mom, a full-fledged theist—but, she said, "I think it will do nothing but stress her out."[10]

Some young unbelievers fear that a stressed-out parent might fire back with criticism or worse. "My parents would not approve and would be very disappointed in me," said Emily, age nineteen, from Rhode Island. "I can imagine my father saying I'm a revolting teen, going against society for the sake of doing so. I can picture them shaking their heads belittlingly, muttering that I'll get over it in time, when I grow up."[11]

Some parents might do more than simply disapprove; they might cut off funds or impose religious discipline. "I'm a freshman in college and dependent financially on my parents," said an ex-Muslim unbeliever with the screen name Godless. "If I tell them [I'm an atheist], they could do anything from disowning me to forcing me to live at home, to sending me to India to attend some sort of religious camp."[12]

And some parents might take even more extreme measures. Rainer206, a Somali American, said, "I haven't told my family. If I did, they'd probably try to kill me at worst or at the very least, try to get me to leave the country and return to the 'homeland' for some serious re-education. I probably will not tell them until I am fully independent of them, if ever."[13]

WAIT UNTIL SOMEDAY

Kawaiigurl1234, the teenager afraid of stressing out her mom by confessing her atheism, has decided to do it—but not yet. "The time isn't right. I mean, to her, I am just a kid and she might not take me seriously. But I know I can't keep this bottled inside me and never tell her. I want to tell my whole family someday. But today is not the day."[14]

Like Kawaiigurl1234, you might want to wait before telling your parents how you feel. James, in Virginia, said, "I've been putting off raising the issue, partly to allow enough time to pass that they probably wouldn't feel like they 'failed to raise me properly.'"[15]

Many young unbelievers wait until they're away at college to reveal their beliefs. Unless it's a Bible college, a university can be a good place to find nontheists who can give you emotional support if your family reacts badly. "Most of the people I was surrounded by [in college] were agnostic or atheist," said Kay, a young atheist in Illinois. "Now, it's almost amusing to me when I meet people who aren't."[16]

If you plan to wait before revealing your unbelief, be careful not to wait too long. "You might be able to keep it a secret for a while," said psychologist Diana Walcutt, "but sooner or later, there will be some kind of blowup [between you and others], and it will come out in a way that you *don't* want."[17]

The Subtle Approach

Some unbelievers don't hide their feelings about God and religion, but they don't go out of their way to declare them publicly either. They just drop hints. "I don't like identifying as an atheist," said Emily, the nineteen-year-old Rhode Islander who envisioned her father calling her revolting. "It's so much easier to simply tell people that you don't go to church and leave it at that."[18]

Some unbelievers use this indirect method to ease the way for announcing their atheism. "I didn't necessarily tell my mom right away," said Allison, a twenty-one-year-old in Oregon. "I just stopped going to church. This appeared normal, as I'd always tried to skip church by 'sleeping in' on Sundays."[19]

But the indirect method may be so subtle that some people may not realize that you're trying to tell them how you feel. Allison said that when she finally revealed her atheism, her mother was heartbroken.

Friends, Relatives, and Doctors

If you're thinking about revealing your unbelief, get advice from unbelievers who've already done it. If you don't know any, see this book's appendix for a list of unbeliever groups.

You can also go to other people you trust, whether they're unbelievers or not. "If you have a relative, teacher, or school counselor who you think would be supportive," said Susanne Werner of the American Humanist Association, "talking to him or her may be helpful."[20]

Psychologist Diana Walcutt, who specializes in anxiety, depression, and stress, suggested that a therapist can help you find the best way to tell people.[21] A school nurse or guidance counselor may be able to help you find a good therapist who will assist for free or for the minimal money that teenagers have on hand.

If you're particularly worried about telling certain individuals—for instance, your parents—try confiding in someone who knows them.

"Start with one person—whoever is the one you trust will be the most receptive, understanding, and discreet," said Richard Wade. "That person might be able to help you determine who, when, how, and if you should tell someone else."[22]

The Decision Maker

In the end, the only one who can decide what to do is *you.*

That's a big help, isn't it? But consider: the people whose reactions mean the most to you are probably the people you know best. So you're best equipped to predict how they'll react if you tell them your beliefs.

Think about how they usually respond to big news. If you broke a promise, showed them a lower-than-usual grade, or introduced them to a bad boyfriend or girlfriend, did they react reasonably? Or did they shout, weep, hit you, make harsh demands on you, or kick you out? If they shouted/wept/hit/demanded/kicked, did they eventually calm down, or did they stay upset?

And if they did any or all of those things, did those reactions hurt more than keeping your secrets hidden and feeling like a liar and hypocrite?

No one but you can decide.

9

How Do You Tell
Your Parents?

The sad thing about coming out for me is that I often act like
my atheism is something I have to apologize for. It's certainly not,
but I do often have to brace myself for the worst.

TEEN ATHEIST (SCREEN NAME), BLOGGER[1]

So you're going to tell Mom, Dad, or both that you're an unbeliever.
You've imagined how they will respond, you've examined your own
needs and feelings, and you've talked over the situation with someone
else you trust.

What's the safest way to spill the news?

Preparing, Part I:
Get Ready, Get Set . . .

You can start by preparing your parents slowly, step by step. Lori
Howard, president of Idaho Atheists, has said that her most important

advice to young unbelievers is "to take their time and not make hasty decisions."[2]

"As far as family goes, my deconversion happened gradually but openly," said a young unbeliever named Matt. "When I questioned doctrine or the Bible or the pastor, they were there. As I came to various conclusions on the road to nonbelief (for example, that the Bible is clearly not literally true), I shared these conclusions with them. By the time I left Christianity, they knew exactly why and how. They wish I was still a believer, but they know why I'm not and respect it."[3]

While you're getting the family used to your viewpoint, you can also prepare for your life after the announcement. If you're worried that your parents might throw you out of the house:

▶ Reach out to trusted relatives and friends to see if you can stay with any of them.

▶ Look online for nearby shelters that accept runaway teenagers. (This book's appendix lists a few sources of information.)

▶ Build up your savings. "I came out to my parents after I was eighteen," said Nicole, age twenty, from Virginia, "specifically after my savings account had been set up in my name and was no longer controlled by my mother."[4]

Preparing, Part II:
The Facts Shall Set You Free

Accumulate lots of ammunition. In the case of freethinkers,
agnostics, and atheists, the ammunition is knowledge.

Blair Scott, board member, American Atheists[5]

"Be prepared for the possibility of some relatives trying to give you arguments for why you should continue believing," said Austin Cline. He has been the expert on atheism and agnosticism for About.com, and he underwent his own deconversion in college.[6]

When it comes to arguments for religion and against atheism, said Cline, "you needn't be able to thoroughly refute them all, especially at the time of your announcement, but it would be good if you could demonstrate that these arguments aren't rock solid and that doubt about them is reasonable. In doing so, you can establish that not believing is itself reasonable and that you aren't being perverse or rebellious."[7]

Later chapters of this book detail some useful counterarguments.

Preparing, Part III:
The Time and the Place

Ever been sent to the principal's office? Then you know how just being in the right (or wrong) place can make you feel nervous. And if you've ever been rushed to do anything, you know that doing things hastily can lead to mistakes.

To tell your parents about your unbelief, pick a place where they feel comfortable and secure. Chris Jarvis, an atheist and an expert negotiator (he works as a sales manager), added that it should be a spot where "you will have [their] full attention."[8]

Consider getting your parents out of the house. "Ask them to meet you at a coffee shop or in the student union. Semipublic places often help everyone keep control of their emotions," said atheist psychologist Darrel Ray, an expert on deconversion.[9] Jarvis added, "Sometimes a car journey is a good place to do this, or a long dog walk or a fishing trip. Somewhere where the other person can't immediately call on reinforcements ('You wait while I get your Father!') or shut down the conversation."[10]

As for scheduling, think about when your parents are most receptive. "Do not start such an important conversation in the kitchen while Mom or Dad is doing something else," said Ray.[11] If Dad's grumpy in the morning but mellow after a big dinner, or if Mom is rushed and busy Monday through Friday but relaxed during the weekend, schedule your talk accordingly.

In addition, Jarvis said, "[Budget] enough time to have a discussion, and also [enough time] for the other person to cool down and assimilate what you have told them."[12] Many young atheists and agnostics have reported that the "I'm an unbeliever" talk can last well over an hour.

THE POWER OF CALM

If dealing with your parents upsets you, it's best to keep in control. "You don't want to look nervous and uncertain," said About.com's Austin Cline. "That only opens the door for your family not taking your atheism too seriously."[13]

Just as bad as nervousness is anger. "Do *not* lose your temper," said psychologist Diana Walcutt. "No matter how you present [your unbelief], they won't be happy, but neither will you if it comes out in a big fight."[14]

To replace anger and anxiety with calm and confidence, do something that you already do constantly: breathe. Here is a typical method for relaxing yourself:

1. Sit comfortably.

2. Inhale slowly through your nose for four or five seconds, letting your belly fill with air.

3. Exhale slowly through your mouth. The exhaling should take at least as long as the inhaling—longer, if possible.

4. That's one breathing cycle. Repeat it at least three more times.

5. If you make it to ten cycles, you should be noticeably more relaxed than you were when you started.[15]

You can also replace negative emotions by editing your thoughts. Angry thoughts can make you angrier; nervous thoughts can make you more nervous. Here's how to handle them.

1. Watch yourself. Keep track of the triggers—the comments, situations, or experiences—that push you into worry or fury. If you know the triggers, you can probably avoid them, ignore them, or overcome them.

2. When you notice yourself having negative thoughts, stop them. You can argue with the thoughts (*Aw, c'mon, Dad's not literally going to kill me*), interrupt them (*Dammit, Mom—whoops, I better stop there*), or block them (*Okay, self, control yourself*).

3. Insert positive thoughts: *Nah, Dad won't kill me. He'll be pissed, but he's been pissed before, and I've survived—and this time, I'm ready for him.*

4. Focus on your goal—to reveal your unbelief as painlessly as possible. The more that you think about what you have to say and how you'll say it, the less you'll focus on things that scare or enrage you.[16]

Another way to keep yourself in control combines deep breathing and positive thinking: meditation. Many (or even most) types of meditation require you to set aside your worries and irritations and insert calming thoughts.

Exercise can be useful too. "Many people find physical activity helps burn up some of that [teenage] stress," says the Women's and Children's Health Network Teen Health website.[17] Tai chi and yoga are known to be especially good at pulling people toward calm and confidence.

Telling, Part I:
Getting an Ally

The last chapter recommended asking a friend, relative, or counselor when and if you should reveal your atheism. Your ally can also come with you when you reveal it. "Having a go-between often is very helpful in sensitive issues like this," said Diana Walcutt.[18] "Once you have one person inside, then get them to do the work with the others," added Chris Jarvis, the sales manager and negotiator. "Let them become your spokesperson, your defender."[19]

This ally may even be—surprise!—one of your parents. It's often best to come out to one at a time. If you approach both simultaneously, "fearful religious parents will feed off of one another's fear, and soon you will be overwhelmed and feel like they are ganging up on you," said Darrel Ray.[20]

Instead, said Jarvis, "if your Dad is likely to explode, get your Mum on [your] side. She'll know how to deal with him, and the reverse if it's your dad you've 'come out' to."[21]

Telling, Part II:
Using Honor and Respect

You want your parents to accept your ideas on God and religion. If Mom and Dad were to belittle you, you'd probably be upset, and you wouldn't want to listen to anything that they'd say.

So don't attack their religion, even if you hate it. Jarvis said, "If you set your worldview up as somehow superior to theirs, you're done for. Sides will be taken and war will break out."[22] Instead, "let them know that you love them and know that what you may say could be upsetting," said Ray. "Do not criticize their religion, just express your own ideas."[23]

There's an additional advantage to showing compassion and maturity. As About.com's Cline said, "In taking the high road, you will also be showing that being an atheist doesn't make you an immoral and rude person."[24]

Telling, Part III: The Terrible Word

"Finding out a relative is an atheist is like finding out
they committed suicide, but worse." Actual quote
from my family from today.

Malphael (screen name), age 27[25]

"Be careful about the word 'atheist,'" said Kelly Richardson, a therapist who works with teenagers.[26]

Advice columnist Richard Wade explained, "The 'A' word, 'atheist,' terrifies and enrages many otherwise calm and rational people. People have attached all sorts of silly, scary, and upsetting ideas to that word."[27]

Fortunately, Wade said, there are alternatives. "Saying, 'Mom, I don't really believe in God' might get a much milder reaction than 'Mom, I'm an atheist.'"[28] American Atheists board member Blair Scott added, "You can use 'friendly' terms like *freethinker* or *agnostic* instead of the dreaded 'A' word if you think that will help your family and friends deal with it."[29]

Improving Your Chances

When it comes to telling your parents about your unbelief, no method is guaranteed. Even if your parents' own priest, rabbi, minister, or imam were to approve your unbelief, some parents would still find it intolerable. The most that this chapter's advice can do is improve your chances of getting a sane, fair hearing.

So get ready, get set . . .

10

How Will Your Parents React?

I told my mom I was an atheist the same night I came out as bisexual . . . . I remember her being much more brokenhearted over my atheism than my alternative sexual orientation.

ALLY, AGE 21, OREGON[1]

The word is out! Your parents know that you don't believe in their religion. Things are going to get real.

The Wrath of God

What's the most common Mom/Dad reaction to the news that their kid is an unbeliever? It's probably anger. And it comes out in a variety of ways.

"My mom barely talks to me (she only yells at me for being an atheist now)," said Atothetheist on the *Thinking Atheist* online forums.[2] Nicole, a twenty-year-old from Virginia, also faced yelling—"Shouting matches

with my mother were more frequent than ever"—and more: "I was forbidden to identify as an atheist within the house."[3]

And other parents use other methods: "I was too old for corporal
punishment," said Joel, age nineteen, from Maryland (we first met him
back in chapter 5), "but that didn't stop the constant guilt trips and the
threats of God forsaking me."[4]

To Calm the Rage

If your parents get mad, keep in mind that you may have scared them,
hurt their feelings, or otherwise hit them where they're vulnerable.

Religion probably means a lot to your mom and dad, and they've put a
lot of care and work into making it mean a lot to you. Now you've turned
your back on it. If your folks believe that the godless are immoral or that
unbelief equals contempt for theists, they believe that godless world is
their enemy—and you've joined it. Your parents may assume that your
rejection of their lifelong guidance makes them bad parents. They may
even believe that you're going to hell.

No wonder they're upset, and no wonder they're attacking you. You're
the one who upset them.

To calm them, start by letting them rant. Teachers and other people
who deal with angry parents say that many a furious parent will calm
down only after saying everything on his or her mind—especially if
the person they're mad at seems willing to listen.[5] Don't roll your eyes,
cross your arms, or make any gesture or facial expression that looks
hostile.

And definitely don't interrupt. Nobody likes getting cut off in mid-
rant.

When Mom or Dad reaches a stopping point, you might ask if you can
go to the bathroom or get a drink of water—particularly if your parents'
anger is making you angry too. Anger-management experts say that
taking a break and walking away can calm down a fury.[6] While you're
out of the room, try the deep breathing or other relaxation exercises

from the last chapter. You'll help yourself, and your absence can give Mom and Dad time to cool off.

If your parents ask about your unbelief, answer honestly but not harshly. That can be a delicate tightrope to walk, especially if your attitude toward religion is honestly harsh. Still, try to phrase things in the kindest way possible—for instance, "I have a hard time agreeing with everything that the Bible says" rather than "The Bible's a lying crap sack."

Finally, remember your goal: to help your parents respect your viewpoint. So pay them the respect that you want them to give to you, and hear them out.

Tears

Sadness is another common parental reaction to the news that a teenager has gone godless.

"I finally told my mom [that I'm an atheist] a few days ago," said a young unbeliever named Mike. "[Today,] I came in and found my mom lying on the sofa crying. I told her that I was sorry that my choices made her feel that way but that it was my decision, and that I wasn't going to lie to the pastor and bishop. She hasn't stopped crying since. My dad came up to my room and told me that I had made a bad decision and lost the only person that loved me."[7]

Seth, another young atheist, ran into a similar experience: "I was about thirteen or fourteen when I told my parents I was an atheist. The reaction of my mother and what she said to me still hurts me today. After I told her she said, 'Seth, I should have raised you better and made you go to church more.' I had no idea what to say . . . . When I tell people I am an atheist at family functions . . . the room goes silent, with my mom sitting in a chair with her face in her hands."[8]

Michele, a twenty-year-old in Ohio, faced a response that was outwardly calmer but possibly more devastating. "My parents are Catholics in name only . . . [but] my mother has plainly stated she feels like a failure for raising a child without faith."[9]

Moving Past Tears

Sadness is tough to handle—maybe even tougher than anger, because a parent exploding in anger can seem strong, but a parent dropping tears seems wounded, and you did the wounding.

How can you help your parents lift the sadness away? Your parents may be willing to tolerate (or ignore) your viewpoint if you compromise here or there. You might promise not to argue religion with particularly devout relatives or family friends. A seventeen-year-old with the screen name bu2b said that he appeased his Mormon mom by agreeing to keep an open mind and talk to her church leaders about his unbelief.[10]

You might even go along with some of your parents' rituals. Said Deborah Mitchell, who writes the blog *Kids without Religion*, "I will still attend church with [my mother], but I will not participate as a believer, only as a person who respects other's traditions. I sit and stand on cue, but I do not say the prayers."[11]

Since your parents are already unhappy with you, don't give them a reason to get unhappier. "Keep your school grades up, diligently do your family duties and chores, and generally stay out of trouble," said Richard Wade. "You don't want your atheism being blamed for failures in such areas."[12]

Finally, give your parents time to heal. Now that you've told them about your godlessness, you don't have to say anything more about it unless they bring up the subject.

Beyond the First Conversation

My dad did not take the news too well . . . . He told me that it was silly and got quite angry/upset with me. [But] over the course of a few months, I had a lot of talks with him, and now he accepts my beliefs.

John, age 21, Australia [13]

"It might take [your parents] a while to be cool with who you are and what you believe," said therapist Kelly Richardson.[14] In the process, they may want to talk to you. "You may have to explain things over time," said American Atheists' Blair Scott.[15]

"I told my dad I was agnostic when I was sixteen," said a college student in Texas who posts as nateychan. "At first, he was very pissed off . . . . We had a loud argument about everything that didn't end well." Time passed; nateychan went to college. "Over winter break I agreed to go to church to appease my grandparents (who don't yet know I'm a nonbeliever). As we were leaving, my Dad said, 'How are you?' and I said, 'Eh, I don't belong here.' And he said, 'Well, maybe you will.' So I feel like he still harbors the hope that I'll come back . . . but I feel like it's obvious to both of us that we're choosing to ignore the monster in the closet. And maybe that's for the better. He may not like it that I'm not Christian, but we get along; and I prefer this to hiding who I am."[16]

Waiting for relatives to accept your unbelief isn't easy, but it can pay off. "As time goes on and you remain true to your convictions," atheist advice columnist Richard Wade said, "your family will have to face the reality that this is where you stand."[17]

If They Deny It

You can shout "I'm an atheist!" in your parents faces in a dozen languages—and they can ignore you.

Denial of the facts—it's a common response to getting painful news.

A sixteen-year-old unbeliever with the screen name sunkissed said, "I *think* my mom knows, but when I told her, I'm pretty sure she thought I was kidding."[18]

"I have told my parents in the past that I don't believe in God, but I guess they [thought] I was just being rebellious," said Mike, age sixteen.[19]

When Trevor, age eighteen, told his mom that he was an atheist, his mother flatly disagreed. "She continued dismissing my atheism as something I only 'think' I am; a 'phase,' something childish that she reckons I'll abandon at the first sign of trouble."[20]

Other parents don't deny that their kids have embraced godlessness; they just act as if it's not there. "[My parents and I] only stay in touch because we've agreed that we won't discuss my atheism," said JulietEcho, age twenty-three. "They can only accept me as a daughter by ignoring major parts of who I am."[21]

If your parents deny or ignore your unbelief, the safest course may be to let them. Their refusal to accept the truth may annoy you, but it may be their way of keeping themselves from getting terribly upset with you. They may already have enough reasons to get mad or sad (trouble seems baked into the teenager–parent relationship even when religion isn't an issue), so why give them another? You can hash out the issue with them later, when you're no longer living on their income and under their roof. Maybe when you're no longer so entangled with each other, they'll be able to accept your viewpoint more easily.

THE OTHER RELATIVES

What about relatives other than Mom and Dad? They may react badly to the news that you're an unbeliever.

Fortunately for my peace of mind, my younger sister started showing signs of nonbelief at about the same time in her life that I did, so I had someone with similar views to talk to without having to worry about it getting back to my parents or teachers.

—JAMES, EARLY TWENTIES, VIRGINIA[22]

My nana actually begged me to lie to her and tell her that I was agnostic [rather than atheist]. I refused. We haven't spoken since.

—MEAGHEN, AGE 25, CANADA[23]

*One of my aunts by marriage heard I was an atheist and asked me
a list of questions like she was examining an extraterrestrial. What do
I do in times of need? How do I protect myself from evil spirits?*

—MICHELE, AGE 20, OHIO[24]

*[My little sister] gets everything she wants, but when I want something
(a new CD or book) I don't get it b/c Mom and Dad say they don't have
any money (b/c they spend it all on my sister). And then my sis turns to
me and says I don't get anything b/c I'm an atheist, and Mom and Dad
agree; they actually say 'Well, maybe you shouldn't worship the devil
and you would get stuff.'*

—ATHEIST PRINCESS (SCREEN NAME), AGE 15[25]

▽ ▽ ▽

But some siblings and other relatives can be a comfort.

*My younger brother . . . was shocked when I told him [I was
an atheist] but hasn't been judgmental about it. Of all my family,
I appreciate his reaction the most. He's fourteen now and the only
person in my family with whom I can discuss religion rather than
have religion lectured at me.*

—NICOLE, AGE 20, VIRGINIA[26]

*[My Catholic confirmation] was an absolute disaster . . . . [Others being
confirmed] were there because they wanted to be there and then you
had me, who was a nonbeliever and was only there 'cause she was
forced there by her parents . . . . I explained how I felt that night to my
sister and she understood, so that made me feel better.*

—JESSICA, AGE 15, CONNECTICUT[27]

There was one very open-minded [relative] in the ways of religion that
I could talk to about my atheist ways . . . . Any chance I got to [be
with him] was the time of my life. We drank, smoked weed, watched
low-budget horror movies, . . . discussed World War I and II, and
laughed about [. . .] Christianity [. . . .]

—BRANDON, AGE 25, NORTH CAROLINA[28]

▽ ▽ ▽

Bottom line: your siblings and other relatives can give you endless pain about your unbelief—or endless support. Be as careful and sensitive in telling them as you are in telling your parents.

Religion Down Your Throat

When your parents hear that you've rejected religion, they may react by insisting on more religion.

"I knew I was an atheist when I was twelve," said Cassidy, who's fourteen. "Recently, my brother (he is thirteen) told my mother he wanted to leave the Mormon faith, with no success. And just today, my mother told me that she is going to start forcing me and my brother to start going to church again."[29]

"I considered myself nonreligious in middle school, and my mother's response was to throw me into a Catholic high school," said Alex, age eighteen.[30]

Some parents don't push religion at you as much as they try to push atheism away. "My mom is trying to convert me," said Josh55, who's thirteen. "My mom won't let me go to the Atheist Nexus or any other atheist websites, sometimes I have to read the Bible, and my mom won't let me say *atheist*."[31]

Why would parents make extra efforts to impose religion when their efforts up to this time have backfired and helped you turn atheist? Some parents may feel that you went atheist because they didn't impose enough religion, so their answer is to impose more. Other parents just don't know what else to do.

Handling the Holiness

What can you do if your parents demand religious observance?

Some experts recommend obedience. "If remaining in your parents' home has advantages that outweigh having to participate in meaningless rituals," said Cliff Walker, editor of the website Positive Atheism, "then you do well to play the game . . . . In Oregon, where it gets very cold, hundreds of grown men spend an hour singing religious songs and listening to religions sermons just to be able to eat and perhaps sleep at the Rescue Mission. Sure it's degrading, but it all depends on what you want."[32] (The Rescue Mission probably doesn't absolutely insist that the homeless attend religious services, but you get the point.)

Going to church doesn't have to be all bad. "Try using the trips as a learning experience," said Austin Cline of About.com.[33] Richard Wade has recommended playing anthropologist or psychologist: "Observing the church members and their ideas as would a scientist in the field might provide you just enough intellectual distancing to reduce your resentment and frustration."[34]

You can try negotiating too. "After my parents got over the initial shock and talked the situation over, they formulated a compromise," said Caleb, an eighteen-year-old Oregon unbeliever. "I would no longer be required to attend church every week, but I would have to go to a 'critical thinking' class every Monday night."[35]

Or try saying no. "[My mother] tries to get me to read the Bible, but I politely refuse," said Liz, age nineteen.[36] This is a risky strategy, though, and you probably should use it only if you're sure your parents won't punish you for it.

The Surprising Response

When I came out [as an atheist], my folks were pretty cool about it.
They greatly disapprove of me being atheist, but they still accept me.

Brandon, age 18, California[37]

Some parents react to their teenagers' coming out with the most surprising response of all: they don't mind.

Coolbus (the screen name for an Australian unbeliever in his late teens) didn't want to reveal his atheism to his church-going dad: "Father is a deacon; if I tell him, he will probably die inside," he said at first.[38] But when they got into a debate on religion, "I realized he knows I am an atheist . . . . [Didn't] rage at me or disown me. Everything went better than I expected. Feel like some weight has been lift[ed] up off my shoulders."[39]

Revealing the truth can even pull you closer to your parents. "Growing up in Tehran, Iran, [my father] was surrounded by Muslim culture but came to the same conclusion that I have," said Drew, a twenty-year-old unbeliever from Texas. "It's a common ground that's actually brought us together as father and son."[40]

Sometimes, parents are split: one will be upset, the other will take the news easily. A seventeen-year-old agnostic from Australia, who posts under the name PYOOnGDOOng, said that his mom "is either crying or getting super aggressive about why I don't believe anymore;" but "Dad is at least reasonable and can understand that I just want to make an informed decision."[41] The father of eighteen-year-old Arkansas unbeliever, Dylan, "teared up and said something like 'If you really don't believe, then I've failed as a father' and acted truly hurt." But "my mother was a much different story . . . . It turns out she doesn't really accept Christianity as the truth either."[42]

Some parents even deconvert. "My mom took the news quite well," said John, a twenty-one-year-old Australian quoted earlier. Although she was a believing Catholic, "she talked to me about why I chose [atheism] and fully accepted my choices. Since then, I have managed to get her to read *The God Delusion* and a few other [atheist] books. She now classifies herself as an agnostic."[43]

What to Do Next?

One last thing: if you need more advice, check the "Getting Help" section of this book's appendix. The resources there can help with challenges ranging from finding a nontheist therapist to dealing with violent parents. Revealing your godlessness to your parents—and facing their reaction—can demand a lot of guts. Many unbelievers wait until deep into adulthood to take the chance. Some never try at all. Getting through the experience as a teenager is an achievement.

So even if your parents punish you and you're sure that you've made a terrible mistake, give yourself some credit. You're in good company with other young unbelievers who spoke up and risked retaliation.

They've survived. You will too.

11

How Will Your Friends React?

I'm going into my sophomore year of high school next year (grade 10) and this will be my first year as an open atheist. Most of my good friends know and either choose not to talk about it [or] don't care, or a few are even atheist themselves. My problem is the other students.

TYLER THE SKEPTIC (SCREEN NAME), AGE 15, ALABAMA[1]

Now that you've told your parents, telling your friends and classmates should seem easy by comparison. But that's like saying that it's easier to climb the Alps than the Himalayas. Either way, you risk a lot of sharp crags.

Before you tell your friends, assess how they'll take the news. Advice columnist Richard Wade said that their age can matter: "The older teens get, the more independence they gain to have friends and belong to groups who are supportive of their views."

Location matters too. "Where there is much religious diversity, as in cities, there tends to be more acceptance for being different," Wade said.

"However, even among the most liberal religious groups, atheists can still sometimes be treated as pariahs."[2]

EEK! An Atheist!

"They were flabbergasted."[3]

"They stared at me like I had just [thrown] a chair at them."[4]

"Their eyes widened. I could see the look on their faces. They wanted to ask if we ate babies."[5]

These are reactions that some young unbelievers got after they revealed their godlessness to classmates.

Evan, a nineteen-year-old atheist from Ohio, had a typical experience. A friend asked, "What's your religion? Do you believe in God?" Evan had deconverted only recently and hadn't yet spoken out about his faithlessness—but faced with such direct questions, "I took a deep breath and responded, 'I have no religion. I do not believe in a god or any deities.'" In response, "my friend had an expression on his face I'll never forget for as long as I live. It was the type of face you see in horror films, when the character is frozen in shock and fear."[6]

What can you do if your friends go into shock?

Most young unbelievers don't do much; they don't have to. Shock usually doesn't last long, and people usually come out of it on their own.

It's after they get over the shock that real trouble can begin.

Preach It!

I had problems with people trying to convert me, and I don't like being
rude to others, so it is very difficult for me to tell someone to
go away and leave me alone.

Marty, age 21, Canada[7]

Leena was a seventeen-year-old in Colorado. When a religious friend of hers discovered that Leena was an atheist, "she then started explaining about God and why one should believe in him," Leena said. "Although I told her I'd rather not discuss the subject, because I knew, with my short fuse, I would start arguing with her about religion, she continued talking about God anyway."[8]

Leena's gone through a common teen atheist experience: other teenagers may try to convert you. "It was as if I had a sign that said 'I am an atheist, come save me' on my back," said Barry, a sixteen-year-old Oklahoman. "I became more of an outcast than I had already been."[9]

"Most of the time, these kinds of people mean well and just want what they think is best for you," said a sixteen-year-old in Arkansas who blogs as the Ginger Atheist. "If you encounter these kinds of people, don't be insulted but be flattered, because they genuinely think that they are helping you. Just gently decline the invitation, and don't bring it up again."[10]

The Shunning

Have I lost friends because of my heretic ways? Of course.

Brandon, age 25, North Carolina[11]

"Last night I was hanging out with a friend of mine when the subject turned to religion," said Samantha, a teenage unbeliever in Illinois. After bombarding Samantha with questions about her atheism, she "left early instead of sleeping over as planned."[12] Samantha added, "It aggravates me that because I don't have a 'set' religion, she doesn't want to be friends."[13]

Plenty of young unbelievers have gone through similar experiences.

Luke, age seventeen, was chatting online with friends and mentioned that he favored gay marriage and other things that the Bible opposes. "[My friends] asked if I was an atheist. And being the honest bastard that I am, [I] said I was. Ever since then, they've all been ignoring me."[14]

Michelle, in Wisconsin, said that when she refused to stand for the Pledge of Allegiance because it uses the phrase *under God*, and her classmates realized that she was an atheist, "students whom I considered companions stopped talking to me."[15]

"I am frustrated by the amount of people who have chosen to delete me from their friend list on Facebook after finding out on Facebook I'm an atheist," said Maggie, a high school senior in Indiana. "This week, I went to one of my friends' open houses. Then after attending, she messages me without knowing I'm an atheist and tells me that the Lord will bless [me] in my future after high school. Then today I logged on Facebook and found out she had deleted me as her friend."[16]

Losing friends is never easy. Here are a couple of ways to handle the problem.

▶ You can try to win your friends back, but it may take some work. "If you really want to repair your friendships with these people," said blogger Teen Atheist, "prove that despite your differences in beliefs, you are still a good and compassionate person. As they would say, 'Turn the other cheek.' Hopefully, they'll warm up to you and figure out that not all atheists are vicious, ill-intentioned demons."[17]

▶ Take comfort in knowing that anyone who'd let religion break a friendship probably isn't someone to keep as a friend anyway. Luke said about the ex-friends who started ignoring him, "Even if I did become their friends again, I probably wouldn't ever respect them the same way."[18] And Teen Atheist asked, "Why would I want to be friends with someone if it meant that I'd always be wondering in the back of my mind if he secretly hates me?"[19] Samantha seemed to have adopted this viewpoint for the friend who walked out on her sleepover. "I'm not sobbing over the loss of her . . . . I'll just stick with the friends that like me for me."[20]

Angry Antiatheists

Remember the last chapter's section on angry parents? Now, meet some angry teenagers.

Jessica, a teenage unbeliever in Virginia, said that when she mentioned her atheism to some classmates, "They started calling me a devil worshipper. Told me, a thirteen-year-old girl, I was going to be tortured in hell for eternity."[21]

David, a twenty-year-old in Massachusetts, remembered his sophomore year in high school, when he went up against a student named Mike. "Mike was a football player and a very devout Christian. He was twice my size, would be very loud, and would constantly threaten me with either hell or physical pain."[22]

Standing up for your rights seems particularly likely to inflame teenage rage. Casey, an eighteen-year-old high school senior in Wisconsin, objected to his public school's holding graduation in a church. When his family sued the school district to put the ceremony somewhere unreligious, his fellow students turned on him. "Everyone would always ask, in an accusing tone, 'What's your problem?'" Casey has said. "They would tell me I was being ridiculous and that I just wanted attention."[23]

A lawsuit is a serious matter, so it's understandable that people could get upset. But even something as innocent as setting up a school club can spark a fury.

When Joaquin, an eighteen-year-old in Illinois, put up a display in the school cafeteria inviting students to join him and other atheists in the school's new unbelievers' club, most students were perfectly civil. A few, though, were not. "One of the girls even said to my good friend Clacos that he had no morals," Joaquin reported. Sometimes, the anger got physical. "By the end of this period, we were pushed back with our table a good foot."[24]

Duncan, age sixteen, tried to start an atheist club at his high school in Alabama. Some students didn't like the idea. "One threatened to shoot me and every other atheist with a shotgun," he's said. Another tried to choke him, but "I kinda kicked him, and he never touched me again."[25]

If you run into anger, and you don't want to kick anyone, what can you do?

You can go to your school's authorities. Duncan did; he got his school's principal to sponsor his club. "Our kids have a right to meet. And they have a right to establish a club," Duncan's principal said. "I could see where there would be resistance, but it's not really a question, because it's the law."[26]

The authorities may not be helpful, though. Jessica said that when she went to her guidance counselor about her classmates' calling her devil worshipper, the counselor didn't believe her.[27]

Whatever you do, don't return hate for hate. "Responding in a hateful manner only makes things worse," said atheist therapist Darrel Ray. "One of the best things is just to be polite, listen, and not respond. Just nod your head and say, 'Thank you.' It kind of takes the fun out of it for them when they can't make you upset. Being the coolest, calmest person in the room is a powerful thing and gives you a big advantage."[28]

An approach like that worked for David, the high school sophomore confronted by the football-playing-Christian Mike. "I always talked him down [from heights of anger]. It was how I survived in high school. [I] was always terribly nice to all of my bullies and would often talk circles around them."[29]

Who? What? When? Where? How?

If I told most people that I was an atheist, I would be treated like the poor lost soul who strayed from the path of righteousness.

At best, my identification as [an atheist] would elicit a confused "why?"

Ian, age 24, Connecticut[30]

If you let people know that you don't believe in God, you may confuse them. And they may ask questions.

Some of the questions will be challenges. Remember Joaquin, the eighteen-year-old who set up a display advertising his high school atheist club? He said that one girl "came up and flatly said: 'That's bullshit! If God ain't real, how you breathin'?'"[31] (Later chapters of this book will give you answers to the most common challenges.)

Other questions will be genuine attempts to understand you. Young atheists and agnostics have run into questions about morality, life after death, the origin of the universe, and so on.

Be kind to the questioners, even the ones who challenge you. Answer their questions calmly and honestly. If you don't know the answers, say so. After all, admitting that you don't know every cosmic truth is a main difference between unbelievers and believers.

THE DATING POOL

I had a very close male friend who I was very much interested in, and he told me that, while we spent a lot of time together, and he enjoyed being around me and was attracted to me, that he could never date me because I was going to hell.

Kary, age 26, Illinois[32]

"It may sound horrible," said Christine, a twenty-three-year-old unbeliever in Ontario, Canada, "but I do not think that I could have a close personal relationship with a person who believed in organized religion."[33] No matter how attracted you are, it's often hard for unbelievers to date believers.

"I tried dating a Conservative Jew once," said Emily, a nineteen-year-old in North Carolina. "[I] should have seen before I started that it wasn't going to work out." Their religious differences grew so wide that "I can no longer converse with him without someone antagonizing the other."[34]

Mark, a twenty-four-year-old in England, had been dating his Christian girlfriend for three years. "One day, she just asked me out of the blue why I was an atheist." When he explained his distrust of Christianity and the Bible, she grew upset. "We have agreed to just leave the subject alone and not talk about it. I have to say I would rather talk about it because I know she has doubts, which is healthy, but she won't talk about it because she's scared that she won't like where she ends up. Long term, I don't think it'll ever really work out [between us]."[35]

Relationships for unbelievers seem to work better when both partners feel the same way. Nineteen-year-old Emily from Rhode Island, whom we first heard from in chapter 8, said: "I got lucky with dating—my boyfriend is also an atheist. It's a relief that I don't have to feel like I need to explain my beliefs to him."[36]

To find unattached (and cute) unbelievers, see if your school has a freethinkers club. If it doesn't, consider starting one. You can also try online unbeliever forums, but be careful. As you know, not everyone online is what he or she says.

What if you can't find an unbeliever to love and you're attracted to a devout theist instead? Do you have any chance at all to build a decent relationship?

Yes. "I dated a confessing Catholic for over a year, and I recall only one argument about religion," said a young unbeliever named Matt.[37]

But religion is like politics, sex, or any other topic where people have strong feelings: a relationship is easier when both people in it agree.

The Safe Haven

I have actually had a lot of people ask me if it's weird to be such close friends with [an atheist], because our faiths are so different, and honestly I don't think it is! In fact, I think it makes us closer.

Mickey, a Mormon high school freshman, Utah[38]

A few pages ago, there was the story of Joaquin, who invited students to join his school's atheist club. Some students got mad and others were curious, but the majority had another reaction. "Throughout the entire day, close Christian friends came by and gave us high fives, hugs, and bro fists."[39]

Tolerance, acceptance, and even genuine warmth are among the most common reactions to the news that someone is an agnostic or atheist.

"To my own friends that are Bible-toting Southern Baptists or United Methodists, I am often seen as sort of a playful blasphemer," said Emily, the nineteen-year-old, from North Carolina. "They feel affection for me and I for them, and religion has very little to do with it."[40]

"In high school, I never felt out of place in terms of religion or lack of [it]," said Emily from Rhode Island. "My friends and I had more important things to talk about, like the latest Harry Potter book, impossible homework assignments, and who we wanted to ask to the next school dance."[41]

Other kids are even going through their own deconversions. "Surprisingly, when I began to open up about my atheism to my classmates, I found a lot of them were also battling against their former belief that God was an absolute truth that had to be accepted," said Aidan, age eighteen, from Ontario. "A surprising number of them were starting to turn into agnostics or atheists. Seeing that, I had more confidence to continue to express my beliefs and hold fast to them."[42]

Some people may not be completely accepting at first. Still, if you remain firm but friendly, they may come around. "I told my friends fairly early about my beliefs," said Liz, a nineteen-year-old unbeliever. "One or two tried to bring me back to Christianity, but once they saw my reasons and my resolve, they accepted it. In fact, one of my friends continued to ask me questions about my beliefs and has actually admitted to me to being agnostic."[43]

Never forget, though, that accepting your unbelief may be hard for believers. You may have to avoid certain touchy topics. "The majority of my friends are believers and attend religious ceremonies frequently," said Aidan. "The best way to deal with them is by not discussing anything religious around them."[44]

Off to College

[Atheists and agnostics] mentioned that college allowed them
to have contact with people who were more accepting, that
college offered them a helpful opportunity to talk to others, that
being away from home made things easier, and that it was
easier to exercise their identity in college.

Heather Downs, atheism researcher[45]

You'll probably find more acceptance for unbelief in college than in high school. About one in six college students has no religious preference.[46] Less than half of all college students—40 percent—follow religious teachings in everyday life.[47]

Liz, a nineteen-year-old unbeliever, has found the change from high school to college refreshing: "I must say, there are many more atheists in college than there were in high school. I enjoy attending my classes and asking about people's religions, and have wonderful discussions, even with those who are religious."[48]

If you're suddenly among people who accept you and you no longer feel that you have to fight for your beliefs, you may even feel free to enjoy religion. "When I came to Amherst [College], I was pretty eager to share my opinions and to challenge people to think beyond their religion," one student has said. "I've really eased up over the years . . . . I'm starting to think about what good things religion brings."[49]

Not all schools and students are equally open to unbelief, though. "In religion classes, it becomes a struggle to not be named the bad guy simply for bringing up the atheist point of view," said nineteen-year-old Emily from North Carolina. "I want to engage in meaningful and respectful discussion or nothing at all."[50]

So if you're in high school: study up, get the grades, earn the scholarships and grants, and choose a college that will welcome you and your godless viewpoint. (The last chapter of this book names some of them.)

To Speak Up or Not?

If you choose to come clean with your classmates about your godlessness, do it carefully and kindly. At the same time, try not to be timid or apologetic. After all, there's nothing wrong with being an atheist or agnostic. By now, you've probably accepted that as a fact.

And if all goes well, your friends will accept it too.

12

How Do Unbelievers Handle Hostile Teachers, Principals, and Classmates?

Who is to determine what prayer shall be spoken and by whom? Legally, constitutionally or otherwise, the state certainly has no right.

REVEREND MARTIN LUTHER KING JR. ON PRAYER IN PUBLIC SCHOOLS[1]

Some teachers or school administrators demand prayer in school, censor atheistic opinions, oppose campus clubs for godless students, or insist on teaching biblical creationism instead of evolution. How should you handle them?

If you don't know, take heart. Other teenagers and young adults have faced these problems, and they've often won.

But it wasn't easy.

Here are some of their stories.

Pray or Disobey?

Maybe you will [be] gangbanged before we throw you out of
one of our cars. WE WILL GET YOU—LOOK OUT!

Actual threat issued to Jessica Ahlquist, teenage atheist
who opposes school prayer[2]

Prayer may cause more friction between schools and unbelievers than any other issue.

A famous case involves atheist Jessica Ahlquist. In the fall of 2009, she was a freshman at Cranston West High School in Cranston, Rhode Island. When she entered the school auditorium, a friend pointed out a banner about eight feet high and three feet wide. The banner, titled "School Prayer," began with *Our Heavenly Father* and ended with *Amen*.[3] "I was surprised to see it and didn't think that my school would have something like that," she said later.[4]

Jessica was an atheist but kept the fact quiet. "The shyest girl in school," as she's described herself,[5] worried that she'd lose friends if they knew.

Still, she couldn't stay silent about the banner. "It seemed like it was saying, every time I saw it, 'You don't belong here.'"[6]

Jessica protested the banner at school board meetings and started a Facebook page to call for its removal. Her father supported her; on April 4, 2011, he and the American Civil Liberties Union's Rhode Island affiliate sued the school district on her behalf to bring the banner down.[7]

In school the next day, "People who had never talked to me before were judging me and calling me names," Jessica said. "I went home crying."[8] Her Twitter account received messages including, "I hope there's lots of banners in hell when you're rotting in there, you atheist f***."[9] A state representative called Jessica an "evil little thing" on a radio talk show.[10]

The attacks kept on for months—but civil rights organizations ranging from the Hugh M. Hefner Foundation to the Touro Synagogue

Foundation gave Jessica awards for speaking out.[11] Atheist groups have raised over $40,000 in college scholarship money for her.[12] And in February 2012, the school board agreed to remove the banner.[13]

Jessica said that the experience has been hard, but it strengthened her. "I've become more comfortable with myself as a result. I've met people more like me, with similar interests and ideals." And, she concluded, "I've also discovered my voice and my passion."[14]

A Devotional for Your Diploma

My graduation from high school is this Friday. I live in the Bible Belt of the United States. The school was going to perform a prayer at graduation, but due to me sending the superintendent an email stating it was against Louisiana state law and that I would be forced to contact the ACLU if they ignored me, they ceased it. The school backed down, but that's when the shitstorm rolled in.

Damon Fowler, posting as SeriousMoad, high school atheist[15]

One of the most common venues for school prayers is the graduation ceremony. An especially notorious one sprang up in 2011 in Bastrop, Louisiana.

Damon Fowler was set to graduate Bastrop High School on May 20, 2011.[16] But, as he said in the quote above, the school's graduation ceremony traditionally included a prayer. Damon lobbied the school district to substitute a moment of silence instead, and he won.

He won the battle, that is. He would face a war before graduation.

A Bastrop High teacher criticized Damon in the local newspaper as "a student who really hasn't contributed anything to graduation or to their classmates."[17] At a school event the night before the graduation, Damon said, he saw people "staring at me, calling me names, talking about me behind my back."[18] Even Damon's fundamentalist Christian parents were apparently furious at him; according to Damon's brother, Jerrett, his mother "cut [him] off from all communication," including messages from his relatives. What's more, Jerrett added, "He has gotten death threats already and threats of bodily harm if he shows up to graduation."[19]

Damon got through the graduation safely. But another student, who was supposed to introduce the ceremony's moment of silence, ignored the rules and led the crowd in reciting the Lord's Prayer.[20]

Damon left Louisiana less than a week after his graduation. He moved in with his sister, who lived in Texas. Sympathizers sent him more than $15,000 for a college scholarship fund.[21] A year later, when another Bastrop High atheist came out to demand a prayer-free graduation, Damon called on his own supporters to help the young atheist.[22]

"I will continue the fight," Damon has said. "I'm not backing down, and I will continue to stand for constitutional rights as long as they're violated."[23]

KNOW YOUR RIGHTS: THE SUPREME COURT ON RELIGION IN SCHOOL

> Neither a state nor the federal government can set up a church.
> Neither can pass laws which aid one religion, aid all religions,
> or prefer one religion over another. Neither can force nor influence
> a person to go to or to remain away from church against his will
> or force him to profess a belief or disbelief in any religion.
>
> *Hugo Black, Supreme Court Justice*[24]

Here are some key cases where the Court made history for anyone who goes to an American public school.

McCollum v. Board of Education, March 8, 1948

On public schools teaching religion: "A state cannot consistently with the First and Fourteenth Amendments utilize its public school system to aid any or all religious faiths or sects in the dissemination of their doctrines."[25]

Engel v. Vitale, June 25, 1962

On schools establishing official prayers: "Government in this country should stay out of the business of writing or sanctioning official prayers and leave that purely religious function to the people themselves and to those the people choose to look to for religious guidance."[26]

Abington Township School District v. Schempp and Murray v. Curlett, June 17, 1963

On mandatory Bible reading in schools: "The place of religion in our society is an exalted one, achieved through a long tradition of reliance on the home, the church, and the inviolable citadel of the individual heart and mind. We have come to recognize through bitter experience that it is not within the power of government to invade that citadel, whether its purpose or effect be to aid or oppose [religion]."[27]

Lemon v. Kurtzman, June 28, 1971

On government funding of religious education: "Government is to be entirely excluded from the area of religious instruction and churches excluded from the affairs of government. The Constitution decrees that religion must be a private matter for the individual, the family, and the institutions of private choice."[28]

Wallace v. Jaffree, June 4, 1985

On a law authorizing teachers to hold a moment of "silent meditation or voluntary prayer": "[The law] was intended to convey a message of state approval of prayer activities in the public schools . . . [and therefore] violates the First Amendment."[29]

Lee v. Weisman, June 24, 1992

On prayer at graduation ceremonies: "No holding by this Court

suggests that a school can persuade or compel a student to participate in a religious exercise. That is being done here [in this case], and
it is forbidden by the Establishment Clause of the First Amendment."[30]

Santa Fe Independent School District v. Doe, June 19, 2000
On prayer before school football games: "School sponsorship of
a religious message is impermissible . . . . The delivery of such a
message—over the school's public address system, by a speaker
representing the student body, under the supervision of school fac-
ulty, and pursuant to a school policy that explicitly and implicitly
encourages public prayer . . . is invalid."[31]

Shut Up, Unbeliever!

The Christian faith cannot rule the United States. It is unconstitutional.
Religion and government are supposed to be separate.
"No Rights," by teenage atheist Krystal Myers[32]

In 2012 Krystal Myers was a high school senior in Lenoir City,
Tennessee, a suburb of Knoxville. She was an honor student and an editor of the Lenoir City High School newspaper. She was also an atheist.[33]

"My rights as an atheist are severely limited when compared to other
students who are Christians," she wrote in an opinion piece for her
paper. She pointed out:

▶ The school allowed Christian youth ministers on campus to
   interact with students.

▶ Football games, graduation ceremonies, and school board
   meetings included prayers.

▶ At least one teacher wore a crucifix T-shirt on the job and encouraged students to join a Christian club.[34]

When Krystal submitted her article, titled "No Rights: The Life of an Atheist," school officials refused to publish it "because of the potential for disruption in the school."[35] Krystal went public, telling the *Knoxville News Sentinel* that the school was censoring her.

The newspaper ran "No Rights" plus a story about Krystal. Within twelve hours, the paper's website had received nearly two hundred comments, most of which supported Krystal.[36]

Less than a month after the newspaper ran Krystal's story, the school board announced that it would stop opening its meetings with prayer, and the high school promised to stop prayers at football games. There wasn't much progress on Krystal's other complaints—but she promised to keep fighting.[37]

AN UNBELIEVER IN A RELIGIOUS SCHOOL

My high school experience was ruined because
my mom forced me into a school to "find religion."
All that decision has done is make me
run farther away from religion.
Alex, age 18, Missouri[38]

Most teenage unbelievers go to public schools, where no teacher is supposed to preach religion. But what if you're an unbeliever in a church, mosque, or temple's religious school?

You could have a hard time.

Matt, a sixteen-year-old Pennsylvanian, said that at his school, "All of the guidance counselors relate every issue and solution to God, and never actually try to help you with your problem."[39]

"Last Thursday, we were discussing . . . the rosary (the prayers and everything about it, how it got together, etc.)," said ANS, from Australia, "and my friend made a funny remark about the rosary, and my religion teacher (hardcore Christian) did not have any of it. He sent him to RTC (Responsible Thinking Class) with the reason 'disrespectful.'"[40]

Enri, from Ecuador, told this story: "My Bible teacher (yes, every day we are preached [to] about how wonderful God is) said that atheist[s], Catholics, Buddhists, gays, bisexuals, lesbians and transgenders are all going to hell. And I stood up and said exactly this: 'What is your problem? OK, I get it, you are homophobic. But why throw Buddhists, atheists, and Catholics in there too?' . . . And then the teacher started screaming a crapload at me about how whatever isn't Christian belongs to the devil."[41]

Not all religious schools and teachers are so bad. When Enri's Bible teacher sent him to the principal for mouthing off, he discovered that "the principal is quite open-minded and nice, he let me go with only a warning about challenging other people's beliefs."[42] And Matt, the student with the unhelpful guidance counselors, found that his religion teacher treated him fairly, even when Matt argued with the man: "After class, he talked to me, saying that it was really good of me to stand up for what I think, and that he wishes the other students would be more like me."[43]

Hitting with a Club

Becoming my school's number one enemy didn't take a single insult,
a single disruption in class, or a single disciplinary action.
Instead, it took seven simple words: "I want to start an atheist club."

Micah White, high school atheist[44]

Micah White was a student at southeast Michigan's Grand Blanc High School—and an atheist. But he kept his beliefs to himself until he read a letter in the school newspaper from a student who wanted GBHS's biology classes to teach creationism.

The letter angered Micah into action. The school had a Bible club, so he decided to start an atheist club.[45]

Micah needed approval from the assistant principal but didn't get it: "He told me that our club could meet within the school, but we wouldn't be able to solicit members" like other student groups. Micah pointed out that the school was violating the federal Equal Access Act, which guaranteed all groups the same privileges. He said that the assistant principal replied, "Stop worrying so much about the law, and worry about what Grand Blanc High School allows."[46]

Micah asked the citizens group Americans United for Separation of Church and State for help. The group threatened to sue GHBS, and Micah got his club.[47]

His fight grabbed national media attention. He chatted with host Bill Maher on the ABC television talk show *Politically Incorrect*, and he wrote "Atheists under Siege," an opinion article about his adventure, for the *New York Times*.[48]

What did Micah learn from his exploits? "Never be afraid to stand up and say what you believe."[49]

The Evolution of Education

Some theists don't like the theory of evolution. Evolution's long, slow march contradicts the Bible's declaration that God built the world in a week. Some theists try to make schools criticize the theory, stop schools from teaching it, or make schools teach doctrines that fit the Bible's story.

That's where Zack Kopplin comes in. Zack may or may not be one of the millions of unbelievers (he doesn't publicly discuss his beliefs), but he's been their ally in keeping biblical ideas out of science class.[50]

Zack was a sophomore at Baton Rouge Magnet High School in Louisiana in 2008, when the state passed the Louisiana Science Education Act (LSEA).[51] The law would "assist teachers, principals, and other school administrators to create and foster an environment within public elementary and secondary schools that promotes critical thinking skills, logical analysis, and open and objective discussion of scientific theories being studied including, but not limited to, evolution."[52]

Thinking, analysis, and discussion are good things. But the law was suggested by the Louisiana Family Forum,[53] a group working "to persuasively present biblical principles in the centers of influence."[54]

Zack believed that the LSEA was a step toward teaching creationism instead of evolution. He fought back: he led a rally against the LSEA at the state capitol,[55] testified against the law before the Louisiana Senate Education Committee,[56] recruited more than seventy Nobel Prize winners to ask the state government to repeal the law,[57] and created a petition that amassed more than seventy-five thousand signatures to "tell Louisiana to teach real science in public schools, not creationism."[58]

And he failed. The LSEA stayed on the books, and evolution vanished from Louisiana's science curriculum.[59]

Still, Zack didn't quit. Now a college student, he's still lobbying to repeal LSEA. "This is a much larger fight than just Louisiana," he's said. "This is a fight against the American problem of science denial and antiscience legislation. And whether we win or lose in Louisiana, we're going to keep fighting."[60]

The Preacher Teacher

In 2006 Matthew LaClaire was a sixteen-year-old junior at Kearny High School in Kearny, New Jersey. His history teacher was a Baptist youth pastor.[61] "If you reject [Jesus], you belong in hell," he told his students during class.[62] He also denounced Muslims, nonbiblical education, and "deviant sexual behavior."[63]

Matthew, who was raised in the godless beliefs of Ethical Culture[64] (see chapter 4), complained to the school's principal and the head of its history department. But Matthew's teacher denied preaching in class.

Then Matthew pulled out some CDs. He had been secretly recording his teacher.[65]

About a month later, the story hit the news.[66] Most of the Kearny High community opposed Matthew. He even received a death threat.[67]

Eleven weeks after the news broke, the school board took action—against Matthew. The board banned recording in class without the teacher's permission.[68]

Matthew sued the school district (with help from his parents and the American Civil Liberties Union) for penalizing him and not protecting him from students who harassed him.[69] About three months later, the suit was settled. The settlement included training for teachers in the separation of church and state, plus a statement by the school board praising Matthew.[70] (At least one board member kept publicly criticizing him, though.[71])

Matthew went on to college, became a board member of the Secular Student Alliance (an unbeliever group),[72] and has been a frequent guest host on the unbeliever radio show *Equal Time for Freethought*.[73]

"I received a remarkable education at Kearny High School, though not the kind of education I anticipated," Matthew said later. "The experience has strengthened my understanding of citizenship, friendship, trust, adaptability, humor, conformity, determination, empathy, honesty, maturity, reason, and many other values."[74]

What Have We Learned Today?

If teachers or administrators want to inject religion where it doesn't belong, you can fight back. And you can win—at least some of the time.

13

Can You Celebrate Christmas? And Other Holiday FAQs

Holidays are the simple part. I pretend that they don't have any religious connotation and just enjoy the time spent with my family.

MEAGHAN, AGE TWENTY-FIVE, ALABAMA[1]

If you're an unbeliever, you probably don't find much spiritual or religious meaning in Christmas, Hanukkah, the Muslim Eid al-Fitr, the Buddhist Vesak, and other holidays—but Christmas carols are fun to sing, flaming Hanukkah candles make a pretty sight, and the feasts on the Eid and Vesak are tasty. If you want to participate in these holidays, are you a hypocrite? And if you don't want to participate but your family forces you to, what can you do?

Celebrating Christmas—Yes or No?

I celebrate Christmas because I believe in the messages it brings.
Peace on earth, good will toward man, all of it.
I believe in every last bit.

Luis, age 17, Tennessee[2]

"Isn't Christmas about Jesus?" asked Hazel, an eighteen-year-old atheist (raised Jewish) from New York. Her answer: "Well, not to me. Excuse me if I'm about to go totally Hallmark on all of you, but to me, Christmas is a holiday of giving and love. Whoa, that sounded super cheesy, but it's true!"[3]

A lot of unbelievers feel the way that Hazel does.

Some people might say that you have no right to celebrate Christmas if you don't believe in Christianity. But, said Alex, an eighteen-year-old unbeliever from England, "we should be allowed [to] enjoy the beauty of Christmas just as we can enjoy the beauty of religiously inspired works of art. The beauty is real, even if the object of inspiration is not."[4]

And Greg Epstein, the humanist chaplain at Harvard University, has no problem if his school's teenagers and twentysomethings enjoy holiday gift giving, carols, or Christmas trees—or, for that matter, Hanukkah lights: "Religion doesn't own singing, and religion certainly doesn't own candles and trees and presents."[5]

Besides, in the words of Luis, the godless seventeen-year-old Tennesseean quoted at the top of this section, "Nobody has a right to tell me what I can and can't do on December 25th."[6]

P.S. If you don't want to follow holiday traditions but your family insists on them—for instance, if your parents drag you to church—you may want to follow the advice from chapter 10 about dealing with parents who force their kids to attend religious services. Ask to negotiate more palatable activities when you can, obey your parents when you must, and look for elements of the services that can entertain you.

ANTIHYMNS: THE UNBELIEVER'S TOP 30

If an unending flood of Christmas carols starts getting you down, fill your headphones with these sacrilegious tunes. They come recommended by popular unbeliever websites such as *Friendly Atheist*, Think Atheist, and Atheist Nexus.

Some songs popular among atheists and agnostics are more anti-God than strictly atheist or agnostic. If a song criticizes God, then the song admits that God exists, which isn't the usual godless viewpoint. But many unbelievers like these songs anyhow.

Let's start the music.

Ani DiFranco, "What If No One's Watching": Fast-moving folk-punk song full of doubt about God.

A Perfect Circle, "Judith": Heavy metal that stages an assault on God for ruining a blameless believer.

Bad Religion, "American Jesus": This propulsive number attacks connecting religion with patriotism.

Bad Religion, "Atheist Peace": A punk tornado, it's godlessness you can slam-dance to.

Billy Joel, "Only the Good Die Young": A bouncy rocker that tries to seduce a religious girl.

Corporate Avenger, "The Bible is Bull****": Aggressive electronica that denounces holy books.

Death Cab for Cutie, "I Will Follow You into the Dark": A ballad of love after death, without heaven or hell.

Depeche Mode, "Blasphemous Rumours": Gloomy electronica that doubts God's love and mercy.

Frank Zappa, "Jesus Thinks You're a Jerk": A catchy yet acidic satire of TV preachers.

Godsmack, "Bad Religion": A grungy rejection of a corrosive, corrupting way of life.

Holly Near, "I Ain't Afraid": A gospel-style song denunciation of religions and preachers.

John Lennon, "God": A bluesy denial of God, Jesus, and other icons.

John Lennon, "Imagine": A melodic vision of peace without religion.

Marilyn Manson, "The Fight Song": An industrial-metal refusal to obey a nonexistent deity.

Metallica, "Leper Messiah": A nasty blast at a greedy, hypocritical preacher.

Metallica, "The God that Failed": Heavy metal that calls faith a "mind-clouding monster."

Modest Mouse, "Bukowski": A spooky tune that denounces God as a control freak.

Motörhead, "(Don't Need) Religion": A thrashy rejection of faith and prayer.

Muse, "Thoughts of a Dying Atheist": An eerie rocker about an unbeliever's last hours.

Nine Inch Nails, "Heresy": Industrial rock with an agnostic message.

Patti Smith, "Gloria": Classic rock that defies Christianity.

Randy Newman, "God's Song": A satire that ridicules people for following God.

Red Hot Chili Peppers, "Shallow Be Thy Game": A funk-punk scream against religion.

Rush, "Faithless": A somber call for hope rather than faith.

Rush, "Freewill": An anthemic rocker about believing whatever you want.

Tim Minchin, "White Wine in the Sun": A sweet, witty Christmas song for unbelievers.

Tool, "Opiate": A guitar-and-drum extravaganza that compares a god to a sex criminal.

Tori Amos, "God": A propulsively rhythmic declaration of disappointment with God.

Various artists, "It Ain't Necessarily So": A languid seducer makes agnosticism sexy, by classic songwriters George and Ira Greshwin.

XTC, "Dear God": A gentle, lyrical refusal to believe.

Grace before Meals

What do you do when you're an atheist and your
family is going around the table before Thanksgiving dinner,
praising the gods, people, and things they are grateful for?
Do you stay silent? Do you pretend to thank God? . . . Of course
not. Atheists have plenty to be thankful for—without the need
to include anything supernatural.

*Hemant Mehta, Secular Student Alliance
advisory board chairman* [7]

On Thanksgiving and other special days, both religious and secular, many families say grace or another prayer before a meal. And many unbelievers wonder what to do about it.

If the people at your Thanksgiving say a prayer that you find too religious, you may not like it—but consider just sitting through it. "Passive 'participation' is a minimum that most atheists should be willing to accept," said Austin Cline, About.com's expert on all things atheist and agnostic. "It doesn't take anything to be quiet while others are praying."[8]

If someone calls on you to say grace, you don't have to mention God. There are unbeliever versions that many theists can accept. You can find some at secularseasons.org/celebrations/graces.html. Possibly the most popular is this humanist grace written by Bill Logan, a New Zealand therapist and celebrant (someone who officiates at weddings, funerals, and other occasions).[9]

For what we are about to receive
let us be truly thankful
. . . to those who planted the crops
. . . to those who cultivated the fields
. . . to those who gathered the harvest.

For what we are about to receive
let us be truly thankful
to those who prepared it and those who served it.

In this festivity let us remember too
those who have no festivity
those who cannot share this plenty
those whose lives are more affected than our own
by war, oppression and exploitation,
those who are hungry, sick and cold.

In sharing in this meal,
let us be truly thankful
for the good things we have
for the warm hospitality
and for this good company.

Amen.[10]

Holidays without Holiness

Do unbelievers need their own holidays?

Some say yes, some say no. Among those who say yes, here are some popular celebrations.

The winter solstice is the year's shortest day, when the sun is at its weakest and lowest in the sky. It takes place on December 21 or 22, depending on the year.[11] People have celebrated it as the beginning of the time when the days are supposed to get longer and warmer.[12] Solstice activities include meals, parties, and charitable giving.[13]

Another big day is the first Thursday in May. In 1952 President Harry Truman signed a law: "The President shall issue each year a proclamation designating the first Thursday in May as a National Day of Prayer on which the people of the United States may turn to God in prayer."[14]

About fifty years later, humanist groups responded by decreeing the same day as the National Day of Reason.[15] The goal of this effort, say its organizers, "is to celebrate reason . . . and to raise public awareness about the persistent threat to religious liberty posed by government intrusion into the private sphere of worship."[16] Unbeliever groups have marked the day with parties, speeches, meals, and blood donation drives.[17]

Possibly the most popular unbeliever day isn't strictly for the godless but for anyone who respects science: Darwin Day. The event's organizers call it "an international celebration of science and humanity held on or around February 12, the day that Charles Darwin was born on in 1809."[18] Humanists and fans of science throw Darwin birthday parties and other celebrations.[19]

Another time when unbelievers gather is late September, the time of Banned Books Week and the fall equinox. The equinox—September 22 or 23, depending on the year—is the date when day and night are equally long, and it's traditionally the beginning of autumn.[20] Banned Books Week (the last week of September or thereabouts) is the book world's event to expose and oppose censorship.[21]

Earth Day, Human Rights Day, the spring equinox, the summer solstice—some unbelievers commemorate these days too. And there are other holidays as well. When you don't have a religion to tell you when to party, you can pick any day you want.

Day after Day

As far as dealing with other people's judgments and Christian holidays [as a teenager], I mostly kept to myself and still enjoyed having family around on holidays like any sane person would.

Brandon, age 25, North Carolina[22]

The safest solution for religious holidays may be to take the activities as easy as you can. Enjoy the activities that you like, minimize your participation in the ones that you can't stand, and look for tolerable ways to handle the ones that you can't escape.

Finally: give religious people the same respect that you'd like them to give you. You may find their rituals insane, but if you show believers that you care about how they feel, they might let you handle holiday traditions in your own way.

Even if that way is opting out of holidays altogether—or enjoying every tradition.

ARGUING
ATHEISM

14

How Can You Handle Arguments against Your Being an Atheist?

I've heard it all . . . freak, infidel, heretic, ignorant, weirdo, faggot, little bitch, *etc., etc. The list of offensive names goes on and on. I really just wanted someone to have a very intelligent and calm conversation with me about religion and my beliefs of nonbelieving.*

BRANDON, AGE 25, NORTH CAROLINA[1]

Sooner or later, you'll run into arguments that try to talk you out of unbelief. You'll probably need answers.

This chapter covers some arguments that attack you personally, tells you how to get ready for them, and supplies ideas to counter them. Choose among these chunks of advice carefully and use your best judgment to adapt them to your needs. (If you need to deal with arguments against unbelief in general, see the next chapter.)

Getting Ready, Part I: Know, Know, Know

Master your rhetorical skills. Train yourself to use simple words and
short sentences. Practice speaking. Be comfortable speaking to large
groups of people. Master your body language, vocal tonality, and
speaking pace. Project confidence and comfort. Be loud.

Luke Muehlhauser, author of the blog
Common Sense Atheism[2]

Before you debate a theist, it's best to know how. If you can find a debate
club or class, join it. You'll get practice at organizing an argument and
at thinking on your feet.

And at gathering information: "Study your little butt off about both
[religion] and the arguments against it, because that will always be your
best defense. I find that I know more about my family's religion than
they do," said Wendy, posting as Wendyloh, a twenty-five-year-old
atheist. "They can't use their own Bible against me."[3]

That's a lot of study. Fortunately, you can file the reading list down.
You should read the Bible, for instance, but you don't have to read
all of it. The first five books of the Hebrew Bible (Exodus through
Deuteronomy) and the first four books of the Christian Bible (Matthew,
Mark, Luke, and John) come up in debates more than, say, the pound-
ingly dull First Chronicles.

If you don't have enough knowledge to win a debate, your best move
may be to stay out. "I have made it a point since high school *not* to get
into debates unless I'm confident that I know what I'm talking about,"
said Angus, a twenty-one-year-old unbeliever from Colorado.[4]

What should you do if you find yourself without enough knowledge
to outtalk theists? "If they have a point that you cannot defend against,"
said Mark, a fourteen-year-old atheist with experience in debating
hard-core fundamentalists, "acknowledge that you do not know, and
continue on."[5]

Getting Ready, Part II: The Proper Mood

We all face similar problems, and would like to represent
ourselves and atheists at large in a manner that is convincing
and respectable . . . . By doing so we advance atheism in general
and protect our fellow atheists from harmful repercussions.

Kevin, posting on the Think Atheist forum[6]

In any debate, your behavior matters.

"Always stay calm," said Kevin, the unbeliever quoted above and
an experienced debater. "Getting angry at your debate opponent will
not serve your purpose and will undermine your point."[7] In particular,
according to About.com atheism and agnosticism expert Austin Cline,
"be patient when you hear the same argument for the millionth time."[8]

In addition to keeping your temper, watch your tone. "Don't talk
down to people," added Bryan, a nineteen-year-old Maryland atheist
with debate experience. "Smug certainty is going to get the conversation
nowhere."[9] David Smalley, host of the unbeliever radio show *Dogma
Debate*, emphasized that avoiding snark is especially important for
young unbelievers, "where any arrogance or attitude, even if you're right,
will be blown off as teenage rebellion."[10] Instead, said Andrew on the
atheist blog *Evaluating Christianity*, "Show respect for your opponents,
even as you demolish the substance of their arguments. Given that the
public perception of atheists is that we're a bunch of arrogant jerks, you
should try extra hard to be as minimally jerky as you can."[11]

WALKING AWAY

I really dislike being an advocate [for atheism] when I'm just trying to
do my homework or whatever.

Emily, age 20, Illinois[2]

Maybe you don't enjoy duking it out verbally. Good news: You don't have to. If someone insults you for your atheism, you can try saying something like, "You've got your beliefs, and I've got mine. No need to be nasty about it. Live and let live."

When should you accept a challenge, and when should you walk away? The answer can depend on whom you're facing and how much he or she can hurt you. If disagreeing with your mom makes her ground you and arguing with a classmate makes him pound you, then you might consider finding people who are more willing to listen.

Another time to get away: When debate seems pointless. "I learned a long time ago that there is no arguing with a deeply religious person," said Meaghen, age twenty-five, from Alabama.[13]

"You're Too Young to Decide"

I got this one from my Aunt: "Oh, you're an atheist? Well, you're
only sixteen, you're too young to make that kind of decision!"
But my little sister who is only thirteen gets, "What's that, sweetie?
You're Catholic Christian and accept the Lord Jesus Christ
as our savior? You're smart!"

Nathonamore, posting on Reddit's r/atheism forum[+]

Now that you're ready to debate, let's get into the points that people might say about you.

"The biggest problem our religious neighbors seem to have is my age," said Aubriel J, who's fifteen. "They tell my parents they raised me completely wrong and insist that I am simply too young to be atheistic. I have researched both science and theology. I've read two of [Richard] Dawkins' books. I know more scripture than most Christians I know. I am not ignorant in the least. Besides, no one seems to have a problem with calling small children Christians and bringing them to church. Why is it any different? Should there be an age requirement to irreligiosity?"[15]

"You're too young" is easy to refute. "I am an atheist and seventeen," said Kyle, writing on the Think Atheist website. "Many of my peers believe that at the age of seventeen, I am too young to make such a decision. To which I respond, 'If I am too young to decide there is no god, then aren't you too young to decide there is one?' This is the moment when they get quiet and just kind of stare at me for a short while before walking away, accepting defeat."[16]

"You're Just Rebelling"

My parents say I'm "trying to be a rebel" and am "confused because I'm in my teenage years," and I know that's bull****.

Joshua, posting on the Think Atheist Godless Teens forum[17]

Some theists think that teenagers become atheists or agnostics because they're rebellious. If you've read chapter 5, you know that rebellion isn't usually why a person refuses religion. But how can you prove it?

You can try to turn the conversation away from yourself and toward the theist who's calling you rebellious. Let's call this theist Theo—or Thea: "Well, Thea, why don't you tell me why you believe in God, and I'll tell you why I don't." This approach shows that you're willing to listen, it lets you explain your side, and it can turn an interrogation into a conversation.

You can also ask, "What do you think I'm rebelling against?"

▶ If Thea says that you're rebelling against your parents, then you might mention ways in which you're a good son or daughter.

▶ If Thea says that you're rebelling against God, you can ask how you can rebel against God if you don't think that he exists.

▶ If Thea says that unbelievers in general (and not just you) are rebelling, you can ask how she knows the thoughts of people she's never met.

This topic, by the way, is where patience and calm come in especially handy. If you respond in a sane, reasonable way, you'll show that you're anything but rebellious.

"You're Just Being Trendy"

> The "atheism is just trendy" trope is essentially a way of trivializing atheism and the atheist movement . . . without actually taking the trouble to point out anything that's wrong with it, or to engage in debate with people who are part of it.
>
> *Greta Christina, atheist blogger*[°]

"You're just being trendy" says that teenagers become unbelievers because they think that unbelief is cool. This argument is a lot like, "You're just rebelling." A person who says it is presuming to know how you think and feel. So you can respond by displaying maximum maturity. Show Theo or Thea how much thought and time you've put into arriving at your viewpoint.

Besides: A hat is trendy. A skirt style is trendy. But a conviction about the nature of the universe, its origins, and humanity's place in it—that's more than just a trend.

"You're Just Confused / Lost / Going through a Phase"

> I was explaining [to some theists] my personal history with religion (i.e., I was raised in a Methodist household but never subscribed

to the idea of an omnipotent being, even as a young child), and
discussed the research I had done on many major world religions,
and how that ultimately helped lead me to agnosticism. Their
response was essentially, "Oh, everyone goes through an atheistic/
agnostic phase at some point in their life, usually during college."
I then explained that I've been an atheistic agnostic since before
I knew what those words meant.

Sharad, Virginia[9]

If Theo the theist says that you're confused, lost, or going through a
phase, he's implying that your unbelief is weak and won't last long. He
thinks you'll come around to believe what he believes.

The "confused/lost/phase" argument is like denial, one of the parental
reactions in chapter 10. That chapter told you to parry denial with more
denial—that is, to ignore it. The same treatment could also work with
"confused/lost/phase."

But if you can't ignore it, here are a couple of possible responses:

▶ In implying that you'll turn religious someday, Theo is saying that
he can see your future—but no one can do that. How can Theo?

▶ Since Theo expects you to turn religious, you can ask why he's
bothering to preach to you (or argue with you). After all, he
expects that you'll eventually come out of your godless condition
all by yourself.

"You Don't Know Enough about Religion to Reject It"

There are at least two versions of this objection: "You haven't studied
religion" and "You haven't experienced the presence of God."

You can dispute the "you haven't studied" line by, well, studying.
Nothing shields you from attack like knowledge.

"You haven't experienced God" is a statement that you don't have to dispute, because it actually supports the unbeliever viewpoint. The fact that you've never seen, heard, or met God is probably one reason why you doubt his existence. Now, if you used to be religious, you may have encountered something that you believed was God. But if you've thought about the situation since then, you may have decided that it was something else, like your own emotions and imagination. And you can say so.

Believing in Unbelief—and in Yourself

However you respond to people who say ugly things about you, you might use some concluding advice from Wendy, the atheist who told you to study your little butt off. "Know what it is that you are convinced of and what you DO believe, whether it be science or some other philosophy. I always tell people that 'I know I may not be right, and there is a slim chance you may be right. But in the limits of my own understanding, I am simply not convinced that there is a god or gods.'"[20]

15

How Can You Handle Arguments against Atheism in General?

Common myths about atheists include: All atheists are arrogant, immoral, rebellious, and/or intolerant; all atheists really believe in (the Christian) God and are simply in denial; all atheists are depressed and believe life is meaningless.

URBAN DICTIONARY¹

All atheists aren't arrogant, immoral, rebellious, intolerant, and/or depressed. Most atheists are just as nice and well-adjusted as other people.

But how do you prove it?

"Atheists Are Immoral"

"Atheists are immoral" is so common a gripe that this book has already given a chapter to it. Here are some ways that unbelievers have debated it.

Some unbelievers fight the accusation by pointing at themselves. When a theist blogger called atheist teenagers "young people under the influence of evil," and added "there is no question in my mind that [speaking up for atheism] is the Devil at work,"[2] a teenage unbeliever with the screen name Klimberly answered, "Dude, it's not like we're evil people trying to dominate the world . . . . We're human beings who are different from you, respect that as many of us respect you."[3]

This approach can get the other side to give in a little bit. In a debate on God and atheism, Frank Turek (coauthor of *I Don't Have Enough Faith to Be an Atheist*) said that people need God to explain what's moral. Christopher Hitchens, author of *God Is Not Great: How Religion Poisons Everything*, answered, "For me it's enough to be willing to love my fellow man and perhaps hope that my fellow man or woman will give me some of the same consideration." Turek conceded the point: "You know morality, it's written on your heart. You don't need the Scripture to know right from wrong." (Turek insisted that God is the one who wrote morality onto Hitchens's heart, though.)[4]

Other faithless folks take a more philosophical approach. *Common Sense Atheism* blogger Luke Muehlhauser encountered a young Christian who asked, "Without God, how can you have any morality?" She meant that without God to lay out objective moral facts (principles that should rule human behavior as firmly as the law of gravity rules falling rocks), people will create subjective morals—that is, they'll make their own rules. "Most philosophers, of course, don't think that adding a cosmic dictator to reality gets you objective moral facts," Muehlhauser answered.[5]

Farrell Till, editor of *The Skeptical Review* magazine, added: "How can one determine what 'objective' morality is? From the Bible? If so, a lot of subjectivism will be involved in reading and interpreting it."[6]

And finally: "The ethical behavior of man is better based on sympathy, education, and social relationships [than on God], and requires no support from religion. Man's plight would, indeed, be sad if he had to be kept in order through fear of punishment and hope of rewards after death." That's from someone whom both believers and unbelievers respect: Albert Einstein.[7]

"Atheists Have Committed Terrible Crimes"

This one has a lot of variants: "Atheism has killed more people than religion." "Atheism leads to communism, and communists like Josef Stalin, and Mao Zedong have murdered millions." "Hitler was an atheist."

As it happens, Hitler wasn't an atheist (see chapter 1), and some atheists have been as saintly as Stalin and Mao were evil (see chapter 3). In addition, said atheist author Richard Dawkins, "What matters is not whether Hitler and Stalin were atheists but whether atheism systematically *influences* people to do bad things. There is not the smallest evidence that it does."[8]

In addition, some theists have been as murderous as Stalin or Mao. Look up Prince Vlad III of Wallachia, also known as Dracula; Czar Ivan IV of Russia, alias Ivan the Terrible; and King Leopold II of Belgium.

Even God has called for slaughter (see Numbers 31:17–18, 1 Samuel 15:2–3, Hosea 13:16, Isaiah 13:13–16, and Deuteronomy 7:1). The blogger Conversational Atheist has advised atheist debaters to say, "We both agree, the God of the Bible is as immoral as Hitler and Stalin, right?"[9]

"Atheist Life Has No Meaning"

The meaning we [atheists] find in life is a lived experience . . .
[and] I believe it is possible to radically transform our experience
of the world for the better.

Sam Harris, atheist author, debating religion with pastor Rick Warren[10]

"Some of the questions that friends who are believers ask me, with a certain fear in their voice, are 'But how can your life have any meaning?',

'Isn't your life pointless?', and 'Why try? Isn't it just going to end anyway?'" said Karen, an atheist who's lived in both the American Midwest and Australia.[11]

Fortunately for Karen, her fellow unbelievers have answers. Chapter 3 of this book addresses the topic briefly. Here's some additional commentary that may come in handy:

"Meaning doesn't come from without"—that is, from God or any other force outside of humanity—said Massimo Pigliucci, City University of New York philosophy professor. "It is constructed by us through our reflections on the world and our interactions with fellow human beings."[12]

Atheist scientist Carl Sagan pointed out that if you want to find meaning in your life, "do something meaningful."[13] As Freedom from Religion Foundation copresident Dan Barker put it, "As long as there are problems to solve, hunger to lessen, inequality to eradicate, knowledge to gain, and beauty to create, there will be plenty of meaning in life."[14]

Here are some answers that teenagers and young adults have given when theists have confronted them with "atheist life is meaningless":

"'How can you live a good life knowing there is no point after you die?'" asked Case, a high school student in West Virginia. "Whenever I am asked this question, I think of how good my life has been without any religious intervention."[15]

"Some people say that believing that one day I will no longer exist must be depressing, but I disagree," said Nicole, age twenty. "It makes life more precious, because it's all that we have."[16]

"I don't claim to know an overarching 'Meaning of Life.' I think that life is only what you make of it," said twenty-three-year-old David McAfee in *Mom, Dad, I'm an Atheist*, his advice book for young unbelievers. "We should find ways to make this life happy and satisfying, without regard to the unknowable nature of an afterlife."[17]

"Atheists Are Intolerant"

The chief deficiency I see in the skeptical movement is its
polarization: Us vs. Them—the sense that we have a monopoly
on the truth; that those other people who believe in all
these stupid doctrines are morons; that if you're sensible,
you'll listen to us; and if not, to hell with you. This is
nonconstructive. It does not get our message across.

Carl Sagan, atheist scientist[°]

The charge of intolerance is tough to fight, because it's sometimes true.

Atheist author Sam Harris has recommended what he calls "conversational intolerance." "Bad beliefs should be criticized wherever they appear in our discourse—in physics, in medicine, and on matters of ethics and spirituality as well."[19]

"Am I intolerant because I oppose the teaching of 'scientific creationism' or mandatory prayers in the public schools?" asked Keith Parsons, an atheist professor of philosophy at the University of Houston. He concluded, "If these things make me intolerant of religion, I'll just have to accept the label."[20]

"We just need to get rid of religion," atheist author and entertainer Penn Jillette has said.[21] Many atheists agree, as you can tell from the popularity of antireligion books such as Christopher Hitchens's *God Is Not Great*.

If a theist says that these unbelievers are intolerant, consider this: millions of Christians, Muslims, and other theists want everyone to believe as they do. Every day, many of them write and preach for it. If they succeed, they will have eliminated other beliefs, especially atheism. If it's acceptable for theists to want everyone to believe as they do, is it intolerant for nontheists to want the same thing?

As it happens, unbelievers generally aren't intolerant of religion. A report from Connecticut's Trinity College said that most people without faith feel "skepticism rather than overt antagonism toward religion."[22]

Some unbelievers actually like religion. Res, a college student in Colorado, said, "Religion helps people, absolutely no doubt about it. Leading a theistic life can allow someone to believe in something greater than themselves, and it also helps alleviate fears of death. Followers of a religion have been known to do great things for others, in the name of their faith."[23]

And many unbelievers stand against any kind of intolerance, including atheist intolerance of religion. Chris Stedman, Harvard University's twenty-five-year-old assistant humanist chaplain, has written about college students "[who] were atheists but declined to call themselves that or get involved in organized atheism precisely because they saw it as divisive, mean-spirited, and in contradiction with their personal values."[24] For instance, the Idaho State University group Freethinkers, Atheists & Agnostics for Religious Tolerance is devoted to "advancing dialogue . . . between nontheism and religion."[25] (And yes, the group's name abbreviates as FAART. Real mature, guys.)

So if someone tells you that atheists are intolerant, you can point out that many of them are actually friendly to religion.

"You Can't Prove God Doesn't Exist"

Hermione looked outraged [and shouted,] " . . . You could claim that anything's real if the only basis for believing in it is that nobody proved it doesn't exist!" "Yes, you could," said Xenophilius. "I am glad to see that you are opening your mind a little."

J. K. Rowling, Harry Potter and the Deathly Hallows[26]

"You can't prove God doesn't exist" might come your way as "No one can prove a negative." How you answer it depends on whether you're a positive/strong/hard atheist or a negative/weak/soft atheist. (You can check the definitions in chapter 1.)

If you're negative/weak/soft—or, for that matter, agnostic—you can say that "You can't disprove God" doesn't apply to you. You're not claiming to disprove God's existence; you're just unsure of it (the agnostic position). Or you can say that you don't see enough evidence to convince you (the negative/weak/soft atheistic view).

You can also offer comments like the one from a young English unbeliever who goes by the screen name Princeling: "It is true, I cannot prove to you God does not exist any more than you can prove to me he does. You can try, if you like. But you won't succeed any more than I would in doing the opposite."[27] Another young unbeliever, who calls himself Bazzy, provided this challenge: "Can you prove to me there are no fairies at the bottom of my garden? No, you can't. Just because you cannot disprove a given idea does NOT imply that it becomes an absolute truth."[28]

The most famous version of this argument is called *Russell's Teapot*, from atheist author Bertrand Russell: "If I were to suggest that between the Earth and Mars there is a china teapot revolving about the sun in an elliptical orbit, nobody would be able to disprove my assertion, provided I were careful to add that the teapot is too small to be revealed even by our most powerful telescopes. But if I were to go on to say that, since my assertion cannot be disproved, it is intolerable presumption on the part of human reason to doubt it, I should rightly be thought to be talking nonsense."[29]

"NO ATHEISTS IN FOXHOLES": TRUE OR FALSE?

"There are no atheists in foxholes" is a popular antiatheist cliché. It means that if you put anyone in enough danger, he'll ask God for help. (A foxhole is a pit that soldiers dig and hide in to protect themselves from enemy bullets and bombs.) In other words, no one is really an atheist.

But it's not true. Ask the Military Association of Atheists and Freethinkers, an organization of unbelievers in uniform—hundreds of them.[30] At least eight MAAF members have won the Bronze Star medal for "meritorious achievement or service . . . in connection with military operations against an armed enemy."[31] And the United States Department of Veterans Affairs honors deceased military atheists by allowing them or their families to choose a symbol of atheism (a stylized drawing of an atom with the letter A at the nucleus) for their headstones in military cemeteries.[32]

ATHEIST HEADSTONE SYMBOL

"What if You're Wrong?"

I would rather go to hell than worship a megalomaniacal tyrant.

Kelly O'Connor, atheist, debating Pascal's wager[33]

Let's talk about death. Some theists say that you've got four ways to bet on the endless nap.

1. You believe in God, but your belief is wrong: God's not real, and there's no afterlife. When you die, nothing happens to you.

2. You're a believer, and you're right: God's real, and he wants everyone to believe in him. When you die, God invites you to heaven for believing.

3. You don't believe in God, and you're right: No God, no afterlife. When you die, nothing happens to you.

4. You're an unbeliever, but you're wrong: God's real, and he wants everyone to believe in him. When you die, God kicks you into hell for not believing.

Believers can't lose the bet: Either they go to heaven, or nothing happens to them. But unbelievers can lose everything. The safest bet is to believe, isn't it?

Not so fast.

This line of logic is called **Pascal's wager**, after the theist mathematician who came up with it. It was first published back in 1669,[34] and theists have been using it ever since.

Pascal's wager asks, "What if atheists are wrong?", so some unbelievers counter it by asking believers if they themselves are wrong. "I [was] once in a debate with my Catholic friend," said a college-age unbeliever from Indonesia who goes by the screen name Brother P. "He used [the] Pascal wager argument and bid on Jesus, but then I told him it's useless because there are many gods across all religions, not just one god—the Christian god." So why not worship all gods? "We cannot worship all gods because there [are] at least two gods [who say,] 'Worship just me or burn' (Christian & Islam)."[35]

Even some theists don't like Pascal's wager. Christian blogger and minister Bob Robinson has said, "I want a faith that is based on more than Pascal's wager. In fact, anybody who says they are a Christian because they might as well—since the alternative is worse—really doesn't have true faith."[36] Evangelical pastor Douglas Wilson has pointed out, "The Christian faith does not hold out any hope whatever to the hypocrites or the poseurs . . . who want to go up to the pearly gates and then pretend that they can buffalo God, . . . [because] God searches the hearts."[37]

Other Challenges

This chapter can't cover every argument against unbelief. A smart theist may offer arguments that you don't expect and you can't squash.

Don't sweat it. Every debater gets stumped from time to time.

But the more you know, the better chance you have of presenting your viewpoint with strength and style.

16

How Can You Handle Arguments for Religion?

If there be an infinite being, he does not need our help—we need not waste our energies in his defense.

ROBERT INGERSOLL, ATHEISM ACTIVIST[1]

Ingersoll has a point, but millions of theists still defend God every day. If they challenge you to respond to their defenses, here are a few countermeasures.

"The Universe Didn't Just Happen; Someone Had to Create It"

What started the universe?

"Many believers like to pose the 'First Mover Argument,' or the 'First Cause Argument,' stating that, since something cannot come from nothing, that a god must exist," said a blogger who goes by Godless

Teen. "However, by their logic, this should apply equally well to a god—how did that god come from nothing?"[2]

A lot of theists answer that God has always existed, but Godless Teen is ready for them: "Believers often say something about God being 'eternal and infinite,' but this doesn't stand up to criticism either. If there are exceptions [e.g., God] to the rule [that something can't come from nothing], then those exceptions can apply equally well to other hypotheses, including ones that do not include God."[3] If God could come from nothing, then so could the universe. In fact, "the laws of physics can explain the universe without the need for a creator," said British cosmologist Stephen Hawking.[4]

If that answer isn't satisfying, there's always the answer that Bazzy, a young atheist quoted in the last chapter, gave in an online debate: "If you are asking me to tell you where the universe came from if God did not create it, well then, I can't answer that. To current science, that fact is unknown. But to assume that because our current scientific knowledge cannot prove something we should believe that a magical being is the cause of it, is completely absurd."[5]

And even the evangelical Christian website Biologos admits, "There is certainly reason to be skeptical about the common-sense intuition that everything must have a cause."[6]

"The Universe Is Too Well Designed"

Even if you can account for how the universe was born, theists may challenge you about how it works today. For instance: "The world of nature is too complex to have developed by chance" or "The universe is so fine-tuned to support life that the only explanation is that God did the fine-tuning."

Some unbelievers counter this viewpoint by noting that the universe didn't need God to make it complex; the universe has been around for billions of years and covers an infinite expanse. A lot of complex structures can grow in that much space and time, and no one's proved that a deity made them.

As for the argument that God designed the universe for life: "Most of the universe is rather inhospitable to life," atheist cosmologist Lawrence Krauss said in debating Christian physicist Ian Hutchinson and Christian political columnist Dinesh D'Souza. Krauss added that the universe doesn't exist in order to house living creatures. The universe got along just dandy without them until they evolved to fit the universe.[7]

Other unbelievers point out that even if the universe does have a designer, he or she isn't the wise, benevolent deity that most religions worship. "The moral design of nature is as bungled as its engineering design," said Harvard University psychology professor Steven Pinker. "What twisted sadist would have invented a parasite that blinds millions of people or a gene that covers babies with excruciating blisters?"[8]

JOKE AWAY THE ARGUMENTS

One way to deflate theism is with a few good jokes. So here are some funny lines from unbelievers, humorists, and unbeliever humorists. Even if they don't make theists laugh, you might get a giggle out of them yourself.

One horse-laugh is worth ten thousand syllogisms. It is not only more effective; it is also vastly more intelligent.

—H. L. MENCKEN[9]

Calling atheism a religion is like calling bald a hair color.

—DON HIRSCHBERG[10]

Not only is there no God but try finding a plumber on Sunday.

—WOODY ALLEN[11]

*If God created man in his own image, how come
I'm not invisible?*

—DAVID POWERS[12]

*Born again?! No, I'm not. Excuse me
for getting it right the first time.*

—DENNIS MILLER[13]

*It's fair to say that the Bible contains equal amounts
of fact, history, and pizza.*

—PENN JILLETTE[14]

*You have to make fun of any religion that would let you have
sixteen kids and say it's God's will.*

—KATHY GRIFFIN[15]

*One of the proofs of the immortality of the soul is that myriads have
believed in it. They have also believed the world was flat.*

—MARK TWAIN[16]

*If you're going to war over religion, now you're just killing people
in an argument over who's got the better imaginary friend.*

—RICHARD JENI[17]

*If Jesus had been killed twenty years ago, Catholic school
children would be wearing little electric chairs around their necks
instead of crosses.*

—LENNY BRUCE[18]

*I believed in a virgin birth, and a guy lived in a whale, and a woman
came from a rib. But then something happened that made me doubt
all of it: I graduated sixth grade.*

—BILL MAHER[19]

I'm completely in favor of the separation of Church and State.
My idea is that these two institutions screw us up enough on
their own, so both of them together is certain death.

—GEORGE CARLIN[20]

If there really is a God who created the entire universe with all of its
glories, and He decides to deliver a message to humanity, He will not use,
as His messenger, a person on cable TV with a bad hairstyle.

—DAVE BARRY[21]

Life in Lubbock, Texas, taught me two things. One is that God loves
you, and you're going to burn in hell. The other is that sex is the most
awful, dirty thing on the face of the earth, and you should save it
for someone you love.

—BUTCH HANCOCK[22]

"I Know from Experience that God Is Real"

Some theists say that God has to exist because they've met him. Can anyone refute their firsthand eyewitness testimony?

Yes.

"The feeling of having met God must not be confused with the fact of having met God," said Gordon Stein, author and editor of atheist books such as the *Encyclopedia of Unbelief*,[23] debating Presbyterian minister Greg Bahnsen. "We cannot use our own feelings as if they were valid information about the world. They are feelings that we have inside of us, but you cannot demonstrate them to another person. They cannot be used as evidence."[24]

Recent brain studies hint that if you've met God, the meeting may literally be all in your head. Religious experiences may be connected to epilepsy of the temporal lobe (a part of the brain involved in processing sounds and images), shrinking of the hippocampus (a part of the temporal lobe crucial to memory), and other conditions that can produce hallucinations.[25]

These theories don't mean that a theist who talks about meeting God is brain damaged. But they can explain the theist's experiences without saying that God caused them.

"Religion Is Good for You"

This claim is tough to answer, because people who regularly practice religious activities such as prayer tend to be happier and healthier than other people.[26] Recently, for instance, Gallup and Healthways (a health and well-being company) announced, "Very religious Americans of all major faiths have higher overall well-being than do their respective counterparts who are moderately religious or nonreligious." Atheists and agnostics score the lowest of all.[27]

But wait, there's more: "Jews and Mormons have the highest well-being of any of the faith groups"—and Muslims outscore most Protestants.[28] If a theist of, say, a Protestant faith asks you to believe in his or her god in order to live a happy, healthy life, then you can ask that person to become Jewish, Mormon, or Muslim for the same reason.

In addition, said young atheist author David McAfee (*Mom, Dad, I'm an Atheist*), "[Religion] doesn't accomplish anything that secular therapies cannot."[29]

"Religion Does a Lot of Good"

Many agnostics and soft atheists don't dispute this argument. "I think organized religion does a lot of good things, mostly in the form of materialistic, things like providing monetary aid, and metaphysical things, like providing incentives to do good," said Adi, an atheist college student from New Hampshire.[30]

But some atheist debaters have argued that religion has also been involved in a lot of evil. Ancient Mayans committed countless murders as sacrifices to their gods, Christian crusaders spent centuries slaughtering Middle Eastern Muslims, extremist Muslims have committed suicide bombings against infidels, and so on.

In addition, some unbelievers argue that religion itself is bad since it encourages people to accept faith over reason, and superstition over science. "Faith is the great cop-out, the great excuse to evade the need to think and evaluate evidence," atheist scientist Richard Dawkins has said.[31]

Don't Expect to Deconvert Anyone

> Don't feed yourself illusions that if you argue with anyone,
> you'll be able to change his or her mind. The only person who can
> change someone's mind is himself.
>
> *Mark, age 14*[32]

Will the arguments in this chapter change a theist's mind?

A truism among some preachers is "you can't argue people into heaven." It works the other way too: you can knock down one defense of religion after another, but you probably won't make a theist rise and shout, "You're right! I'm going to abandon my faith!"

But you may convince him that his arguments for religion won't work on you.

17

How Can You Make Arguments for Atheism?

For me to believe something, you have to be able to prove that it's true. You can't prove that there is a God, therefore I don't believe that there is one. My logic is very simple, it bewilders me why so many people are offended and confused by it.

LYNN, POSTING AS GURLGODDESS, AGE 14[1]

"Why don't you believe in God?"

That's a question that you may have to face over and over, so you may need some good answers.

The most honest answer is your personal one. Explain your deconversion simply—and, if possible, calmly. If you never had a religion and therefore never went through a deconversion, you can explain that you've gotten along fine without faith, and you don't see much need for one.

The story of your life may not satisfy some theists. If you want to give them something more, here are a few arguments that atheists and agnostics often use.

The Argument from Evil

I reject God because my own biological father is far better of a person to me than [God] ever was.

Katherine, age 15[2]

The **argument from evil** is probably the most popular argument for God's nonexistence. It says that the God of the major religions—who knows everything, can do anything, and loves humanity—wouldn't let evil things happen to people. Since evil things do happen, the religions' God can't be real. A classic version of this argument, sometimes credited to the Greek philosopher Epicurus, goes like this:

Is God willing to prevent evil but not able?
Then he is not omnipotent.
Is he able but not willing?
Then he is malevolent.
Is he both able and willing?
Then why is there evil in the world?
Is he neither able nor willing?
Then why call him God?

But theists have a variety of arguments against this argument, and unbelievers have arguments against the arguments. Here are a few.

Theist argument #1: Most of the evil in the world is caused not by God but by people. Why does God let them do evil? Because stopping them would mean something even worse: reducing or removing their free will and freedom to act.[3]

Atheist response: Sometimes, reducing free will might not be so bad. Russian ruler Josef Stalin murdered millions of his own people. They probably wouldn't have minded if God had cut off Stalin's freedom to turn them into corpses. Besides, giving people the freedom to do evil doesn't explain why God allows (or causes) natural evils such as plagues, floods, earthquakes, cyclones, droughts, famines, and tsunamis.

▽▽▽

Theist argument #2: God has good reasons for letting evil exist—but we humans can't understand them. "When a parent takes an infant to the doctor for a regular vaccination to prevent some childhood disease, it's because the parent cares for and loves that child," said Wayne Blank, author of the website *Daily Bible Study*. "The young child, however, will almost always see things very differently. When the doctor's needle goes into that little arm, the child will often cry out . . . . Just as an infant cannot possibly understand the motives of its parent while it is still only a child, so, too, we cannot appreciably comprehend God's will."[4]

Atheist response: We're not babies, and God's not a human parent. He's all-wise, so he can reveal his reasons in ways that we can understand. And he's all-powerful, so he can make us smart enough to figure out his reasons. Since he can't (or refuses to) do these things, we're back where we started: with something that's not the all-powerful, all-knowing, all-caring deity of the religions.

▽▽▽

Theist argument #3: God allows evil so that we can learn to fight it and overcome it. As a result, we'll become stronger, smarter, more moral, and better in general.[5]

Atheist response: If God has allowed evil as part of a plan to make us better, he should see by now that his plan isn't working. Millions of people behave terribly every day.

▽ ▽ ▽

Theist argument #4: It's okay for God to allow evil because he'll pay back the victims of evil after they die. "Heaven will bring far more than compensation for our present sufferings," Christian minister and author Randy Alcorn has written.[6]

Atheist response: If God can reward people in heaven for suffering from evil, why not reward them on earth?

The Argument from Unbelief and Divine Hiddenness

The **argument from unbelief** is all about you, the unbeliever. Your existence reveals something illogical about God's existence. Here's how it goes:

1. Religions say that God is all-powerful.

2. Religions also say that God wants everyone to believe in him.

3. Since God is all-powerful, he can help everyone believe.

   a. For instance, he can provide undeniable proof that he exists.

   b. Or he can reach into our minds and make us believe.

4. Nevertheless, many people don't believe.

5. It doesn't make sense that the omnipotent Almighty wants something but doesn't get it.

6. So the religions' version of God doesn't make sense.[7]

Again, theists are ready with responses.

Theist argument #1: God's already given us undeniable proof of his existence. After all, he's provided an awe-inspiring universe, plus the Bible.[8]

Atheist response: Not everyone trusts the Bible or agrees that the existence of the universe proves the existence of God. If God wants his evidence to convince people, why doesn't he provide better evidence?

$$\triangledown \ \triangledown \ \triangledown$$

Theist argument #2: God is eager for us to believe in him, but he doesn't force us to believe because he's even more eager to have us come to him of our own free will. In that view, God is generously putting aside his own desire for our belief, letting us choose whether or not to believe.[9]

Atheist response: This one has an argument all its own. It's similar to the argument from unbelief, and it's called divine hiddenness.

1. Religions say that God loves everyone.

2. And he wants everyone to believe that he exists.

3. And he can show everyone that he exists.

4. So if you want to believe that God exists, he'll enable you to believe it.

5. But many people who've wanted to believe in God—and have exercised their free will to seek him out—have found themselves unable to believe. (A few of them are in chapter 5.)

6. Since these people have willingly sought God but still couldn't believe in him, he must have hidden himself from them.

7. But hiding from willing believers is not the behavior of an all-powerful god who loves people and wants them to believe in him.

8. So the religions' version of God doesn't exist.[10]

▽ ▽ ▽

Theist argument against divine hiddenness: If God doesn't reveal himself to us but instead makes us search for him, the process of searching will turn us into better people.[11]

Atheist response: If a spiritual searcher seeks God, doesn't find him, and becomes an atheist, does the search make the atheist a better person than a theist who has always believed and never sought God?

▽ ▽ ▽

Of course, all arguments about God's motives are guesswork. No one knows why a supreme being would want all of us to believe but allow millions of us not to.

The Paradox of the Stone

Can God create a stone so heavy that he can't lift it?

If he can't create such a stone, then he can't be all-powerful. If he can create it but can't lift it, then again he isn't all-powerful. And if he isn't all-powerful, then the religions are wrong when they that say he is. Their version of God doesn't exist.

This argument, known as the paradox of omnipotence or the **paradox of the stone,** is a favorite of many unbelievers.[12] Theists, of course, deploy arguments against it.

Theist argument #1: The paradox reveals our limits, not God's. We can't imagine God doing the impossible, but our failure to imagine it doesn't mean that he can't do it.[13]

Theist argument #2: God, being perfectly wise, is perfectly logical. So it's not his nature to perform acts that are as logically absurd as the paradox of the stone.[14]

Atheist response: The theists' answers are based on guesswork about God. And guesswork has never proven anything, let alone the existence of God.

THOUGHTS FROM ATHEIST THINKERS

To sum up or spice up your arguments, you may want to quote a few of the wisest unbeliever authorities. Here are some quotes that could come in handy.

All thinking men are atheists.

—ERNEST HEMINGWAY, NOBEL PRIZE–WINNING NOVELIST[15]

There was a time when religion ruled the world. It is known as the Dark Ages.

—RUTH HURMENCE GREEN, ATHEIST AUTHOR[16]

What do I care for [God]? Justice is a matter between men, and I need no god to teach me it.

—JEAN-PAUL SARTRE, NOBEL PRIZE–WINNING PHILOSOPHER AND PLAYWRIGHT[17]

All national institutions of churches, whether Jewish, Christian, or Turkish, appear to me no other than human inventions, set up to terrify and enslave mankind, and monopolize power and profit.

—THOMAS PAINE, AMERICAN REVOLUTIONARY[21]

Religion is an illusion, and it derives its strength from the fact that
it falls in with our instinctual desires.

—SIGMUND FREUD, PIONEERING PSYCHIATRIST[18]

The fact that a believer is happier than a skeptic is no more to the point
than the fact that a drunken man is happier than a sober one.

—GEORGE BERNARD SHAW, NOBEL PRIZE–WINNING PLAYWRIGHT[19]

I'm an atheist, and that's it. I believe there's nothing we can know
except that we should be kind to each other and
do what we can for other people.

—KATHARINE HEPBURN, OSCAR-WINNING ACTRESS[20]

The Argument from Minds and Brains

Why do we have brains? Why is the source of our intelligence, emotions, consciousness, and identity a three-pound lump of meat? Especially a lump like ours. Atheist scholar Richard Carrier has written, "[The] brain . . . is very delicate and easily damaged . . . a considerable handicap, the cause of needless misery and death and pointless inefficiency—which is not anything a loving engineer would give us, nor anything a good or talented engineer with godlike resources would ever settle on."[22]

God doesn't have a physical brain himself; he's pure spirit. Since God is all-wise, his mind must be superior to our fleshy brains. Why didn't God, who loves humanity and created us in his own image, give us this superior kind of mind? And since he didn't give us this kind of mind, doesn't that mean that he's not as powerful, wise, or loving as his followers say he is?

Theist argument: There's more to the mind than the brain. A soul isn't just chemicals pulsing through flesh.[23]

Atheist response: Most of the science says that our thoughts and feelings come from our delicate, pulpy pounds of meat. Until someone proves otherwise, we will continue to disbelieve in God.

The Lack of Evidence

I am an atheist because I have a scientific approach to almost everything except music, and I believe there must be evidence to accept a theory. There's absolutely no evidence suggesting there is a higher power, only speculation.

Dan, young unbeliever, England[24]

Unbelievers use the lack of evidence argument a lot. They doubt or deny God's existence because they just don't see enough proof.[25]

Theist argument: The absence of evidence isn't evidence of absence. That is, humanity's inability to detect God's existence doesn't prove that God doesn't exist.

Atheist response: The "absence of evidence isn't evidence of absence" argument is like the "you can't prove that God *doesn't* exist" argument (from chapter 15). If theists expect us to believe that God exists without evidence to prove it, then they should believe other claims that have no evidence. But if someone were to make such a claim—for instance, a Flying Spaghetti Monster runs the universe—theists would demand evidence before they'd believe it. If there's no evidence, they'd disbelieve it. And that's how we feel about God.

The Simple Answer

Often, we look at the beauty of life and believe it was designed by a higher being. The complexities of life, love, beauty, and

> eloquence [are] answered with simplicity [like "God did it all"];
> but why? Why should the answer be simple if the question and
> the outcome are complex? That's why I am an atheist; because a
> simple answer to a complex question just isn't enough.
>
> *Dylan, age 15, New Zealand*[26]

The lack of evidence, the meaty brain, the heavy stone, divine hidden-ness, the existence of unbelievers, the existence of evil: Unbelievers have given lots of reasons not to believe in the religions' Supreme Being. If this chapter's lines of logic are useful, then use them. Or come up with your own.

As long as you believe what you say and can defend it with facts and logic, you should be able to stand up to anyone who challenges you.

IV.

THE REST OF YOUR LIFE

18

What If You Turn from Atheist to Believer?

If I were not an atheist, I would believe in a God who would choose to save people on the basis of the totality of their lives and not the pattern of their words.

ISAAC ASIMOV, NOVELIST[1]

Do you ever feel the tug of religion?

If you do, you're not alone. More than half of all people raised as atheists are likely to change their viewpoint, according to the authoritative Pew Forum on Religion & Public Life.[2] Even people who start religious and become atheist may turn back to religion.

The Classic Method

Some people find God in a flash. Amy M, a blogger in Idaho, said that she was an atheist until one day during her middle teens. "I happened to look up into the sky, and for the barest moment I felt something—something powerful, something bigger than myself. And I knew that there was *some*thing out there that I might as well call God."[3]

How do you get that splash of enlightenment? A lot of teenage atheists try praying—or just showing up in church. Teenage atheist Marc Hessel accepted an invitation to attend church, where, he said, "I felt a wave of warm, intense light enter throughout my entire body, [and] I felt the Holy Spirit for the first time in my life."[4] And that was it: Marc instantly went Christian.

Lacey Mosley, lead singer of the metal band Flyleaf, was an atheist until age sixteen, when her grandmother forced her to attend church. Mosley suddenly underwent mysterious experiences and feelings that she's described as supernatural. They opened her to Christianity.[5]

On the website fishthe.net, which offers "testimonies of the saving power of Jesus Christ," an ex-atheist named Shaun reported that as a teenager, unbelief wasn't satisfying him. "I began to feel like I was suffocating from the inside," he said. So he joined some Christians for prayer. "Then it happened! There was a violent rushing wind from above. It seemed to occupy all the space in the room and penetrated both my eardrums, but no damage was done. My whole body was filled with this powerful but gentle wind. The suffocating stopped and I could breathe properly again." Shaun interpreted the experience as proof of God's presence.[6]

Most teenage unbelievers who turn to God don't report anything nearly so dramatic, though.

The Power of Friendliness

Often, young unbelievers turn to religion after they meet friendly theists. According to youth pastor Rick Bartlett, teenagers raised without religion "are not looking for an apologetic for the faith, at least not overtly. Instead, they are looking for [something] safe and welcoming."[7]

A young woman who calls herself Lissa said that she spent her first eighteen years without religion. "I went off to college, and a roommate was LDS [a member of the Church of Jesus Christ of Latter-Day Saints, also known as the Mormons] and invited me to go to church with her while I was bored out of my mind on a Sunday. I went and was so impressed, I started taking the discussions."[8] It didn't hurt, she admitted, that the missionaries leading the discussions were young, male, and cute. In any event, they listened to Lissa and responded openly to her questions. She eventually joined their church.

Marc, the guy who felt the wave of warm, intense light, found God in church, but how did this atheist get there? He was a high school kid taking classes at a local college. At the campus cafeteria, "[I] noticed a group of Chi Alpha members meeting in the center corner of the cafeteria. One came up to me and offered me a flyer on a Chi Alpha meeting."[9] (Chi Alpha is a network of college and university ministries that works to "reconcile students to Christ."[10]) Marc accepted the invitation and went to church with the Chi Alphas. And the rest you know.

Teachers can be influential too. Chris Bergman was a teenage atheist who won a scholarship to a prestigious Catholic high school. He started debating religion with one of his teachers, Mr. Schneider. "We discussed every question I had about religion." What's more, he never preached at Chris. "It's just that someone took the time to help me realize that [Christianity] made more sense [than atheism]."[11]

The Scientific Method

You may not have a Mr. Schneider to help you get to God. You don't need him, though. Some atheists and agnostics find religion through science.

As a teenage atheist, said physicist Neil McKenzie, "[I] regarded all Christians as rather soft in the head."[12] But like other people of a scientific bent, he was curious about matters such as how energy ordered itself into the laws of physics and how those laws came about from chaos. Eventually, he decided that science had no answer. So he turned to faith—specifically, Christianity.

Jennifer Fulwiler found God through biochemistry. "In my late teens and early 20s, I struggled with depression," she said. "There was some kind of chemical imbalance going on in my brain." But she had a hard time accepting that her emotions, identity, personality, and entire self could be nothing but the interactions of some brain chemicals.[13] Jennifer's thoughts about her mental chemistry "led me to truly open my mind to [the] possibility that there might be something more to life than the material world . . . . I started to think that I just might have a soul." And she found that Christianity helped her accept the idea of a soul.[14]

Atmospheric scientist Roger Edwards found faith through math. "As a child and early teenager, and aspirant to the scientist I would become, I vacillated between atheism and agnostic uncertainty. I was demanding: 'If you're out there, show me the evidence!'"

He found it. Take a deep breath; Edwards is about to get complicated.

"What is the probability that every single living thing, nonliving [thing], and event has assembled from the Big Bang exactly as they have and are now is arranged, from the nearly infinite number of potential atoms (and by extension, molecules) trapped in that singular point? One over that number, of course. How many molecules are there? Infinity. What's one over infinity? . . . 1/[infinity] = zero. Zero. That's the logical probability to me, that every single component of our universe and life all came to be as it is by pure chance—that God didn't do any of it . . . . Therefore, I can make no other conclusion, as a scientific thinker, than the presence of God."[15]

Holy Words?

If you're more of a reader than a scientific calculator, books can get you from atheism to godliness.

"I read the Bible through, from cover to cover, four times during my sophomore year in college for the explicit purpose of finding scientific contradictions in it. By that, I mean statements in the Bible that were false," said John Clayton, a writer and lecturer who travels America talking about Christianity. "I found that I could not find a contradiction." Since he could find nothing that he considered false, he accepted the Bible as true.[16]

A. S. A. Jones, a research chemist who runs a website called Ex-Atheist .com, says that she had always considered the Bible "superstitious baloney." "The Bible didn't make sense to me. But why did it make sense to others?" To answer those questions, she tried reading the Bible "[as] poetry or fiction, and not as a proposal of fact." She came to see it as "the truth about human nature and our efforts to rise above it."[17]

The Bible isn't the only holy book to spark a conversion. Jeffrey Lang, an atheist from age eighteen through his twenties, read the Quran after meeting some Muslims. "You cannot simply read the Quran, not if you take it seriously," he's said. "You either have surrendered to it already or you fight it." Lang fought—but "the Quran was always way ahead of my thinking; it was erasing barriers I had built years ago and was addressing my queries." Eventually, he became a Muslim.[18]

John Daquila, now in his thirties, stumbled over his faith in school. In a class on religions, he read the *Tao Te Ching*, "the classic book of the way of virtue," a Chinese text from about 1500 BCE. The book says that the universe functions according to various rules and that people should find harmony within them. "Reading these texts, I found a more instinctive way of describing a 'higher power,' as not necessarily a man, but a way," Daquila explained. "After that class, I could no longer say I was an atheist."[19]

Other atheists find holiness in stories that old-fashioned preachers would consider sacrilege. Novelist Will Shetterly found his spiritual path through science fiction. "I [used to be] an atheist, but in my teens, I craved some form of enlightenment," he said. "I felt the sacrifice of Frodo in *The Lord of The Rings*, the suffering of Winston Smith in *1984*, and the respect for difference in *Star Trek*'s Prime Directive." From there, Shetterly continued seeking forms of spirituality and eventually became a Unitarian.[20]

REACTIONS AND RESPONSES

I grew up Christian. When I was about twelve I converted to atheism, and now, at fifteen, I've decided to convert to Islam, after a friend of mine introduced me to the religion . . . . First thing I was asked when I told my friends: "So wait, are you some kind of terrorist now?"

Maz, teenage ex-atheist[21]

"Why must you bounce from one extreme to another?"

That's what Anita Mathias's father asked her as tears slid down his cheeks. She'd just told him that she was no longer an atheist but had decided to join the Missionaries of Charity—a devout Catholic group devoted to helping the poor. Mathias's father was Catholic himself, but he didn't want his daughter becoming a nun.[22]

That's the way it is with converts sometimes: they're so happy to have found a new faith that they want to devote themselves to it completely.

A fast U-turn in your beliefs can confuse and annoy everyone around you, even if you're not going so far as to join a monastery. Kirk Cameron, young star of the television sitcom *Growing Pains*, pulled away from people who didn't share his beliefs, including his castmates. By some accounts, the warm, family-like atmosphere on the set grew distant and cold.[23]

Tony Woodlief, a management consultant and writer in Kansas, went from atheist to Christian starting at age sixteen. He joined the Calvinist Presbyterian Reformed Church with so much enthusiasm that "[my] new faith made me want to set straight everyone who was not a Calvinist." In other words, he became a pain in the butt. "I confess," he said, "that I recoil from such people now."[24]

Even if you take it easier on people, they may need time to handle your conversion. When Chris Bergman left atheism, he found that his conversion "threw [my atheist friends] for a loop. They had looked to me as the champion of atheism, and here I was moving over to the enemy's side."[25] Even Christians didn't know what to make of his change. "It took a long, long time for my 'Christian' friends . . . to believe that I actually believed what I said," Chris said. "There was definitely an attitude of 'Oh, well, you're not really a Christian yet.' Like there was some rite of passage that I hadn't completed."[26]

Sometimes, people are just curious and even caring. After John Daquila discovered the *Tao Te Ching*, his friends—mostly atheists and agnostics—"grilled me on the subject. But in a loving way. It was a way for them to make sure I hadn't gotten into some weird cult or [wouldn't] start damning them left and right—that I was still me." Soon, John's friends accepted his new beliefs.[27]

Dealing with unsupportive responses can make your faith waver. Lissa—the college girl who became a Mormon after discussions with missionaries—reported "one short period of [religious] inactivity after my parents' doubt and disapproval were expressed, which was followed by a feeling of loss." But, she added, "I finally picked [my faith] back up again and haven't dropped it since."[28]

How Long Does It Take?

Even if your discovery of faith hits like lightning, accepting and understanding it can take a long time.

John Daquila said that his abandonment of atheism and discovery of spirituality came in a burst; but after the burst came "a period of slow, steady consumption of ideas, and formulating of my own [ideas]."[29]

Jennifer Fulwiler had occasional religious thoughts and ideas even during her atheistic childhood; only much later did they join together into a belief in God.[30]

After the blogger Amy M looked into the sky and felt the presence of something big, she couldn't bring herself to identify it as God—at least not right away. "I spent the next several years trying to find a name for what I had experienced," she said.[31]

After Roger Edwards used math to determine that God had to exist, he kept re-examining his conclusion. "I tested and retested the theorem, off and on for months, maybe a couple years, and out spat the same answer every time." After those months of calculation, "faith has slowly settled in and solidified the foundation laid by the initial computation."[32]

What to Believe, Where to Go

To work out exactly what to believe, look into a variety of religions. John Clayton didn't settle firmly into Christianity until after he explored the sacred texts of other faiths—"the Vedas, Koran, Sayings of Buddha, writings of Bahá'u'lláh and Zoroaster," he said.[33]

Young atheist John Jeremiah explored several Christian churches, plus Judaism, Buddhism, and the Nation of Islam. Only after he saw a series of video seminars called *Amazing Facts Millennium of Prophecy* did he find a path that he liked. "The Bible was presented with step-by-step reasoning," he remembered. "In one of the seminar sessions, the speaker proved from the Bible what the true day of worship was. I became convinced the seventh-day Sabbath was the day of worship." After the speaker mentioned that he was a Seventh-Day Adventist, Jeremiah joined the SDA church.[34]

Whatever religion you choose, talk to its ministers, priests, rabbis, or other leaders. "Don't be afraid to explore," said John Daquila. "Ask a lot of questions about how any religion matches your feelings on things as simple as what constitutes 'prayer' [or] what their positions on societal issues are."[35]

When you find a faith, keep in mind that it may not stick. Marc Hessel found Christianity in a burst of light, but he later quit Christianity for Judaism.[36] Devin Rose, an atheist in his teens, became a Baptist in his senior year of college and turned to Catholicism a few years later.[37] And after John Clayton chose Christianity, he went from church to church to find one that suited him. None did, so he devised his own ministry. Nevertheless, he's said, "I am still trying to find that true church."[38]

Now What?

Now that I am a Christian, I do have moods in which the whole thing
looks very improbable: but when I was an atheist, I had moods
in which Christianity looked terribly probable.

C. S. Lewis, novelist[39]

If you feel the stirrings of faith, pay attention. Maybe they'll lead you to beliefs that'll fulfill you for the rest of your life.

Or maybe not. If you find out that religion isn't right for you, you can always quit.

That's one thing that belief and unbelief have in common: they're both waiting for you whenever you want to turn to them.

19

What's Your Future Going to Look Like?

> *By the twenty-first century, religious believers are likely to be found only in small sects, huddled together to resist a worldwide secular culture, a prominent sociologist of religion said here last week. In a luncheon talk at the New School for Social Research, Peter L. Berger, whose works are well regarded in religious and academic circles, said . . . "The traditional religions are likely to survive in small enclaves and pockets . . . . People will become so bored with what religions have to offer that they will look elsewhere."*
>
> PETER L. BERGER, *NEW YORK TIMES*, FEBRUARY 25, 1968[1]

What's next for you and other young unbelievers?

Well, as the prediction that opens this chapter indicates, it's hard to foresee the future of belief and unbelief. But let's try.

Alive and Growing

In the future, expect to see more unbelievers.

"People claiming no religious affiliation constitute the fastest growing religious minority in many countries throughout the world. Americans without religious affiliation comprise the only religious group growing in all fifty states." That's the finding of two mathematicians and a physicist who've studied the populations of both theists and nontheists.[2]

Meanwhile, psychologist Nigel Barber has studied countries that cross what he calls the "atheist threshold," where at least half of the people don't believe in God, don't find religion important in their daily lives, or both. "The entire world population," Barber has said, "would cross the atheist threshold by about 2038."[3]

Unbeliever Universities

If your future includes college (or if you're already in college but are looking to transfer to another school or to pursue postgraduate studies), you may want a campus that's friendly to unbelievers.

The Princeton Review, a company that helps students with test preparation, ranks colleges by categories such as campus life—including religious life. The schools where students are least religious tend to cluster in the northeast, particularly New York (Vassar College, Bard College, Skidmore College, Sarah Lawrence College, State University of New York—Purchase College) and Massachusetts (Emerson College, Bard College at Simon's Rock, Worcester Polytechnic Institute).

The Pacific coast is well-represented too: California (Pomona College, Pitzer College, California Institute of Technology), Oregon (Reed College, Lewis & Clark College), and Washington (Evergreen State College). You can find others in Colorado (Colorado College), Ohio (Kenyon College), Wisconsin (Beloit College), Arizona (Prescott College), and Michigan (Kalamazoo College).[4]

If you want to know where not to apply, the Princeton Review lists schools that are explicitly religious. They include Brigham Young University (Mormon, in Utah), Thomas Aquinas College (Catholic, California), Wheaton College (nondenominational Christian, Illinois), University of Dallas (Catholic, Texas), and Grove City College (nonde-nominational Christian, Pennsylvania). Other schools don't have a specific faith but have a lot of religious students, such as Hillsdale (Michigan) and Texas A&M College Station (Texas, obviously). Some of the most religiously strong are historically African American colleges such as Spelman (Georgia), Hampton (Virginia), and Tuskegee (Alabama).[5]

THE VOICE OF THE SECULAR STUDENT

People keep saying, "Oh, you students are the future. You're the future of the movement." Actually, [we're] the present.

Sarah Moglia, Secular Student Alliance event specialist[6]

"The [atheist] movement can look pretty bad to many young atheists," said Vlad Chituc, former president of Yale's chapter of the Secular Student Alliance, the largest American organization of college and high school unbeliever clubs. He has been frustrated with atheist leaders who insult theists, oppose any bit of religion in public life, and insult anyone who disagrees—even their fellow unbelievers.[7]

But things may be changing.

For one thing, college and high school atheist groups are including a wider variety of unbelievers than they used to. "We are really devoted to making the secular-student movement more diverse, because a lot of complaints that we hear is that atheism is an old white-man's thing. And we're trying to show that it's not," said the Secular Student Alliance's Sarah Moglia in 2012.[8] Atheist and agnostic women, people of color, gays, lesbians, bisexuals, transgender people—they're all calling for their fellow unbelievers to hear their viewpoints.

The broadening range of voices may be having an effect. About a year after Moglia made her comments, Vlad Chituc went to a student leadership conference for unbelievers. He found the young and the faithless surprisingly willing to accept his desire to work with people of faith.

"If the future of atheism," Chituc said, "is in the young leaders I met, laughed with, raged with . . . stayed up until 6 AM to get diner food with, almost once or twice cried with, [and] argued about philosophy with . . . then that's an atheism I want to be a part of."[9]

On the Job

After college, of course, comes a career. Which careers are friendliest to unbelievers?

Godlessness is strong in the sciences. One study a few years ago noted that more than half (51.8 percent) of scientists working in American colleges and universities have no religion, compared to only one seventh of the American people as a whole. The same study found that among scientists, physicists seem especially likely to say that they don't believe in God and that there's very little truth in religion.[10]

Thinking about going into medicine? Psychiatrists tend to be more godless than other doctors. More than one in three psychiatrists (35 percent) doesn't believe in God. Less than one in four other doctors (23 percent) would say the same.[11]

There's not a lot of information about unbelievers in other fields. But if you aim for a job with a lot of responsibility, discrimination may follow you. A university-level study of hiring has found that when participants in the study had to choose between an atheist job candidate and a religious one, "participants significantly preferred the religious candidate to the atheist candidate for a high-trust job."[12]

Once you've got a job, there's a chance—a small chance, but a chance—of discrimination at work. In a 2012 survey, one in nine atheists (10.9 percent) reported that fellow workers or classmates rejected, avoided, isolated, or ignored them four or more times because of their atheism. On the bright side, nearly two-thirds of the atheists (63.7 percent) said that they had never run into those problems.[13]

Atheism Plus

Many of us have decided that "not believing in any gods"
isn't enough. Many of us have decided that we're no longer willing
to work with people who say we're stupid, who say we're lazy,
who say we're freaks of nature.

Greta Christina, Atheism Plus supporter[+]

More than disbelief

One new trend in unbelief that may be a part of your future is called **Atheism Plus** or Atheism+.

It began in August 2012 with Jen McCreight. As a member of the Secular Student Alliance's board of directors and president of Purdue University's Society of Nontheists, Jen attended and organized events for unbelievers.[15] She felt warmly welcomed—"until I started talking about feminism." She detailed experiences of atheists (both male and female) harassing atheist women and girls, up to and including threats of rape.[16]

"It's time for a new wave of atheism," Jen declared, "a wave that isn't just a bunch of 'middle-class, white, cisgender [having the same gender as an adult as you had at birth], heterosexual, able-bodied men' . . . . It's time for a wave that cares about how religion affects *everyone* and that applies skepticism to *everything*, including social issues like sexism, racism, politics, poverty, and crime."[17]

Within two days, Jen's post attracted 762 comments—more than her previous eleven posts combined—and most of them supported her.[18] The day after her post, she announced Atheism Plus for people who are "atheists *plus* we care about social justice, atheists *plus* we support women's rights, atheists *plus* we protest racism, atheists *plus* we fight homophobia and transphobia."[19]

Soon, websites were boiling with comments on Atheism Plus and on its supporters—everything from "a bunch of frauds . . . [who] bitch about nonexistent misogyny"[20] to "Atheism Plus is good. And I don't just mean 'good' in the sense of 'morally right.' I mean 'good' as in 'good for the health and future of atheism.'"[21]

Atheism Plus may become a big step in the evolution of godlessness, or it may fade. Its future depends on unbelievers themselves.

And Now . . .

In 2009, comedy writer Ariane Sherine, with help from Richard Dawkins and the British Humanist Association, launched a campaign of bus and subway ads saying, "There's probably no god. Now stop worrying and enjoy your life."[22]

That's good advice whether God exists or not.

The life of an unbeliever isn't always easy, but it can be very enjoyable. Unless society changes radically, the future will include millions of people who don't believe in God, so you won't be alone. You may face criticism and even discrimination, but you can whip these problems just as other unbelievers have.

Now take the advice of Ariane Sherine's ads, and go enjoy your life!

Acknowledgments

The first person who deserves credit for this book's existence is my agent, Paul Levine. He worked with publisher after publisher until we found the right house and the right contract, and he helped me through the stresses of negotiations and renegotiations.

Nicole Geiger, Lindsay Brown, and Sheila Ashdown, my editors, have been remarkably patient and insightful. As an editor myself, I have high standards for our job and contempt for those who don't do it well. Nicole, Lindsay, and Sheila do it very, very well.

Hemant Mehta deserves great thanks. When he spread the word about this book through his blog, the *Friendly Atheist*, dozens of young unbelievers stepped up to answer my interview questions. Without their answers, this book would be much weaker. Without Hemant, I wouldn't have had their answers.

Thanks also to everyone whom I've quoted in this book. Writing it meant digging into hundreds of first-person accounts—often painful ones—and I appreciate everyone who has shared his or her story.

My family and friends could not have been more supportive over the years when I was conceiving, proposing, researching, and writing this book. Among the kindest and strongest have been those who profess strong religious faith. I've often thought that people who are secure in their faith don't need to feel defensive or threatened by other views, and my experience in writing this book makes me feel this way more than ever.

My darling, Lea Hernandez, and her daughter, Summer, have lived with me through most of the time I was writing this book. As my binders full of research piled up on the kitchen table and I struggled to find clear, fair ways to explain complex, controversial stories, Lea and Summer were always completely on my side. I couldn't ask for better companions.

Finally, I thank my parents, Marvin and Seena Seidman. They demonstrated by words and behavior that any person who shows kindness, generosity, and an open mind deserves respect, regardless of the person's religion or lack of it. If God exists, I hope that he or she blesses my parents. I bless them too.

Appendix: More Information about Unbelief

The information listed below includes websites, organizations, and other resources. Keep in mind that the world changes fast, particularly online, and that any of these resources can go out of business at any time. And don't believe everything that you read. Be a smart unbeliever and check it out first.

The Basics Online

Several websites and blogs provide solid facts about atheists, agnostics, and their beliefs (or lack of them). The most comprehensive is **About .com's Atheism and Agnosticism** section: atheism.about.com. Other trustworthy sites:

- ▶ **100 Facts Every Atheist Teen Must Know:** atheismfacts.org

- ▶ **Atheism Resource:** atheismresource.com

- ▶ **Fun Trivia: Atheism and Agnosticism:** funtrivia.com/en /Religion/Atheism-and-Agnosticism-12341.html

- ▶ **Positive Atheism:** positiveatheism.org

▶ **Teens without God:** kidswithoutgod.com/teens

▶ **The Secular Web Library:** infidels.org/library

The Basics in Print

Quite a few books cover the world of unbelief. Some of them are for teenagers and young adults in particular.

▶ *Mom, Dad, I'm an Atheist: The Guide to Coming Out as a Non-Believer* by David McAfee (Dangerous Little Books, 2012)

▶ *The Young Atheist's Survival Guide: Helping Secular Students Thrive* by Hemant Mehta (Patheos Press, 2012)

And these books cover unbelief in general:

▶ *Breaking the Spell: Religion as a Natural Phenomenon* by Daniel Dennett (Viking Press, 2006)

▶ *The God Delusion* by Richard Dawkins (Houghton Mifflin, 2006)

▶ *God Is Not Great: How Religion Poisons Everything* by Christopher Hitchens (Twelve Books, 2007)

▶ *Letter to a Christian Nation* by Sam Harris (Knopf, 2006)

▶ *The Portable Atheist: Essential Readings for the Nonbeliever* by Christopher Hitchens (Da Capo Press, 2007)

▶ And an unbeliever classic: *Why I Am Not a Christian* by Bertrand Russell (available in various editions)

Getting Help

If your parents, school, classmates, or anyone else gives you grief about your unbelief, you may need help. Here are some good sources of guidance:

▶ In the **"Ask Richard"** advice column, retired marriage and family therapist Richard Wade helps young unbelievers solve problems with friends and family: patheos.com/blogs /friendlyatheist/category/richard-wade.

▶ The site **Godless Teens** has useful information too: godlessteens.com.

▶ If you need to speak to a therapist about quitting religion, the **Secular Therapist Project** lists counselors who can help: seculartherapy.org.

▶ For any kind of problem, not just one tied to unbelief, **Teen Line** (teenlineonline.org) calls itself "a confidential telephone helpline for teenaged callers . . . . If you have a problem or just want to talk with another teen who understands, then this is the right place for you!" It operates every evening from 6:00 to 10:00 PM Pacific Coast time (9:00 PM to 1:00 AM East Coast time). The phone numbers are 800-852-8336 (in California) and 310-855-4673 (elsewhere).

▶ If your parents get so upset at your unbelief that they start hitting, you can try **Safe Horizon**. The group helps to protect victims of violence, including young ones: safehorizon.org. Its domestic-violence hotline is 800-621-4673.

▶ If you're thinking about leaving home (or if you've already left), there's the **National Runaway Safeline** (800-786-2929). Its website has a section for youth and teenagers: 1800runaway.org.

▶ If you must leave home, you can check the **AtheistHavens** page on Reddit, which helps "young adults that are kicked out or disowned by their family due to their atheism." The members offer "couches to crash on, warm meals to share, someone to lean on, and someone to listen": reddit.com/r/AtheistHavens.

And here are some resources for keeping yourself feeling all right when the stresses of the unbelieving life start to get to you.

▶ The **Anxiety Coach** offers breathing exercises to calm panic attacks: anxietycoach.com/breathingexercise.html.

▶ The United Kingdom's **Patient** website suggests muscular and deep-breathing exercises for relaxation: patient.co.uk/health /relaxation-exercises.

▶ **Empowered Teens & Parents** suggest positive self-talk is key to staying strong in difficult situations: empoweredteensandparents. com/parenting/learning-positive-self-talk.

▶ **RN Central** lists one hundred ways to be more positive—and reap the benefits that kind of thinking brings: rncentral.com /nursing-library/careplans/100_positive_thinking_exercises_to _incorporate_into_your_life.

▶ The **National Education Association** may be able to help you deal with angry parents: nea.org/home/12800.htm.

▶ **ShareCare** offers a list of activities to calm yourself down when you're angry: sharecare.com/question/as-teen-calm-down-angry.

The News

Here are some news organizations and aggregators that track stories about unbelievers fighting for their place in the world and the theists trying to stop them.

▶ *The New York Times* (probably America's most prestigious newspaper): topics.nytimes.com/top/reference/timestopics /subjects/a/atheism

▶ *The Huffington Post* (online news and opinion site): huffingtonpost.com/news/atheism

▶ *The Guardian* (a prominent British newspaper): theguardian.com /world/atheism

▶ **Alltop** (headlines from various unbeliever sites): atheism.alltop.com

▶ **Fox News** (this conservative channel is sometimes unfriendly to unbelief but devotes a section of its website to it): foxnews.com /topics/issues/atheism.htm

▶ **The Freethinker** (international news about unbelievers): freethinker.co.uk

Opinions and Arguments

Once an atheist news event gets reported, the unbeliever community reacts. Here are few popular sites where prominent unbelievers offer not just news but also opinions, insights, and sometimes calls to action:

▶ **Atheist Revolution** focuses on Christian extremism and the atheist movement's struggles with it: atheistrev.com.

▶ **Daylight Atheism** offers headlines and opinions on religious morality, American politics, secularism, and other topics for unbelievers: patheos.com/blogs/daylightatheism.

▶ **Friendly Atheist,** by former Secular Student Alliance chairman Hemant Mehta, is a blog of news and viewpoints: patheos.com /blogs/friendlyatheist

Some popular opinion sites may be especially interesting for young unbelievers because they come from young unbelievers. For instance:

▶ **Teen Skepchick** is a collective of more than a dozen young bloggers, mostly female: teenskepchick.org.

▶ **The Atheist Teenager** comes from a pair of young unbelievers who cover not just atheism but also politics, relationships, and music: theatheistteenager.com.

Unbeliever Radio

You can find atheist/agnostic ideas and opinions on iTunes and elsewhere. These are some of the most prominent unbeliever podcasts:

▶ **Freethought Radio** features interviews with famous atheist authors and other well-known unbelievers: ffrf.org/news/radio.

▶ **Thank God I'm Atheist!** views the news from an unbeliever perspective, with an emphasis on abuses by theists: thankgodimatheist.com/podcast.

▶ **The Angry Atheist** interviews prominent unbelievers and argues against the misconceptions that many theists have about unbelief: angryatheist.info.

▶ **The Thinking Atheist** focuses on themes ranging from the origin of the universe to the unbeliever's approach to Christmas: thethinkingatheist.com/podcast.

Unbeliever TV

YouTube is full of unbelief. Here are some popular atheistic YouTube channels:

▶ **Dark Matter 2525** is cartoon comedy that roasts religion, with animated uploads that make fun of God and his followers: youtube.com/DarkMatter2525.

▶ **Jaclyn Glenn** is a young woman who talks to the viewer with a pretty smile and nasty sarcasm about matters of faith: youtube.com/JaclynGlenn.

▶ **Pat Condell** delivers godless stand-up comedy that aims at religion in general and Islamic extremism in particular: youtube.com/patcondell.

▶ **The Amazing Atheist** calls himself "a professional ranter who yells loudly in empty rooms and puts videos of it on the internet"—and has more than half a million subscribers: youtube.com/TheAmazingAtheist.

▶ **The Atheist Experiece** is a weekly cable access show geared at the non-atheist audience: youtube.com/user /TheAtheistExperience.

▶ **The Richard Dawkins Foundation for Reason and Science** offers talks with some of the world's most prominent unbelievers: youtube.com/richarddawkinsdotnet.

▶ **The Thinking Atheist** features smoothly polished videos about topics ranging from Noah's Ark to giant gatherings of unbelievers: youtube.com/TheThinkingAtheist.

Meeting Unbelievers in Person

The best-known organization for young American unbelievers is the **Secular Student Alliance**. Its website, secularstudents.org, says that the group exists "to organize, unite, educate, and serve students and student communities that promote the ideals of scientific and critical inquiry, democracy, secularism, and human-based ethics."

You can find less formal organizations via **Meetup**, which calls itself "the world's largest network of local groups." Meetup claims more than eight hundred atheist-related groups, with nearly two hundred thousand members at atheists.meetup.com.

American Atheists, a leading national unbeliever group, lists local unbeliever groups on its website: atheists.org. So does the **American Humanist Association**, another widespread group of unbelievers and their allies: americanhumanist.org.

These organizations work primarily in the United States. If you're outside the United States, you can try the **Atheist Alliance International**, which lists international unbeliever groups at atheistalliance.org. So does the **International Humanist and Ethical Union**, at iheu.org.

If you're deconverting, the organization **Recovering from Religion** lists groups of people like you in dozens of cities: recoveringfromreligion.org.

Before you go to a meeting of any group, check to see if it welcomes teenagers. Some groups are strictly for adults, and some meetings take place in bars and other places where people under eighteen or twenty-one aren't allowed to go.

Meeting Unbelievers Online

Most of the groups listed above have forums, Facebook groups, or other ways of hanging out with other unbelievers in virtual space. Check their websites for the most current social spaces.

Here are some other popular virtual hangouts:

▶ **Atheist Empire Yahoo! Group:** dir.groups.yahoo.com/group /atheistempire

▶ **Atheist Forums:** atheistforums.org

▶ **Atheist Nexus:** atheistnexus.org

▶ **Ex-Christian:** ex-christian.net

▶ **R/Atheism:** reddit.com/r/atheism

▶ **Richard Dawkins Foundation:** richarddawkins.net/discussions

▶ **Think Atheist:** thinkatheist.com

Most unbeliever groups are active on social media. Here are some of the most popular atheist and agnostic Facebook pages:

▶ **American Atheists:** facebook.com/AmericanAtheists

▶ **Atheism:** facebook.com/nogods

▶ **Atheist Republic:** facebook.com/AtheistRepublic

▶ **Freedom from Religion Foundation:** facebook.com/4ffrf

▶ **Richard Dawkins Foundation:** facebook.com /RichardDawkinsFoundation

▶ **Sam Harris:** facebook.com/pages/Sam-Harris/22457171014

▶ **The Thinking Atheist:** facebook.com/thethinkingatheist

▶ **We Fucking Love Atheism:** facebook.com/WFLAtheism

And some of the most popular Twitter feeds:

▶ **Almightygod:** @almightygod

▶ **American Atheists:** @AmericanAtheist

▶ **Atheist QOTD:** @AtheistQOTD

▶ **Daily Atheism:** @AtheistQ

▶ **Daniel Dennett:** @danieldennett

▶ **Godless Spellchecker:** @GSpellchecker

▶ **Richard Dawkins:** @RichardDawkins

▶ **Sam Harris:** @SamHarrisOrg

▶ **Think Atheist:** @ThinkAtheist

Be careful, though: not everyone online is whom he or she pretends to be. Don't give away personal information—particularly your address or phone number—to anyone online.

Money for College

Being an unbeliever can help you pay for school. There are a number of scholarships for atheists and agnostics.

American Atheists offers the $2,000 **O'Hair Scholarship** and the $1,000 **President's Scholarship** for "students who demonstrate atheist activism in their communities and schools," according to the organization's website. There's also the $1,000 **Chinn Scholarship** for activism in equality for lesbians, gays, bisexuals, and transgender people (LGBT), but you don't have to be LGBT to win. These scholarships are available to college students and to high school students entering college in the upcoming year. More information is at atheists.org/scholarship.

The Freedom from Religion Foundation's **Michael Hakeem Memorial College Essay Contest** awards college students up to $3,000 for essays on a topic such as "Why I Don't Believe in God." High school seniors can win the **William J. Schultz High School Essay Award**, which also pays up to $3,000. More information is at ffrf.org.

The American Humanist Association gives students in grades nine through twelve the chance to win up to $1,000 in its **Humanist Essay Contest**. Students can write on nearly any topic related to humanism. More information is at thehumanist.org.

These scholarships are open to students throughout the United States and sometimes elsewhere, depending on the rules. Other scholarships are more limited, like the **Herb Silverman Secular Humanist Scholarship** for students at the College of Charleston, South Carolina (ssm.cofc.edu/scholarships). You can research these scholarships and others at sites such as those listed below. Use the search terms *atheist*, *agnostic*, or *secular* to find the scholarships relevant to you.

▶ **Begin College:** begincollege.com

▶ **College Scholarships:** collegescholarships.com and collegescholarships.org

▶ **Niche:** colleges.niche.com/scholarships

▶ **Sallie Mae College Answer:** collegeanswer.com/scholarships

▶ **Scholarships:** scholarships.com

▶ **Secular Student Alliance:** secularstudents.org/scholarships

▶ **Student Scholarship Search:** studentscholarshipsearch.com

Other grants and scholarships aren't strictly about atheism but reward the kind of mind that rejects blind faith. The James Randi Educational Foundation, for instance, offers thousands of dollars in its **Critical Thinking Educational Scholarship Awards** for students with "[a] plan for building critical thinking skills into their chosen field of study": randi.org.

Good luck!

Notes

A special note from the author: I've listed some of the people here by first name and last name, some by pseudonyms or screen names, and some by first name only. It's all in service of identifying people as they wanted to be identified.

All quotes from the Bible, were sourced through Bible Gateway, https://www.biblegateway.com.

1. Who Are Atheists (and Agnostics and Other Unbelievers)?

1. David Templeton, "My Lunch with Sparky," *Sonoma County Independent*, December 30, 1999–January 5, 2000, http://www.metroactive.com/papers/sonoma/12.30.99/schulz2-9952.html.

2. Susan Page, "2008 Race Has the Face of a Changing America," *USA Today*, March 11, 2007, http://usatoday30.usatoday.com/news/washington/2007-03-11-politics-diversity-cover_N.htm; Jeffrey M. Jones, "Some Americans Reluctant to Vote for Mormon, 72-Year-Old Presidential Candidates," Gallup News Service, February 20, 2007, http://www.gallup.com/poll/26611/Some-Americans-Reluctant-Vote-Mormon-72YearOld-Presidential-Candidates.aspx.

3. Fox News / Opinion Dynamics Poll, "Supreme Court Justice John Paul Stevens Recently Announced He will Resign . . . ," Polling Report, Inc., April 20–21, 2010, http://www.pollingreport.com/court.htm.

4. Pope Benedict XVI, "Pope's Holyroodhouse Speech Transcript," The Richard Dawkins Foundation for Reason and Science website, September 16, 2010, http://old.richarddawkins.net/articles/518808-pope-s-holyroodhouse-speech-transcript.

5. Kimberly Winston, "One Scouts Ban Remains Intact: Atheists," Religion News Service website, May 30, 2013, http://www.religionnews.com/2013/05/30/one-scouts-ban-remains-intact-atheists.

6. Robert Evans, "Atheists Face Death in 13 Countries, Global Discrimination: Study," Reuters, December 9, 2013, http://www.reuters.com/article/2013/12/10/us-religion-atheists-idUSBRE9B900G20131210; *FreeThoughtPedia*, "Laws and Other Rules against Atheists and Agnostics," last modified November 23, 2010, http://www.freethoughtpedia.com/wiki/Laws_and_other_rules_against_atheists_and_agnostics.

7. Nina Shepherd and Mark Cassutt, "Atheists Identified as America's Most Distrusted Minority, According to New U of M Study," *UM News*, March 28, 2006, http://www1.umn.edu/news/news-releases/2006/UR_RELEASE_MIG_2816.html.

8. Gary Wolf, "The Church of the Non-Believers," *Wired* 14, no. 11 (November 2006), http://www.wired.com/wired/archive/14.11/atheism_pr.html.

9. Clarence Darrow, "Why I Am an Agnostic," *Short Works of Clarence Darrow* (Charleston, SC: BiblioBazaar, 2009), 45.

10. CassieCasey, "Agnosticism," TeenageWriters.com forum, December 16, 2006, http://teenagewriters.com/forum/archive/index.php/t-7197.html.

11. [Ben] Gaarden, "My Thoughts," *Astral Pulse* (forum), April 24, 2005, http://www.astralpulse.com/forums/welcome_to_world_cultures_traditions_and_religions/my_thoughts-t18710.0.html;msg161689#msg161689.

12. *Merriam-Webster*, s.v. "freethinking," accessed January 1, 2014, http://www.merriam-webster.com/dictionary/freethinking.

13. Michael Martin, "Atheism on the Rise in U.S.," *Tell Me More*, National Public Radio, August 14, 2009, http://www.npr.org/templates/story/story.php?storyId=111885128&ft=1&f=1003.

14. Isaac Asimov, *It's Been a Good Life* (Amherst, NY: Prometheus Books, 2002), 21.

15. "About Humanism," American Humanist Association, accessed January 1, 2014, http://www.americanhumanist.org/Who_We_Are/About_Humanism.

16. Tim LaHaye and David Noebel, *Mind Siege: The Battle for Truth* (Nashville, TN: Word Publishing, 2000), 35.

17. Ayn Rand, *Anthem* (London: Cassell, 1938), part 11, http://www.gutenberg.org/cache/epub/1250/pg1250.txt.

18. Chris Mooney, "Not Too 'Bright,'" The Committee for Skeptical Inquiry website, October 15, 2003, http://www.csicop.org/specialarticles/show/not_too_bright.

19. Stephen Colbert, "Bart Ehrman," *The Colbert Report* website, June 20, 2006, http://www.colbertnation.com/the-colbert-report-videos/70912/june-20-2006/bart-ehrman.

20. Pete Darwin, "Agnosticism = Cop Out . . . ," *The Caudal Lure* (blog), December 9, 2011, http://caudallure.wordpress.com/2011/09/12/agnosticism-cop-out.

21. Bhagwad Jal Park, "Agnostics Are Wimps!," *Expressions* (blog), October 22, 2010, http://www.bhagwad.com/blog/2010/philosophy/agnostics-are-wimps.html.

22. John Draper, "Militant Agnostics," *Cobourg Atheist News*, November 24, 2010, http://www.cobourgatheistnews.com/opinion/atheism/249-militant-agnostics.

23. Frank Apisa, "Agnostic vs. Atheist," *able2know* (forum), June 15, 2006, http://able2know.org/topic/77088-5.

24. Mark Vernon, "How to Be Agnostic," *Philosophers Magazine*, October 29, 2009, http://www.philosophypress.co.uk/?p=785.

25. Psyadam, "Why Agnosticism Is Superior to Atheism," *Raving Atheists* (forum), August 25, 2010, http://ravingatheists.com/forum/showthread.php?p=616950.

26. Ouchichi, "Atheists Suck, Not Atheism," *Newgrounds* (forum), May 18, 2008, http://www.newgrounds.com/bbs/topic/908908/2.

27. Matt, "Have U Noticed, So-Called ATHEISTS Are of 3 Categories!?," *Yahoo! Answers* (forum), accessed January 1, 2014, http://answers.yahoo.com/question/index?qid=20080617115440AA0XfhQ.

28. Stephen Thompson, "Is There a God?," *Onion A.V. Club*, September 6, 2000, http://www.avclub.com/articles/is-there-a-god,1394.

29. Norbert Körzdörfer, "Brad Pitt Interview," *Bild*, July 29, 2009, http://www.bild.de/BILD/news/bild-english/celebrity-gossip/2009/07/22/brad-pitt-interview/inglourious-basterd-star-on-angelina-jolie-and-six-kids.html.

30. CM Punk, Twitter post, October 20, 2012, 12:16 a.m., https://twitter.com/CMPunk/status/259553683803623424.

31. Anita Singh, "Daniel Radcliffe: A Cool Nerd," *The Telegraph*, July 4, 2009, http://www
.telegraph.co.uk/culture/harry-potter/5734000/Daniel-Radcliffe-a-cool-nerd.html.

32. "Militant Atheist Daniel Radcliffe," Bang Showbiz, February 11, 2012, http://www
.bangshowbiz.com/products/showbiz/index.html?id=2012042114018474192&ch=showbiz.

33. Sharon Waxman, "George Clooney, Uncowled," *The Washington Post*, September 28, 1997,
http://www.washingtonpost.com/wp-srv/style/longterm/movies/review97/fgeorgeclooney.htm.

34. George Clooney, interview by Larry King, *Larry King Live*, CNN, February 16, 2006,
http://transcripts.cnn.com/TRANSCRIPTS/0602/16/lkl.01.html.

35. Vauhini Vara, "Just How Much Do We Want to Share on Social Networks?," *The Wall Street
Journal*, November 28, 2007, http://search.proquest.com/docview/399083840?accountid=47391.
Note: This citation was sourced from ProQuest a service available at many libraries where a
library card number can be used to access articles.

36. Wolfhaley [Tyler, the Creator], Spring.me, accessed November 16, 2013, http://new.spring
.me/#!/wolfhaley/q/1979879402; Brendan Frederick, "Q&A: 10 Facts We Learned About
Tyler, the Creator from Formspring," Complex.com, May 10, 2011, http://www.complex.com
/music/2011/05/10-facts-we-learned-about-tyler-the-creator-from-formspring#10.

37. Neil Strauss, "Zac Efron: The New American Heartthrob," *Rolling Stone*, August 23, 2007,
http://www.zefron.com/gallery/displayimage.php?pid=12857&fullsize=1.

38. Laurie Heifetz, "Hairspray's Hebrew Hotties," *Forward*, July 18, 2007, http://forward.com
/articles/11176/hairspray-s-hebrew-hotties-.

39. "'Nones' on the Rise," Pew Research Religion & Public Life Project, October 9, 2013,
http://www.pewforum.org/2012/10/09/nones-on-the-rise/; Larry Shannon-Missal,
"Americans' Belief in God, Miracles, and Heaven Declines," Harris Interactive website,
December 16, 2013, http://www.harrisinteractive.com/NewsRoom/HarrisPolls/tabid/447/ctl
/ReadCustom%20Default/mid/1508/ArticleId/1353/Default.aspx.

40. "State and County QuickFacts," U.S. Census Bureau website, 2011, http://quickfacts
.census.gov/qfd/states/00000.html.

41. Barry A. Kosmin and Ariela Keysar, *American Religious Identification Survey* (ARIS 2008):
Summary Report, (Hartford, CT: Trinity College, 2009), 5, http://commons.trincoll.edu/aris
/files/2011/08/ARIS_Report_2008.pdf; "Religious Composition of the United States," *U.S.
Religious Landscape Survey* (Washington, DC: Pew Forum on Religion & Public Life, February
2008), 12, http://religions.pewforum.org/pdf/report-religious-landscape-study-full.pdf.

42. Ibid.

43. Ibid.

44. "Incorporated Places with 100,000 or More Inhabitants in 2008—Population," U.S.
Census Bureau, http://www.census.gov/compendia/statab/2010/tables/10s0027.xls.

45. "State & County QuickFacts: Idaho," U.S. Census Bureau website, 2013, http://quickfacts
.census.gov/qfd/states/16000.html.

46. "State & County QuickFacts: Maine," U.S. Census Bureau website, 2013, http://quickfacts
.census.gov/qfd/states/23000.html.

47. "State & County QuickFacts: Hawaii," U.S. Census Bureau website, 2013, http://quickfacts
.census.gov/qfd/states/15000.html.

48. "U.S. and World Population Clock," U.S. Census Bureau website, 2014, http://www.census
.gov/popclock; Kosmin and Keysar, *ARIS* 2008, 5.

49. Kosmin and Keysar, *ARIS* 2008, 5; The Pew, *U.S. Religious Landscape Survey* (Washington,
DC: Pew Forum on Religion & Public Life, 2008), 20, http://religions.pewforum.org/pdf
/report-religious-landscape-study-full.pdf.

50. Barry A. Kosmin and Ariela Keysar, with Ryan Cragun and Juhem Navarro-Rivera,
American Nones: *The Profile of the No Religion Population* (Hartford, CT: Trinity College,

2009), 1, http://commons.trincoll.edu/aris/files/2011/08/NONES_08.pdf; The Pew, *Landscape Survey*, 5, http://religions.pewforum.org/pdf/report-religious-landscape-study-full.pdf.

51. Melinda Lundquist Denton, Lisa D. Pearce, and Christian Smith, "Personal Religiosity and Spirituality," *Religion and Spirituality on the Path through Adolescence: A Research Report of the National Study of Youth & Religion* (Chapel Hill, NC: University of North Carolina, 2008): 22–23.

52. "Provo-Orem, Utah, Is Most Religious U.S. Metro Area," Gallup Polotics poll, March 29, 2013, http://www.gallup.com/poll/161543/provo-orem-utah-religious-metro-area.aspx; Frank Newport, "Mississippi Maintains Hold as Most Religious US State," Gallup Poll, February 13, 2013, http://www.gallup.com/poll/160415/mississippi-maintains-hold-religious-state.aspx.

53. Norman Baynes, ed., *The Speeches of Adolf Hitler* (New York: Howard Fertig, 1969), 378.

54. Adolf Hitler speech (delivered to the Reichstag, April 28, 1939), The Propagander website, accessed January 2, 2014, http://comicism.tripod.com/390428.html.

55. Ward H. Lamon, *The Life of Abraham Lincoln: From His Birth to His Inauguration as President* (Boston: James R. Osgood and Company, 1872), 489, https://ia600308.us.archive.org/21/items/abrahamlincoln00lamo/abrahamlincoln00lamo.pdf.

56. Abraham Lincoln, Second Inaugural Address, March 4, 1865, http://www.bartleby.com/124/pres32.html.

57. *Stanford Encyclopedia of Philosophy*, s.v. "Spinoza, Baruch," by Steven Nadler, last modified July 15, 2013, http://plato.stanford.edu/entries/spinoza.

58. Albert Einstein, "Science and Religion," in *Science, Philosophy and Religion, A Symposium* (Conference on Science, Philosophy and Religion in Their Relation to the Democratic Way of Life, Inc., New York, 1941), http://einsteinandreligion.com/scienceandreligion2.html.

59. Mark Twain, *Following the Equator* (Hartford, CT: The American Publishing Company, 1898), chap. XII, http://www.gutenberg.org/files/2895/2895-h/2895-h.htm#ch1.

60. Albert Bigelow Paine, *Mark Twain, a Biography*, vol. 2 (New York: Harper & Brothers Publishers, 1912), 412, http://books.google.com/books?id=FkcLAAAAIAAJ&printsec=frontcover#v=onepage&q&f=false.

61. Mark Twain, *Mark Twain's Notebooks and Journals: Volume III* (1883–1891), ed. Frederick Anderson (Oakland: University of California Press, 1980), 389.

62. "Edison Invents His Own Aeroplane," *New York Times*, December 1, 1910, http://query.nytimes.com/gst/abstract.html?res=9802E3DE1638E333A25752C0A9649D946196D6CF. Note: This citation was sourced from ProQuest, a service available at many libraries where a library card number can be used to access articles.

63. Ibid.

64. Edward Marshall, "No Immortality of the Soul, Says Thomas A. Edison," *New York Times*, October 2, 1910, http://query.nytimes.com/gst/abstract.html?res=9903EEDC1F39E333A25751C0A9669D946196D6CF.

2. Is Atheism a Religion?

1. Guy Raz, "A 'Collision' of Beliefs: Atheist vs. Theologian," *All Things Considered*, National Public Radio, October 25, 2009, http://m.npr.org/news/front/114115179?singlePage=true.

2. James J. Kaufman v. Gary R. McCaughtry and Jamyi Witch, 422 F. Supp. 2D 1016 (W.D. Wis. 2006), accessed January 1, 2014, https://casetext.com/case/kaufman-v-mccaughtry-4#.U6EaPfldWn8.

3. James J. Kaufman v. Gary R. McCaughtry et al., 419 F.3d 678 (7th Cir. 2005), accessed January 1, 2014, http://law.justia.com/cases/federal/appellate-courts/F3/419/678/617423.

4. Janna Seliger, "The Devout Atheist," iBuzzle website, accessed January 2, 2014, http://www

.buzzle.com/articles/the-devout-atheist.html (page discontinued).

5. Bill McGinnis, "Atheism Is the Religion which Says There Is No God," LoveAllPeople.org, accessed January 2, 2014, http://patriot.net/~bmcgin/atheismsays.txt.

6. Brandon A. Cox, "The Religion of Atheism," *Brandon A. Cox* (blog), accessed January 2, 2014, http://www.brandonacox.com/culture/the-religion-of-atheism.

7. John W. Loftus, "Is Atheism a Religion?," *Debunking Christianity* (blog), last modified May 15, 2012, http://debunkingchristianity.blogspot.com/2009/05/is-atheism-religion.html.

8. Jeff Randall, "Is Atheism a (Religion/Faith/Belief System/Etc.)?," *Thinking Critically* (blog), May 3, 2011, http://thinking-critically.com/2011/05/03/is-atheism-a-religionfaithbelief-systemetc.

9. "Tract #16: Is Atheism a Religion?," *I Am an Atheist* (blog), accessed January 2, 2014, http://www.iamanatheist.com/blog/tracts/tract-16-is-atheism-a-religion.

10. David Eller, *Atheism Advanced: Further Thoughts of a Freethinker* (Parsippany, NJ: American Atheist Press, 2007), xvi, http://www.amazon.com/dp/1578840023?tag=wwwdebunkingc-20&camp=14573&creative=327641&linkCode=as1&creativeASIN=1578840023&adid=0CC267Z0NVMC3RJ9NZQ8&.

11. Laura Lond, "Atheism: Godless Religion," Associated Content website, January 25, 2008, accessed 2010, http://www.associatedcontent.com/article/563945/atheism_godless_religion.html?cat=34 (site discontinued).

12. Geoff Mather, email message to author, May 28, 2011.

13. Julian Baggini, "Faith and Reason," *RS Review*, 3, no. 2 (January 2007): 26.

14. Ray Comfort, "The Religion of Atheism," Bully! Pulpit website, March 23, 2011, http://www.bullypulpit.com/raycomfort/2011/03/the-religion-of-atheism.html.

15. Cal Thomas, "The Atheist Wager," *On Faith* (blog), December 28, 2006, http://newsweek.washingtonpost.com/onfaith/panelists/cal_thomas/2006/12/post_2.html (site discontinued).

16. Staks Rosch, "Atheism 101: Does It Take More Faith to Be an Atheist?," Examiner.com, July 17, 2009, http://www.examiner.com/atheism-in-philadelphia/atheism-101-does-it-take-more-faith-to-be-an-atheist.

17. "Do Atheists Have Faith?", Atheist-FAQ.com, last modified February 21, 2014, http://atheist-faq.com/do-atheists-have-faith.

18. Kevin Childs, "What I'm Learning from Atheists (III)," KevinChilds.com blog, April 23, 2010, http://kevinchilds.com/?p=1821.

19. Vjack, "Atheists Do Not Worship Humanity," *Atheist Revolution* (blog), June 9, 2008, http://www.atheistrev.com/2008/06/atheists-do-not-worship-humanity.html.

20. Childs, "What I'm Learning."

21. Ibid.

22. Revelation, "Is Atheism a Religion? Are Atheists Fundamentalists in their Religious Belief System?," Revelation.co, February 1, 2010, http://www.revelation.co/2010/02/01/is-atheism-a-religion-are-atheists-fundamentalists-in-their-religious-belief-system.

23. Charles Darwin, "Variation Under Domestication," *On the Origin of Species* (London: John Murray, 1859), http://www.talkorigins.org/faqs/origin/chapter1.html.

24. John C. Snider, "Podcast #116—Darwin Day vs. In God We Trust," *American Freethought* (podcast), February 18, 2011, http://www.americanfreethought.com/wordpress/2011/02/18/podcast-116-darwin-day-vs-in-god-we-trust.

3. Don't You Need God for a Moral Life?

1. George W. Bush, "Remarks by the President at National Hispanic Prayer Breakfast," White

House Archives, May 16, 2002, http://georgewbush-whitehouse.archives.gov/news
/releases/2002/05/20020516-1.html.

2. Romans 2:14–15

3. Matt Slick, "Can Atheists Be Ethical?," Christian Apologetics & Research Ministry website, accessed January 2, 2014, http://carm.org/can-atheists-be-ethical.

4. Penny Edgell, Joseph Gerteis, and Douglas Hartmann, "Atheists as 'Other': Moral Boundaries and Cultural Membership in American Society," *American Sociological Review* 71 (2006): 227, http://www.soc.umn.edu/assets/pdf/atheistAsOther.pdf.

5. "Worldwide, Many See Belief in God as Essential to Morality: Richer Nations Are Exception," Pew Research Global Attitudes Project, March 13, 2014, http://www.pewglobal .org/2014/03/13/worldwide-many-see-belief-in-god-as-essential-to-morality.

6. Sam Harris, "The Myth of Secular Moral Chaos," SamHarris.org (blog), accessed January 2, 2014, http://www.samharris.org/site/full_text/the-myth-of-secular-moral-chaos.

7. Daniel Florien, "Do Atheists Get Their Morals from the Bible?," *Unreasonable Faith* (blog), March 24, 2009, http://www.patheos.com/blogs/unreasonablefaith/2009/03/do-atheists-get -their-morals-from-the-bible.

8. Byron, email interview with author, April 18, 2010.

9. Olivia, "Moralism and Morality," *Teen Skepchick* (blog), September 14, 2011, http:// teenskepchick.org/2011/09/14/moralism-and-morality.

10. Richard Carrier, "What an Atheist Ought to Stand For," The Secular Web website, last modified 2004, http://www.infidels.org/library/modern/richard_carrier/ought.html.

11. Goparaju Ramachandra Rao (better known as Gora), "Atheism Questions and Answers," June 27, 1973, *Positive Atheism*, http://www.positiveatheism.org/india/gora31.htm.

12. CruxClaire, "Just Another Untrustworthy Atheist," *Teen Ink* blog, accessed January 2, 2014, http://www.teenink.com/opinion/spirituality_religion/article/170845/Just-another -untrustworthy-atheist.

13. "History of American Atheists," American Atheists website, accessed January 2, 2014. http://www.atheists.org/about-us/history.

14. Carrier, "What an Atheist."

15. Richard Dawkins, *The God Delusion* (New York: Mariner Books, 2008), 298.

16. Bertrand Russell, "My Ten Commandments," *Everyman* 3, no. 62 (April 3, 1930): 5–7.

17. Robert Green Ingersoll, *The Works of Robert G. Ingersoll, Vol. 3* (New York: The Dresden Publishing Co., 1902), under "About the Bible," http://www.gutenberg.org/files/38803 /38803-h/38803-h.htm.

18. Ibid.

19. Christopher Hitchens, "The New Commandments," *Vanity Fair*, April 2010, http://www .vanityfair.com/culture/features/2010/04/hitchens-201004.

20. Ibid.

21. A. C. Grayling, *The Good Book: A Secular Bible* (London: Bloomsbury, 2011), 27, http:// issuu.com/bloomsbury/docs/thegoodbook/27.

22. Russell, "My Ten Commandments."

23. Dawkins, *The God Delusion*, 298–9.

24. Bertrand Russell, *The Autobiography of Bertrand Russell: 1944–1969*, (New York: Simon & Schuster, 1969), 534.

25. Dawkins, *The God Delusion*, 299.

26. Russell, *Autobiography*, 534.

27. George Carlin, *When Will Jesus Bring the Pork Chops?* (New York: Hyperion, 2004), 18, http://www.amazon.com/When-Will-Jesus-Bring-Chops/dp/1401301347#rea der_1401301347.

28. Sam Harris and Andrew Sullivan, "Is Religion 'Built Upon Lies'?", *Beliefnet*, January 17, 2007, http://www.beliefnet.com/Faiths/Secular-Philosophies/Is-Religion-Built-Upon-Lies.aspx?p=2.

29. Russell, "My Ten Commandments."

30. Penn Jillette, *God, No! Signs You May Already Be an Atheist and Other Magical Tales* (New York: Simon & Schuster, 2011), 165, http://www.amazon.com/God-No-Already-Atheist-Magical/dp/1451610378.

31. Carlin, *When Will Jesus*, 17.

32. Hitchens, "The New Commandments."

33. Dawkins, *The God Delusion*, 299.

34. Russell, *Autobiography*, 534.

35. Jillette, *God, No!*, 203.

36. Russell, "My Ten Commandments."

37. Hitchens, "The New Commandments."

38. RustinN, "Morality and Religion," *Teen Ink* blog, accessed January 2, 2014, http://teenink.com/opinion/spirituality_religion/article/408256/Morality-and-Religion.

39. Al Stefanelli, "On Morals: Why Atheism Trumps Christianity," posted by nonplussedbyreligion, *The Analyzed Atheist* (blog), accessed January 2, 2014, http://analyzedatheist.tumblr.com/post/9974042323/on-morals-why-atheism-trumps-christianity.

40. Daniel, Catholic School Atheist (Facebook page), February 22, 2012, http://www.facebook.com/catholicschoolatheist/info (site discontinued).

41. Grisham, "Are Religious People More Charitable than Atheists?" Newsvine.com, November 8, 2011, http://grisham.newsvine.com/_news/2011/11/08/8691971-are-religious-people-more-charitable-than-atheists; "Giving Statistics," National Park Service, 2013, http://www.nps.gov/partnerships/fundraising_individuals_statistics.htm.

42. Buster G. Smith and Rodney Stark, "Religious Attendance Relates to Generosity Worldwide," Gallup World Poll, September 4, 2009, http://www.gallup.com/poll/122807/religious-attendance-relates-generosity-worldwide.aspx; Brett Pelham and Steve Crabtree, "Worldwide, Highly Religious More Likely to Help Others," Gallup World Poll, October 8, 2008, http://www.gallup.com/poll/111013/worldwide-highly-religious-more-likely-help-others.aspx.

43. "Religious Americans Often Do Not Support Specifically Religious Charitable Causes," Grey Matter Research & Consulting website, June 6, 2011, http://www.greymatterresearch.com/index_files/causes.htm.

44. "SHARE Opens Fund for Haiti Quake Relief," Center for Inquiry website, January 14, 2010, http://www.centerforinquiry.net/news/share_opens_fund_for_haiti_quake_relief.

45. "Crisis Response," Foundation Beyond Belief website, accessed January 2, 2014, http://foundationbeyondbelief.org/crisis.

46. Institute for Economics & Peace, *Global Peace Index 2013: Measuring the State of Global Peace*, (New York: Institute for Economics and Peace, 2012), 5, http://www.visionofhumanity.org/sites/default/files/2013_Global_Peace_Index_Report_0.pdf.

47. United Nations Office on Drugs and Crime (UNODC), *Global Study on Homicide 2011*, (Vienna: United Nations Office on Drugs and Crime, 2011), 9, http://www.unodc.org/documents/data-and-analysis/statistics/Homicide/Globa_study_on_homicide_2011_web.pdf.

48. UNODC, "Intentional Homicide, Number and Rate per 100,000 Population," UNData website, last updated August 1, 2012, http://data.un.org/Data.aspx?d=UNODC&f=tableCode%3A1#UNODC.

49. "Humanitarian League," Henry S. Salt Archive, accessed August 27, 2013, http://www.henrysalt.co.uk/humanitarian-league.

50. Ben Isacat, *How to Do Animal Rights . . . Legally, with Confidence* (How to Do Animal Rights, 2008), 166, http://www.animalethics.org.uk/How-to-Do-Animal-Rights-2013.pdf.
51. Mohandas Karamchand Gandhi, "The Moral Basis of Vegetarianism" (speech delivered at London Vegetarian Society, November 20, 1931), http://www.henrysalt.co.uk/studies/essays/the-moral-basis-of-vegetarianism.
52. Henry S. Salt, *Seventy Years among Savages* (London: George Allen & Unwin Ltd., 1921), 213, http://archive.org/stream/seventyyearsamon00salt#page/n5/mode/2up.
53. Marit Grave, *Fridtjof Nansen*, trans. Margaret Ellson Davies (Oslo, Norway: Aschehoug, 1994), http://www.frammuseum.no/Polar-Heroes/Main-Heroes/Fridtjof-Nansen.aspx; and Linn Ryne, "Fridtjof Nansen: Man of Many Facets," Metropolitan News Company website, accessed August 27, 2013, http://www.mnc.net/norway/Nansen.htm.
54. Fridtjof Nansen, "Science and the Purpose of Life," *The Hibbert Journal*, 6, no. 24 (1908): 743.
55. "Fridtjof Nansen – Biographical," Nobelprize.org, accessed August 27, 2013, http://www.nobelprize.org/nobel_prizes/peace/laureates/1922/nansen-bio.html.
56. Paul Kurtz and Edwin H. Wilson, "Humanist Manifesto II," American Humanist Association website, 1973, http://americanhumanist.org/Humanism/Humanist_Manifesto_II.
57. Gennady Gorelick, *The World of Andrei Sakharov*, with Antonina W. Bouis (London: Oxford University Press, 2005), under "Chronology," http://people.bu.edu/gorelik/AIP_Sakharov_Photo_Chrono/AIP_Sakharov_Photo_Chronology.html.

4. Are There Atheist-Friendly Religions?

1. This quotation melded elements from various versions and translations: Siddhartha Gautama (Buddha), *The Kalama Sutta*, cited in http://blog.gaiam.com/quotes/authors/Buddha, http://buddhasutra.com/files/kalama_sutta.htm, http://en.wikiquote.org/wiki/Buddha, http://oaks.nvg.org/kalama.html, http://shindharmanet.com/critical/, http://supremeenlightenment.blogspot.com/2009/04/kalama-sutta-buddhas-charter-of-free_28.html, http://web.singnet.com.sg/~sidneys/kalama.htm, http://www.accesstoinsight.org/lib/authors/soma/wheel008.html, http://www.allgreatquotes.com/buddha_quotes.shtml, http://www.buddhanet.net/e-learning/kalama1.htm, http://www.dhammatalks.net/Books5/Bhikkhu_Buddhadasa_Help_The_Kalama_Sutta_Help.htm, http://www.ling.upenn.edu/~beatrice/buddhist-practice/kalama-sutta.html, accessed January 2, 2014.
2. "The Declaration of the Independent: A Poll on Controversial Issues," *The Troy Independent*, February 6, 2011, http://thetroyindependent.org/?p=419.
3. Jon Meacham, "The God Debate", *Newsweek*, April 9, 2007, posted on The Richard Dawkins Foundation website, accessed August 8, 2014, http://old.richarddawkins.net/articles/825-the-god-debate.
4. Charles Darwin, "Recapitulation and Conclusion," *On the Origin of Species*, http://www.talkorigins.org/faqs/origin/chapter14.html.
5. Simon Blackburn, "Morality without God," *Prospect*, March 23, 2011, http://www.prospectmagazine.co.uk/2011/03/blackburn-ethics-without-god-secularism-religion-sam-harris.
6. Elaine Howard Ecklund, "Some Atheist Scientists with Children Embrace Religious Traditions," *Huffington Post* (blog), December 7, 2011, http://www.huffingtonpost.com/elaine-howard-ecklund-phd/some-atheist-scientists-w_b_1133958.html.
7. Ibid.
8. "'Nones' on the Rise," Pew Research Religion & Public Life Project, October 9, 2012, http://www.pewforum.org/2012/10/09/nones-on-the-rise.

9. Craig Groeschel, *The Christian Atheist: Believing in God but Living as if He Doesn't Exist* (Grand Rapids, MI: Zondervan, 2010), 21–22, http://christianatheist.com/files/2010/01/031032789x_samptxt.pdf.

10. Lizette Alvarez, "Fury, God, and the Pastor's Disbelief," *New York Times*, July 8, 2003, http://www.nytimes.com/2003/07/08/international/europe/08PAST.html?pagewanted=all.

11. Godless Girl, "Can You Follow Jesus without Religion?," *Godless Girl* (blog), January 12, 2012, http://www.godlessgirl.com/2012/01/can-you-follow-jesus-without-religion.

12. Olivia, "An Atheist's Awe," *Teen Skepchick* (blog), April 20, 2011, http://teenskepchick.org/2011/04/20/an-atheist%E2%80%99s-awe.

13. Hillel2000, "Revisiting the Religion Post," *American Jewish Teen* (blog), January 28, 2012, http://americanjewishteen.wordpress.com/2012/01/.

14. Pew Research Center, *A Portrait A Portrait of Jewish Americans: Findings from a Pew Research Center Survey of US Jews* (Washington, DC: Pew Research Center's Religion & Public Life Project, October 1, 2013), 74, http://www.pewforum.org/files/2013/10/jewish-american-full-report-for-web.pdf.

15. "SHJ Philosophy," Society for Humanistic Judaism website, accessed November 25, 2013, http://www.shj.org/member.htm.

16. "Western USA Society for Humanistic Judaism Congregations & Communities," Society for Humanistic Judaism website, accessed December 7, 2013, http://www.shj.org/affwest.htm; "Central USA Society for Humanistic Judaism Congregations & Communities," Society for Humanistic Judaism website, accessed December 7, 2013, http://www.shj.org/affcent.htm; "Eastern USA Society for Humanistic Judaism Congregations & Communities," Society for Humanistic Judaism website, accessed December 7, 2013, http://www.shj.org/affeast.htm.

17. Jonathan Zimmerman, "An Atheist's Synagogue Search," *Tablet*, March 7, 2013, http://www.tabletmag.com/jewish-life-and-religion/126217/an-atheists-synagogue-search.

18. vreify, "Atheist Spirituality: Does It Exist?," *Teen Skepchick* (blog), May 21, 2012, http://teenskepchick.org/2012/05/21/atheist-spirituality-does-it-exist.

19. "About Our Unitarian Universalist Association of Congregations," Unitarian Universalist Association website, last modified August 20, 2013, http://www.uua.org/association.

20. John Murray, "Circular Letter of the Universalist General Convention of 1793," *Universalist Quarterly* (October 1875): 446–448, http://universalistchurch.net/universalist-history/1793-convention-circular-letter.

21. "Atheist and Agnostic People Welcome," accessed January 2, 2014, http://www.uua.org/beliefs/welcome/atheism/index.shtml.

22. August Berkshire, "Unitarian Universalists?," Minnesota Atheists website, accessed January 2, 2014, http://mnatheists.org/news-and-media/news/8-local-news/837-unitarian-universalists?tmpl=component&print=1&layout=default&page=.

23. Sierra, under "Letter[s] from Atheist Kids to American Atheist," "Humanism for Kids" page, Witty Humanist Youth website, accessed August 11, 2014, https://sites.google.com/a/wittyhumanistyouth.org/why/kids-page.

24. Kusala Bhikshu, "Do Buddhists Believe in God?," Urban Dharma website, accessed January 2, 2014, http://www.urbandharma.org/udharma3/budgod.html.

25. Austin Cline, "What's Wrong with Buddhism?," About.com (Agnosticism/Atheism), May 28, 2009, http://atheism.about.com/b/2009/05/28/whats-wrong-with-buddhism.htm.

26. John Horgan, "Buddhist Retreat: Why I Gave Up on Finding My Religion," *Slate*, February 12, 2003, http://www.slate.com/articles/arts/culturebox/2003/02/buddhist_retreat.single.html.

27. Grundy, "An Interview with the Arizona Atheist," *Deity Shmeity* (blog), October 8, 2012, http://deityshmeity.blogspot.com/2012/10/an-interview-with-arizona-atheist.html.

28. "Evolution Debate in Kansas," American Geosciences Institute website, last modified December 4, 2006, http://www.agiweb.org/gap/evolution/KS.html; John Hannah, "The Changing Face of Kansas Evolution Instruction—A Timeline of Events (February 2007)," Designed Instruction website, February 14, 2007, http://www.designedinstruction.com/edlog /evolution-ks-ed-events.html; Kansas Science Education Standards, Kansas State Board of Education November 8, 2005, ii, http://web.archive.org/web/20051125163758/http://www .ksde.org/outcomes/sciencestd.pdf.

29. Justin Pope, "Pasta Monster Gets Academic Attention," NBC News website, last modified November 16, 2007, http://www.nbcnews.com/id/21837499/#.UsY3F_RDun8.

30. Bobby Henderson, "Open Letter to Kansas School Board," Venganza.org, accessed January 2, 2014, http://www.venganza.org/about/open-letter.

31. Jordan Schrader, "School: Pirates Are Not Welcome," *Citizen-Times*, March 28, 2007, http://www.citizen-times.com/apps/pbcs.dll/article?AID=200770328123.

32. Gary Nelson, "Flying Spaghetti Monster Takes Up Residence at County Courthouse," *Crossville Chronicle*, March 24, 2008, http://crossville-chronicle.com/local/x960637460 /Flying-Spaghetti-Monster-takes-up-residence-at-county-courthouse.

33. Matthew Day, "'Pastafarian' Wins Religious Freedom Right to Wear Pasta Strainer for Driving Licence," *The Telegraph*, July 13, 2011, http://www.telegraph.co.uk/news/newstopics /howaboutthat/8635624/Pastafarian-wins-religious-freedom-right-to-wear-pasta-strainer-for -driving-licence.html.

34. "Who We Are," Ethical Humanist Society of Chicago website, accessed April 27, 2014, http://ethicalhuman.org/who-we-are.html.

35. "Teen Ethical Leadership Program," New York Society for Ethical Culture website, accessed January 2, 2014, http://nysec.org/teens.

36. "Services," North Texas Church of Freethought website, accessed January 2, 2014, http:// www.churchoffreethought.org/services.php.

37. "FACTS Rituals," First Atheist Church of True Facts website, accessed January 2, 2014, http://www.factschurch.com/facts_rituals.html.

38. "Meetings," Calgary Secular Church website, July 29, 2013, http://www.calgarysecular church.org/2013/07/meetings.html.

39. "About," The Sunday Assembly website, accessed January 2, 2014, http://sundayassembly .com/about.

5. How Do You Become an Atheist?

1. "Facing the Big God Question," *The Bulletin* (Bend, OR), December 18, 2009, http://www .bendbulletin.com/article/20091218/FEAT01/912180331.

2. Nevadagrl435, "My Deconversion (Very Long)," Ex-Christian.net, September 15, 2012, http://www.ex-christian.net/topic/53749-my-deconversion-very-long.

3. Hannah Draper, email interview with author, April 17, 2010.

4. "Agnostic/Atheist Teens, What Religion Did You Grow Up Within?," *BabyFreeFAQ.com* (forum), accessed January 2, 2014, http://www.babyfreefaq.com/adolescent/22441.html.

5. Forwhatiamworth, in "Were You Always an Atheist/Agnostic? Or . . .," *Social Anxiety Support* (forum), March 3, 2013, http://www.socialanxietysupport.com/forum/f162/were-you -always-an-atheist-agnostic-or-143687/index6.html#post1061647065.

6. Tom, reply to query from author on MySpace *Atheist and Agnostic Teens* (group message board), April 11, 2010, (site discontinued, URL unavailable).

7. Elizabeth, email interview with author, April 14, 2010.

8. LS, in "What Convinced You? A Survey for Non-Believers," *Greta Christina's Blog*, November 10, 2011, http://freethoughtblogs.com/greta/2011/11/10/what-convinced-you-a-survey-for-non-believers/#comment-32119.

9. Greylight, "The Path that Led Me Here," Ex-Christian.net, October 26, 2012, http://www.ex-christian.net/topic/54167-the-path-that-lead-me-here.

10. Meatball, in "Why Are You an Atheist," *AtheistForums.org*, August 26, 2008, http://atheistforums.org/thread-1-page-2.html.

11. Fleur, in "Were You Always an Atheist/Agnostic? Or . . . ," *Social Anxiety Support* (forum), February 27, 2013, http://www.socialanxietysupport.com/forum/f162/were-you-always-an-atheist-agnostic-or-143687/index6.html#post1061534953.

12. Mark Turner, email interview with author, April 26, 2010.

13. Bradley Wright, "Why Do Christians Leave the Faith? The Fundamental Importance of Apologetics," *Black, White and Gray* (blog), November 17, 2011, http://www.patheos.com/blogs/blackwhiteandgray/2011/11/why-do-christians-leave-the-faith-the-surprising-importance-of-apologetics.

14. Heather L. Downs, "The Deconversion Experience: A Qualitative Study of Students' Experiences with Leaving a Belief in the Christian God and Identifying with Non-Belief" (doctoral thesis, Center for Human Enrichment, University of Northern Colorado, 2002), 18, http://visibleatheist.files.wordpress.com/2010/01/deconarticle.pdf.

15. Michael, "Ask Teen Atheist #5," *Diary of a Teenage Atheist* (blog), March 27, 2010, http://teenatheist.wordpress.com/2010/03/27/ask-teen-atheist-5.

16. Rainer206, comment on "Muslim Teen, I Am Officially Rejecting My Faith," Reddit *r/atheism* (forum), March 10, 2013, http://www.reddit.com/r/atheism/comments/1a2107/muslim_teen_i_am_officially_rejecting_my_faith/c8tiyf6.

17. Troy, comment on "Teen Poll—Religious, Non Religion, or Atheist, What Is Your Reasoning for Having Your Views?," *Yahoo! Answers Adolescent* (forum), accessed January 2, 2014, http://answers.yahoo.com/question/index?qid=20130325223810AAHVe1D.

18. Nevadagrl435, "My Deconversion."

19. Atothetheist [Steven], *Thinking Atheist* (forum), May 17, 2012, http://www.thethinkingatheist.com/forum/Thread-Teenage-Atheists?pid=116801#pid116801.

20. Isaac Asimov, *Yours, Isaac Asimov: A Life in Letters*, ed. Stanley Asimov (New York: Doubleday, 1995), 316.

21. Tom, under "Letter[s] from Atheist Kids to American Atheist," "Humanism for Kids" page, Witty Humanist Youth website, accessed August 11, 2014, https://sites.google.com/a/wittyhumanistyouth.org/why/kids-page.

22. Joel Collins Sati, "My Moment of 'Uhuru' (Freedom)," *The African Atheist* (blog), accessed January 2, 2014, http://theafricanatheist.tumblr.com/post/23442580701/uhuru-freedom.

23. John Szaszvari, email interview with author, May 20, 2010.

24. Tranquildream, in "Were You Always an Atheist/Agnostic? Or . . . ," *Social Anxiety Support* (forum), October 2, 2011, http://www.socialanxietysupport.com/forum/f162/were-you-always-an-atheist-agnostic-or-143687/index2.html#post1059337788.

25. Scarlett, comment on "What Convinced You? A Survey for Non-Believers," *Greta Christina's Blog*, November 10, 2011, http://freethoughtblogs.com/greta/2011/11/10/what-convinced-you-a-survey-for-non-believers/#comment-37561.

26. Sabrina S, in "Agnostic and Atheist Teens, What Religion Were You Raised with and Why Are You Now Agnostic or Atheist?," *Yahoo! Answers Religion & Spirituality* (forum), accessed January 2, 2014, http://answers.yahoo.com/question/index?qid=20111119115140AAhpDEV.

27. Glass Child, comment on "Were You Always an Atheist/Agnostic? Or . . .," *Social Anxiety Support* (forum), September 20, 2011, http://www.socialanxietysupport.com/forum/f162/were

-you-always-an-atheist-agnostic-or-143687/index6.html#post1061568289.

28. Eaten_by_you, "Oxymoron: Athiest Church," *Atheist Teens' Journal* (forum), December 12, 2005, http://atheist-teens.livejournal.com/58377.html.

29. Sunflower, "Christianity and Anxiety," Ex-Christian.net, November 5, 2012, http://www.ex-christian.net/topic/54270-christianity-and-anxiety.

30. Bradley Wright, "Why Do Christians Leave the Faith? Breaking Up with a God Who Failed Them," *Black, White and Gray* (blog), November 22, 2011, http://www.patheos.com/blogs/blackwhiteandgray/2011/11/why-do-christians-leave-the-faith-breaking-up-with-a-god-who-failed-them.

31. Austin Hunt, "What Age Did You Become an Atheist/Agnostic and Why?," Atheist Nexus website, July 9, 2012, http://www.atheistnexus.org/forum/topics/what-age-did-you-become-an-atheist-agnostic-and-why?xg_source=activity.

32. Kate Hawthorne, "Escaping Indoctrination," Ex-Christian.net, March 25, 2012, http://new.exchristian.net/2012/03/escaping-indoctrination.html.

33. Bradley Wright, "Why Do Christians Leave the Faith? The Problem of Responding Badly to Doubt," *Black, White and Gray* (blog), December 1, 2011, http://www.patheos.com/blogs/blackwhiteandgray/2011/12/why-do-christians-leave-the-faith-the-problem-of-responding-badly-to-doubters.

34. Greylight, "The Path That Led."

35. Paul, comment on "What Convinced You? A Survey for Nonbelievers," *Greta Christina's Blog*, November 10, 2011, http://freethoughtblogs.com/greta/2011/11/10/what-convinced-you-a-survey-for-non-believers/#comment-76829.

36. Darius Morgan, email interview with author, April 14, 2010.

37. Hawthorne, "Escaping Indoctrination."

38. Downs, "Deconversion Experience," 17.

39. Michele, email interview with author, April 19, 2010.

40. Hawthorne, "Escaping Indoctrination."

41. Weareg0d, "I Was Raised by Fundamentalist Christian Parents My Entire Life. I Eventually Became an Atheist, and This Is My Story," Reddit *r/atheism* (forum), March 4, 2013, http://www.reddit.com/r/atheism/comments/19nhs8/i_was_raised_by_fundamentalist_christian_parents.

42. Scarlett, comment "What Convinced You?."

43. Sam Harris, "10 Myths—and 10 Truths—About Atheism," *Los Angeles Times*, December 24, 2006, posted on SamHarris.org, http://www.samharris.org/site/full_text/10-myths-and-10-truths-about-atheism1.

44. Troy, comment, "Teen Poll."

45. Atheist Anon, "Who Am I?," *Classy Atheist* (blog), July 25, 2012, http://classyatheist.blogspot.com.

46. Kay Miller, email interview with author, April 26, 2010.

47. Downs, "Deconversion Experience," 14.

6. How Will Becoming an Atheist Change You?

1. Gary Wolf, "The Church of the Nonbelievers," *Wired* 14, no. 11 (November 2006), http://www.wired.com/wired/archive/14.11/atheism_pr.html.

2. Heather L. Downs, "The Deconversion Experience: A Qualitative Study of Students' Experiences with Leaving a Belief in the Christian God and Identifying with Nonbelief" (doctoral thesis, Center for Human Enrichment, University of Northern Colorado, 2002), 19, http://visibleatheist.files.wordpress.com/2010/01/deconarticle.pdf.

3. Thomas Stooke, "Letter from Thomas," Atheism Central for Secondary Schools website, accessed April 27, 2013, http://www.eclipse.co.uk/thoughts/thomas.htm.

4. Peregrínus, in "Were You Always an Atheist/Agnostic? Or . . .," *Social Anxiety Support* (forum), February 20, 2013, http://www.socialanxietysupport.com/forum/f162/were-you -always-an-atheist-agnostic-or-143687/index5.html#post1061371193.

5. Greylight, "The Path that Led Me Here," Ex-Christian.net, October 26, 2012, http://www .ex-christian.net/topic/54167-the-path-that-lead-me-here.

6. Downs, "Deconversion Experience," 12.

7. Charizard, comment on, "Were You Always an Atheist/Agnostic? Or . . .," *Social Anxiety Support* (forum), September 20, 2011, http://www.socialanxietysupport.com/forum/f162/were -you-always-an-atheist-agnostic-or-143687/#post1059312711.

8. Greylight, "The Path That Led."

9. Downs, "Deconversion Experience," 12.

10. David Blauvelt, email interview with author, April 13, 2010.

11. Bradley R. E. Wright, Dina Giovanelli, Emily G. Dolan, and Mark Evan Edwards, "Explaining Deconversion from Christianity: A Study of Online Narratives," *Journal of Religion & Society* 13 (2011): 8, http://moses.creighton.edu/jrs/2011/2011-21.pdf.

12. J, "J's Transition: From Brownsville Revival to Atheist," *RagingRev.com* (blog), accessed May 2, 2013, http://ragingrev.com/2012/09/your-stories-j-goes-from-brownsville-revival-to -atheism.

13. Freud, in "Were You Always an Atheist/Agnostic? Or . . . ," *Social Anxiety Support* (forum), September 23, 2011, http://www.socialanxietysupport.com/forum/f162/were-you-always-an -atheist-agnostic-or-143687/#post1059318855.

14. Eric Gorski, "Number of Groups for Atheists Skyrockets on College Campuses," *The Boston Globe*, November 27, 2009, accessed May 2, 2013, http://www.boston.com/news/nation/articles /2009/11/27 /number_of_groups_for_atheists_skyrockets_on_college_campuses.

15. Spikedhair95 [Nick], "Being an Atheist Teen is Hard . . .," *AtheistForums.org*, September 19, 2012, http://atheistforums.org/thread-14862.html.

16. Adept, comment on "My 'Crisis' of Faith," *Teen Spot* (forum), February 14, 2007, http:// www.teenspot.com/boards/showthread.php?375406-My-crisis-of-faith.&p=9458634&viewfull =1#post9458634 (site discontinued).

17. like WOAH its Mia!, "Listening to Christian Rock . . . ," Ex-Christian.net, April 11, 2008, http://www.ex-christian.net/topic/23081-listening-to-christian-rock.

18. longhorn_fraz, comment on "My 'Crisis' of Faith," *Teen Spot* (forum), February 14, 2007, http://www.teenspot.com/boards/showthread.php?375406-My-crisis-of-faith.&p=9457795& viewfull=1#post9457795 (site discontinued).

19. ChadOnSunday, comment on "Have the New-Atheists Redefined the Term 'Atheism'?" *CreateDebate* (forum), accessed May 1, 2013, http://www.createdebate.com/debate/show /Have_the_New_Atheists_redefined_the_term_atheism.

20. Dylan Tillman, email interview with author, May 11, 2010.

21. Sunflower, "Christianity and Anxiety," Ex-Christian.net, November 5, 2012, http://www .ex-christian.net/topic/54270-christianity-and-anxiety.

22. Fez, comment on "Were You Always an Atheist/Agnostic? Or . . . ," *Social Anxiety Support* (forum), September 20, 2011, http://www.socialanxietysupport.com/forum/f162/were-you -always-an-atheist-agnostic-or-143687/index4.html.

23. John Szasvari, email interview with author, April 15, 2010.

24. Stefan O'Kula, "Some Teens Say Atheism Rational Choice," *Augusta Chronicle*, November 10, 2009, http://chronicle.augusta.com/stories/2009/11/10/xtr_555109.shtml.

25. Mark Turner, email interview with author, April 26, 2010.

26. John Szasvari, email interview with author, April 15, 2010.

27. Downs, "Deconversion Experience," 14.

28. Matthew Barsden, email interview with author, April 14, 2010.

29. The Sanhedrin, comment on "I Wish I Could Forget the Name Jesus," July 15, 2011, http://www.ex-christian.net/topic/47414-i-wish-i-could-forget-the-name-jesus/?p=679516.

30. Vanessa Sampson, "Walking Away from the Watchtower," *Daylight Atheism* (blog), August 17, 2011, http://www.patheos.com/blogs/daylightatheism/2011/08/walking-away-from-the-watchtower.

31. Aidan Djabarov, email interview with author, April 19, 2010.

7. What If You Were Raised an Atheist?

1. Aidan Djabarov, email interview with author, April 19, 2010.

2. Barry A. Kosmin and Ariela Keysar, with Ryan Cragun and Juhem Navarro-Rivera, *American Nones: The Profile of the No Religion Population* (Hartford, CT: Trinity College, 2009), 6, http://commons.trincoll.edu/aris/files/2011/08/NONES_08.pdf.

3. Vitharr [Evan], comment on "Atheism," *Cultures Shocked* (forum), July 6, 2007, http://www.cultures-shocked.org/forums/showthread.php?860-Atheism&p=31152#post31152.

4. Gralian, comment on "Poll: What Religion Were You Before Becoming an Atheist," *Escapist Magazine*, September 28, 2010, http://www.escapistmagazine.com/forums/read/528.235291-Poll-What-religion-were-you-before-becoming-an-atheist#8359081.

5. Mary Phan, email interview with author, April 14, 2010.

6. Eliane, comment on "Raised as a Theist or Atheist?," *TeenForumz.com*, May 1, 2013, http://www.teenforumz.com/lifestyle-culture/41242-raised-theist-atheist.html#post988974.

7. Stephanie Russell-Kraft, "Growing Up Godless," *Open Salon* (blog), March 5, 2012, http://open.salon.com/blog/srussellkraft/2012/03/05/growing_up_godless.

8. Hemant Mehta, "Whatever Happened to the Young Atheist Whose Family Filed a Lawsuit Against a Christian Rapper and a School District?," *Friendly Atheist* (blog), April 15, 2013, http://www.patheos.com/blogs/friendlyatheist/2013/04/15/whatever-happened-to-the-young-atheist-whose-family-filed-a-lawsuit-against-a-christian-rapper-and-a-school-district; "Public School Holds Christian Rally to Convert Students," YouTube video, 2:54, uploaded by acluvideos, September 23, 2011, https://www.youtube.com/watch?v=QVaMjeTaNDM.

9. Jordan Anderson, "Standing Up for What You Believe In," American Civil Liberties Union website, August 21, 2012, http://www.aclu.org/blog/religion-belief/standing-what-you-believe.

10. Jonathan Anderson v. Chesterfield County School District, Chesterfield County School Board, John Williams, and Larry Stinson, No. unknown (D.S.C. December 5, 2011), 3, submitted by Susan Dunn, Daniel Mach, and Heather L. Weaver, American Civil Liberties Union website, http://www.aclu.org/files/assets/anderson_complaint__filed.pdf.

11. "School District Agrees to Stop Proselytizing Students," American Civil Liberties Union website, January 12, 2012, http://www.aclu.org/religion-belief/south-carolina-school-district-agrees-stop-proselytizing-students.

12. Jonathan Anderson quoted in Ellen Meder, "'God Is Good,' Atheists . . . Bad?," *Morning News*, SCNow website, last modified April 17, 2013, http://www.scnow.com/news/education/article_8e2f2a06-a574-11e2-aa67-001a4bcf6878.html.

13. Heather L. Weaver, "Paying the Price for Defending Religious Freedom in South Carolina," American Civil Liberties Union website, April 17, 2013, http://www.aclu.org/blog/religion-belief/paying-price-defending-religious-freedom-south-carolina.

14. Reilly Hedegaard, "Why I Am a 13-Year-Old Atheist," *The Blessed Atheist Bible Study* (blog), June 5, 2011, http://blessedatheist.com/2011/06/05/why-i-am-a-13-year-old-atheist.

15. Jeannette O., email interview with author, April 13, 2010.

16. Aidan Djabarov, email interview with author, April 19, 2010.

17. "Population: Hardesty, OK," Google Public Data, last modified September 25, 2013, https://www.google.com/publicdata/explore?ds=kf7tgg1uo9ude_&met_y=population&idim=place:4032550&dl=en&hl=en&q=hardesty%20oklahoma%20population.

18. "Hardesty High School," GreatSchools website, last modified May 2, 2014, http://www.greatschools.org/oklahoma/hardesty/635-Hardesty-High-School.

19. "Hardesty Public Schools: Home of the Bison," Hardesty Public Schools website, accessed May 13, 2013, http://www.hardesty.k12.ok.us.

20. Chester Smalkowski, Nadia Smalkowski, American Atheists v. Hardesty Public School District, Texas County, Town of Hardesty, et al., No. unknown (W.D. Okla. August 11, 2006), 5, submitted by Richard R. Rice, American Atheists website, http://www.atheists.org/upload/Smalkowski_Complaint_11Aug2006.pdf (page discontinued).

21. John Stossel, Sylvia Johnson, and Lynn Redmond, "The Black Sheep of Hardesty," ABC News website, May 11, 2007, http://abcnews.go.com/2020/story?id=3164811&page=1.

22. Edwin Kagin, "Smalkowski Case Settled in in Oklahoma," *Blasphemous Blogging: The Blog of Edwin Kagin*, November 9, 2008, http://edwinkagin.blogspot.com/2008/11/smalkowski-case-settled-in-oklahoma.html.

23. Fibonaccimathgenius, "Society's Attitude Towards Atheism," *Teen Ink* website, accessed June 4, 2011, http://teenink.com/opinion/spirituality_religion/article/232955/Societys-Attitude-Towards-Atheism.

24. Christine Smith, email interview with author, April 17, 2010.

25. Noah J. Sexton, "Growing Up as an Atheist: Teen Perspective," Secular Post website, November 14, 2012, http://www.secularpost.net/2012/11/14/gua.

26. Morgaine and Megan H., "Refusing to Hide: Dialogue with a 12-Year-Old Atheist," *Black Sun Journal*, November 13, 2007, http://www.blacksunjournal.com/psychology/1127_refusing-to-hide-dialogue-with-a-12-year-old-atheist_2007.html.

27. Karen Elizabeth McMichael, comment on "AI: Picture Books for Godless Kids," Queereka! website, January 3, 3013, http://queereka.com/2013/01/03/ai-picture-books-for-godless-kids.

28. Ibid.

29. Christopher Shull, email interview with author, April 18, 2010.

30. Hedegaard, "Why I Am."

31. Russell-Kraft, "Growing Up Godless."

32. Nakile, comment on "What Too Many Atheists Don't Get about Christians (Part One)," Reddit *TrueAtheism* (forum), January 12, 2014, http://www.reddit.com/r/TrueAtheism/comments/1v1dih/what_too_many_atheists_dont_get_about_christians/censcjq.

33. "Public Act 095-0680," Illinois General Assembly website, October 11, 2007, http://www.ilga.gov/legislation/publicacts/fulltext.asp?Name=095-0680&GA=95.

34. Ibid.

35. Nadia Malik, "Teen Sues Dist. 214 over New Silence Law," *Daily Herald* (Arlington Heights, IL), October 27, 2007, 3, http://nadiaahmedmalik.blogspot.com/2008/01/teen-sues-dist-214-over-new-silence-law.html.

36. Eric Zorn, "Rep. Monique Davis to Athiest Rob Sherman: 'It's Dangerous for Our Children to Even Know that Your Philosophy Exists!'" Change of Subject, *Chicago Tribune*, April 3, 2008, http://blogs.chicagotribune.com/news_columnists_ezorn/2008/04/rep-monique-dav.html; Illinois General Assembly (meeting), April 2, 2008, mp3, provided by the

Illinois Information Service, Change of Subject, *Chicago Tribune*, April 3, 2008, http://blogs.chicagotribune.com/news_columnists_ezorn/files/DAVIS.mp3.

37. Paul Stanley, "'Moment of Silence' Allowed After Court Rejects Atheist Lawsuit," *Christian Post*, October 21, 2011, http://www.christianpost.com/news/moment-of-silence-allowed-after-court-rejects-atheist-lawsuit-58884.

38. "Breaking News: Supreme Court Says 'No' to Dawn Sherman on 'Moment of Silence' Appeal," *Rob Sherman News* (blog), October 3, 2011, http://www.robsherman.com/news/2011/10/03BN1.htm.

8. Should You Tell?

1. Isiah, "How to Come Out as an Atheist to Your Parents and Family if [You're] a Teen?," *Yahoo! Answers* (forum), accessed June 15, 2013, http://answers.yahoo.com/question/index?qid=20130411222141AAP5CIM.

2. Sgokills, "How to Tell My Mom I'm Atheist?," *Yahoo! Answers Family & Relationships* (forum), accessed May 30, 2013, http://answers.yahoo.com/question/index;_ylt=AuwzCGWVnvqNBm0AAKnoMbnsy6IX;_ylv=3?qid=20130524213249AAwRH7m.

3. RHRN, "15 Year Old Atheist," *Boards.ie* (forum), February 28, 2009, http://www.boards.ie/vbulletin/showthread.php?p=59226359.

4. Darius Morgan, email interview with author, April 14, 2010.

5. Nathan, "Should I Tell My Parents I'm an Atheist?," *Yahoo! Answers Religion & Spirituality* (forum), accessed May 30, 2013, http://answers.yahoo.com/question/index?qid=20130418125407AAx6IHt.

6. Teen Atheist, "Ask Teen Atheist, #2," *Diary of a Teenage Atheist* (blog), May 15, 2008, http://teenatheist.wordpress.com/2008/05/15/ask-teen-atheist-2.

7. ChildrenofSodom, "Coming Out of the Closet," Metal Set Lists website, December 22, 2008, http://www.metalsetlists.com/blog.php?b=29.

8. Nathan, "Should I Tell?"

9. Richard Wade, comment on "Where Are the Young Atheists?," *Friendly Atheist* (blog), December 30, 2009, http://www.patheos.com/blogs/friendlyatheist/2009/12/30/where-are-the-young-atheists.

10. Kawaiigurl1234, "Am I an Atheist, Agonist, or Skeptic," Sodahead website, accessed May 29, 2013, http://www.sodahead.com/living/am-i-an-atheist-agonist-or-skeptic/question-2452913.

11. EmilyC., email interview with author, April 18, 2010.

12. Godless, "#238: If I Tell My Parents I Am an Atheist, They Will Disown Me (or Worse)," *Captain Awkward* (blog), May 2, 2012, http://captainawkward.com/2012/05/02/238-spiritual-crisis.

13. Rainer206, "Muslim Teen, I Am Officially Rejecting My Faith," Reddit *r/atheism* (forum), accessed November 16, 2013, http://www.reddit.com/r/atheism/comments/1a2107/muslim_teen_i_am_officially_rejecting_my_faith/c8tdax2.

14. Kawaiigurl1234, "Am I an Atheist."

15. James, email interview with author, April 17, 2010.

16. Kay Miller, email interview with author, April 26, 2010.

17. Diana L. Walcutt, "I Don't Believe in God; How Do I Tell My Parents?," Psych Central website, September 11, 2009, http://psychcentral.com/ask-the-therapist/2009/09/11/i-dont-believe-in-god-how-do-i-tell-my-parents.

18. Emily C., email interview.

19. Allison Stacey, email interview with author, April 17, 2010.

20. Susanne Werner, "Thoughts on Exposing Your Secular Beliefs," Teens without God website, accessed May 29, 2013, http://kidswithoutgod.com/teens/grow/coming-out.

21. Walcutt, "I Don't Believe in God."

22. Richard Wade, "Ask Richard: Teen Atheist Ponders Coming Out in Religious Family," *Friendly Atheist* (blog), April 2, 2012, http://www.patheos.com/blogs/friendlyatheist/2012/04/02/ask-richard-teen-ponders-coming-out-in-religious-family.

9. How Do You Tell Your Parents?

1. Teen Atheist, "Martha, Part 2," *Diary of a Teenage Atheist* (blog), November 9, 2007, http://teenatheist.wordpress.com/2007/11/09/martha-part-2.

2. Lori Howard, email interview with author, March 7, 2010.

3. Matt Cicero, email interview with author, April 13, 2010.

4. Nicole Schrand, email interview with author, April 19, 2010.

5. Blair Scott, "Do Atheists Hide from Family and Friends?," Alabama Atheist, October 5, 2010, accessed June 6, 2013, http://www.alabamaatheist.org/?p=267 (site discontinued).

6. Austin Cline, "How Do I Reveal My Atheism to My Family? Testing the Waters," About.com (Agnosticism/Atheism), accessed June 17, 2013, http://atheism.about.com/od/atheistsfamily/a/reveal_2.htm.

7. Ibid.

8. Tank [Chris Jarvis], "How to Tell Your Family You Are an Atheist," *Happy Atheist Forum*, June 15, 2010, http://www.happyatheistforum.com/forum/index.php?action=printpage;topic=5111.0.

9. Darrel Ray, "How Do I Talk to My Parents about God?," Teens without God website, accessed June 17, 2013, http://kidswithoutgod.com/teens/ask/how-do-i-talk-to-my-parents-about-go.

10. Tank, "How to Tell Your Family."

11. Ray, "How Do I Talk."

12. Tank, "How to Tell Your Family."

13. Cline, "How Do I Reveal."

14. Diana L. Walcutt, "I Don't Believe in God; How Do I Tell My Parents?," Psych Central website, September 11, 2009, http://psychcentral.com/ask-the-therapist/2009/09/11/i-dont-believe-in-god-how-do-i-tell-my-parents.

15. Allison T. Brill, "Take a Deep Breath . . . and Relax," Massachusetts Commonwealth Conversations Public Health, 2012, http://blog.mass.gov/publichealth/mass-in-motion/take-a-deep-breathand-relax/; David Carbonell, "A Breathing Exercise to Calm Panic Attacks," Anxiety Coach, May 5, 2013, http://www.anxietycoach.com/breathingexercise.html; Lisa Chilvers, "Deep Breathing to Calm Your Mind," Holistic United, accessed June 17, 2013, http://www.holisticunited.com/blog/deep-breathing-to-calm-your-mind/#sthash.ugGWalNb.dpuf; Chelsea Clark, "Deep Breathing a Key to Calm," Body and Soul website, accessed June 17, 2013, http://www.bodyandsoul.com.au/sex+relationships/wellbeing/deep+breathing+a+key+to+calm,12039; Robin Berzin, "A Simple Breathing Exercise to Calm Your Mind & Body," Mind Body Green website, April 1, 2012, http://www.mindbodygreen.com/0-4386/A-Simple-Breathing-Exercise-to-Calm-Your-Mind-Body.html; Tim Kenny and Colin Tidy, "Relaxation Exercises," Patient, last modified November 3, 2013, http://www.patient.co.uk/health/relaxation-exercises; Hara Estroff Marano, "How to Remain Calm During Uneasy Times," *Psychology Today*, last modified November 22, 2010, http://

www.psychologytoday.com/articles/200304/how-remain-calm-during-uneasy-times; Mary Polce-Lynch, "The Quickest, Least Expensive and Most Effective Way to Relax," Virginia Women's Center, September 2012, http://www.virginiawomenscenter.com/services-psychology-deep-breathing.html; Lawrence Robinson, Robert Segal, Jeanne Segal, and Melinda Smith, "Relaxation Techniques for Stress Relief," Help Guide, last modified February 2014, http://www.helpguide.org/mental/stress_relief_meditation_yoga_relaxation.htm; Jordan Shakeshaft, "6 Breathing Exercises to Relax in 10 Minutes or Less," *Time* Health & Family, October 8, 2012, http://healthland.time.com/2012/10/08/6-breathing-exercises-to-relax-in-10-minutes-or-less/#ixzz2WhUavI6g; Andrew Weil, "Breathing: Three Exercises," Dr. Weil website, accessed June 17, 2013, http://www.drweil.com/drw/u/ART00521/three-breathing-exercises.html; Barbara Wood, "Deep Breathing: A Great Health Trick," Lifehack, undated, http://www.lifehack.org/articles/lifehack/deep-breathing-a-great-health-trick.html; Carlos P. Zalaquett, "Breathing Techniques," University of South Florida, accessed June 17, 2013, http://www.coedu.usf.edu/zalaquett/Help_Screens/breath.htm; "Breathing Exercises for Optimum Performance," Human Performance Resource Center, August 2012, http://hprc-online.org/blog/total-force-fitness/files/PS_BreathingVideos_cdm092712.pdf; "Calm Breathing," Anxiety BC, accessed June 17, 2013, http://www.anxietybc.com/sites/default/files/CalmBreathing.pdf; "Deep Breathing to Relieve Acute Stress," University of Pittsburgh Medical Center, accessed June 17, 2013, http://www.upmc.com/services/healthy-lifestyles/acute-stress/pages/deep-breathing.aspx; "Relaxation Technique I—Deep Breathing," Indiana Coalition Against Domestic Violence, accessed June 17, 2013, http://www.icadvinc.org.php53-6.dfw1-1.websitetestlink.com/wp-content/uploads/2012/10/Conf2012-Deep-Breathing.pdf; "Relaxation Techniques: Breath Control Helps Quell Errant Stress Response," Harvard Medical School Family Health Guide, October 2006, http://www.health.harvard.edu/fhg/updates/update1006a.shtml; "Take a Deep Breath and Relax," Common Steps, accessed June 17, 2013, http://commonsteps.org/46562.html; "Take a Deep Breath and Relax," Queen's University, accessed June 17, 2013, http://www.queensu.ca/learningstrategies/grad/stress/module/relaxthebody/TakeaDeepBreathAndRelax.pdf (site discontinued).

16. Abhishek Agarwal, "Anger Management—5 Steps to Successful Temper Control," Global Oneness, accessed June 20, 2013, http://www.experiencefestival.com/wp/article/anger-management-5-steps-to-successful-temper-control (site discontinued); Dean Anderson, "3 Ways to Stop Negative Thinking," Spark People, undated, http://www.sparkpeople.com/resource/motivation_articles.asp?id=614; Debra Beck, "Learning Positive Self-Talk," Empowered Teens & Parents, April 12, 2013, http://empoweredteensandparents.com/parenting/learning-positive-self-talk; Jacques Dallaire, "The Five R's—A Negative Thought Stopping Procedure," Performance Prime, 2012, http://www.performanceprime.com/performance-04_negative_thought_stopping.php; positive teens [Marian D'Angelo], "Latest Updates," Positive Thinking Teens, July 28, 2009, http://positiveteens.wordpress.com; hywo, "Creating a Positive Exercise Experience by Zachary Fiorido," Health Your Way, May 22, 2012, http://www.healthyourwayonline.com/tag/positive-thinking; Todd Goldfarb, "7 Effective Ways to Implement Positive Thinking," We the Change, October 30, 2007, http://www.wethechange.com/7-effective-ways-to-implement-positive-thinking; Carolyn Gregoire, "Positive Thinking Tips: 10 Ways to Overcome Negativity and Become More Optimistic," HuffPost Teen, December 9, 2012, http://www.huffingtonpost.com/2012/12/09/positive-thinking-tips-10_n_2252944.html; Lizzie Heiselt, "3 Steps to Overcoming Negative Thoughts," Babble, March 12, 2013, http://www.babble.com/mom/3-steps-to-overcoming-negative-thoughts; Geoffrey James, "Positive Thinking,: 7 Easy Ways to Improve a Bad Day, last modified June 18, 2012, http://www.inc.com/geoffrey-james/positive-thinking-7-easy-ways-to-improve-a-bad-day.html; Jessica Kieras, "What to Do about Negative Thinking When

Positive Thinking Doesn't Work," Jessica Kieras, January 17, 2013, http://www.jessicakieras.com/negative-thinking-positive-thinking-doesnt-work; Krystal Kuehn, "Staying Positive in a Negative World: 4 Keys to Positive Thinking 4 Life," New Day Counseling, 2008, http://www.newdaycounseling.org/Positive_Thinking.html; Victoria Marano, "7 Simple Strategies on How to Stop Negative Thinking," A Healthy Life, 2011, http://vmarano.tumblr.com/post/4717005654/stopnegativethinking; Remez Sasson, "How to Think Positively," Success Consciousness, accessed June 20, 2013, http://www.successconsciousness.com/think-positively.htm; Mark Tyrell, "How to Stop Negative Thinking in 7 Simple Steps," Uncommon Help, accessed June 20, 2013, http://www.uncommonhelp.me/articles/how-to-stop-negative-thinking; Michelle Uy, "10 Tips to Overcome Negative Thoughts: Positive Thinking Made Easy," *Tiny Buddha*, accessed June 20, 2013, http://tinybuddha.com/blog/10-tips-to-overcome-negative-thoughts-positive-thinking-made-easy; "100 Positive-Thinking Exercises that Will Make Any Patient Healthier & Happier," RN Central, August 19, 2008, http://www.rncentral.com/nursing-library/careplans/100_positive_thinking_exercises_to_incorporate_into_your_life; "Building Self-Esteem: Changing Negative Thoughts," At Health, May 20, 2012, http://athealth.com/topics/building-self-esteem-a-self-help-guide-part-4/; "Challenging Negative Thinking," Reach Out, accessed June 20, 2013, http://au.reachout.com/Challenging-negative-thinking; "Helping Teenagers with Stress," Mental Health Screening, accessed June 20, 2013, http://www.mentalhealthscreening.org/screening/resources/teenagers-and-stress.aspx; "How Can I Change Negative Thoughts I Have about Myself to Positive Ones?," Strength of Us, accessed June 20, 2013, http://strengthofus.org/pages/view/215; "Positive Thinking: Reduce Stress by Eliminating Negative Self-Talk," CNN Health, http://www.cnn.com/HEALTH/library/positive-thinking/SR00009.html.
17. "Stress—Learning to Relax," Women's and Children's Health Network website (Teen Health), last modified August 23, 2012, http://www.cyh.com/healthtopics/healthtopicdetails.aspx?p=243&np=293&id=2210.
18. Walcutt, "I Don't Believe."
19. Tank, "How to Tell Your Family."
20. Ray, "How Do I Talk."
21. Tank, "How to Tell Your Family."
22. Ibid.
23. Ray, "How Do I Talk."
24. Cline, "How Do I Reveal."
25. Malphael, "Finding Out a Relative Is an Atheist Is Like Finding Out They Committed Suicide, but Worse," Reddit *r/atheism* (forum), accessed June 20, 2013, http://www.reddit.com/r/atheism/comments/1g7fwt/finding_out_a_relative_is_an_atheist_is_like.
26. Kelly Richardson, "Be Respectful in Questioning Family's Religious Views," *The Sacramento Bee*, January 25, 2008, K3.
27. Richard Wade, email interview with author, February 22, 2010.
28. Ibid.
29. Scott, "Do Atheists Hide."

10. How Will Your Parents React?

1. Ally Stacey, email interview with author, April 17, 2010.
2. Atothetheist [Steven], July 10, 2012 (7:04 p.m.), comment on mikeacbarnes, "Telling Your Parents You're an Athiest," *Thinking Atheist* (forum), July 10, 2012, http://www.thethinkingatheist.com/forum/Thread-Telling-Your-Parents-You-re-An-Atheist?pid=

181641#pid181641.

3. Nicole Schrand, email interview with author, April 19, 2010.

4. Joel Collins Sati, "My Moment of 'Uhuru' (Freedom)," *The African Atheist* (blog), accessed January 2, 2014, http://theafricanatheist.tumblr.com/post/23442580701/uhuru-freedom.

5. Alain Jehlen, "How Can You Deal with Angry Parents?," National Education Association website, April 2008, http://www.nea.org/home/12800.htm; Howard Margolis, "Listening: The Key to Problem Solving with Angry Parents," *Social Psychology International* 12, no. 4 (November 1991): 329–47, http://spi.sagepub.com/content/12/4/329.abstract; "Tips & Tricks: Dealing with Angry Parents," One-Stop Counseling Shop website, March 21, 2013, http://onestopcounselingshop.com/2013/03/21/tips-tricks-dealing-with-angry-parents; "Dealing with Angry Parents," EducationWorld website, accessed June 24, 2013, http://www.educationworld.com/a_admin/admin/admin474.shtml.

6. "Anger Management for Teens," Middle Earth blog, June 26, 2010, http://middleearthnj.wordpress.com/2010/06/26/anger-management-for-teens; Dominique Jordan, "How to Control Your Temper, BellaOnline website, accessed August 15, 2014, http://www.bellaonline.com/articles/art2596.asp; Heather White, "What Are Anger Management Techniques for Teens?," Livestrong.com, last modified January 11, 2014, http://www.livestrong.com/article/81274-anger-management-techniques-teens; "Anger Management: 10 Tips to Tame Your Temper," Mayo Clinic website, accessed June 14, 2013, http://www.mayoclinic.com/health/anger-management/MH00102/NSECTIONGROUP=1; "Calling All Hotheads: Tips on Keeping Cool in an Angry World," pamphlet, National Crime Prevention Council website, accessed June 14, 2013, http://www.ncpc.org/cms/cms-upload/ncpc/files/hotheads.pdf; Raychelle Lohmann, "As a Teen, How Can I Calm Down When I'm Angry?," Sharecare website, accessed August 15, 2014, http://www.sharecare.com/question/as-teen-calm-down-angry; "Anger Management," Young Men's Health website, last modified June 10, 2013, http://www.youngmenshealthsite.org/anger.html.

7. Mike, "I Just Told My Parents That I'm an Atheist?," *Yahoo! Answers* (forum), accessed June 14, 2013, http://answers.yahoo.com/question/index?qid=20120426183045AAG9i38.

8. Seth Jon Nonnemaker, "My Parents Reaction to Me Saying 'I'm an Atheist,'" Think Atheist website, June 27, 2011, http://www.thinkatheist.com/profiles/blogs/my-parents-reaction-to-me.

9. Michele, email interview with author, April 19, 2010.

10. bu2b, "Need Some Help . . . Told My Parent I Was an Atheist and a Nonbeliever Last Night," *Recovery from Mormonism* (forum), December 14, 2010, http://exmormon.org/phorum/read.php?2,55912.

11. Deborah Mitchell, "Coming Out," *Kids without Religion* (blog), May 1, 2013, http://raisingkidswithoutreligion.net/2013/05/01/coming-out.

12. Richard Wade, "Ask Richard: Teen Atheist Ponders Coming Out in Religious Family," *Friendly Atheist* (blog), April 2, 2012, http://www.patheos.com/blogs/friendlyatheist/2012/04/02/ask-richard-teen-ponders-coming-out-in-religious-family.

13. John Szaszvari, email interview with author, April 15, 2010.

14. Kelly Richardson, "Be Respectful in Questioning Family's Religious Views," *The Sacramento Bee*, January 25, 2008, K3.

15. Blair Scott, "Do Atheists Hide from Family and Friends?," Alabama Atheist, October 5, 2010, accessed June 6, 2013, http://www.alabamaatheist.org/?p=267 (site discontinued).

16. nateychan, "How to Tell Your Parents You're an Atheist," *Flaming Atom* (forum), February 9, 2012, http://forum.flamingatom.com/single/?p=8207732&t=9386086.

17. Wade, "Ask Richard: Teen Atheist Ponders."

18. Sunkissed, comment on "Teens: Atheist Survey?," *Yahoo! Answers Teen & Preteen* (forum), accessed April 7, 2010, https://answers.yahoo.com/question/index?qid=20100328044214AAa

2YMU.

19. Mike, "I Just Told My Parents That I'm an Atheist?," *Yahoo! Answers Religion & Spirituality* (forum), April 27, 2012, http://answers.yahoo.com/question/index?qid=20120426183045AA G9i38.

20. Trevor, "Ask Richard: Parents Rendered Deaf by the Word 'Atheist,'" *Friendly Atheist* (blog), January 31, 2011, http://www.patheos.com/blogs/friendlyatheist/2011/01/31 /ask-richard-parents-rendered-deaf-by-the-word-"atheist".

21. JulietEcho, comment on "Ask Richard: Teen Atheist Suffers Her Parents' Fear and Prejudice," *Friendly Atheist* (blog), January 8, 2010, http://www.patheos.com/blogs/friendlyatheist /2010/01/08/ask-richard-teen-atheist-suffers-her-parents%E2%80%99-fear-and-prejudice.

22. James, email interview with author, April 17, 2010.

23. Meaghen Manders, email interview with author, 2010.

24. Michele, email interview.

25. Atheist Princess, "My Sister Hates Me," Atheist Nexus website, November 23, 2009, http://www.atheistnexus.org/profiles/blogs/my-sister-hates-me.

26. Nicole Schrand, email interview.

27. lemach94 [Jessica], "I'm Free!!," Experience Project *I Am an Atheist* (blog), May 5, 2010, http://www.experienceproject.com/stories/Am-An-Atheist/1020357.

28. Brandon Paugh, email interview with author, April 13, 2010.

29. Cassidy, "How Should I Tell My Mother I'm an Atheist?," Snanswer.com, April 2013, accessed June 3, 2013, http://www.snanswer.com/rthms/how-should-i-tell-my-mother-im-an-atheist.html (site discontinued).

30. Alex Nicole, email interview with author, April 23, 2010.

31. Josh55, "I Just Told My Parents I'm an Atheist," Experience Project *I Am an Atheist* (blog), January 3, 2012, http://www.experienceproject.com/stories/Am-An-Atheist/1979694.

32. Cliff Walker, comment on "Growing Up Atheist in Honduras," *Positive Atheism* website, October 4, 2000, http://www.positiveatheism.org/mail/eml9414.htm.

33. Austin Cline, "My Family Wants Me to Keep Going to Church: Questions about Atheism and Atheists: Going to Church with Family," About.com (Agnosticism/Atheism), accessed May 29, 2010, http://atheism.about.com/od/atheistsfamily/a/church.htm.

34. Richard Wade, "Ask Richard: Young Atheist Out to Religious Parents but Not to Religious Friend," *Friendly Atheist* (blog), December 31, 2012, http://www.patheos.com/blogs /friendlyatheist/2012/12/31/ask-richard-young-atheist-out-to-religious-parents-but-not-to -religious-friend.

35. "Facing the Big God Question," *The Bulletin* (Bend, OR), December 18, 2009, http://www .bendbulletin.com/article/20091218/FEAT01/912180331.

36. Liz, email interview with author, April 14, 2010.

37. Brandon King, "When I Came Out," Atheist Nexus website, July 13, 2012, http://www .atheistnexus.org/forum/topics/when-i-came-out.

38. Coolbus, comment on "Question for Atheists (srs)," *Bodybuilding.com* (forum), January 10, 2011, http://forum.bodybuilding.com/showthread.php?t=130726193&p=608371803 &viewfull=1#post608371803.

39. Coolbus, "Dad Finally Found Out I'm an Atheist," *Bodybuilding.com* (forum), April 9, 2012, http://forum.bodybuilding.com/showthread.php?t=143879031&page=1.

40. Drew Ayling, email interview with author, April 17, 2010.

41. PYOOnGDOOng [Joe], "So I Told My Parents I'm Agnostic . . .," *Bodybuilding.com* (forum), December 21, 2012, http://forum.bodybuilding.com/showthread.php?t=150524083 &page=1.

42. Dylan Tillman, email interview with author, May 11, 2010.

43. Szaszvari, email interview.

11. How Will Your Friends React?

1. Tyler the Skeptic, "First Year as an Out-of-the-Closet Atheist in the Bible Belt?," *Yahoo! Answers Religion & Spirituality* (forum), accessed July 1, 2013, http://answers.yahoo.com /question/index?qid=20120704025618AANaCdZ

2. Richard Wade, email interview with author, February 22, 2010.

3. Sandhya Bathija, "Commencement Controversy," *Church & State* 62, no. 6 (June 2009), https://www.au.org/church-state/june-2009-church-state/featured/commencement -controversy.

4. Jezabel [Jessica], "I Am Atheist," *Teen Ink* blog, accessed July 1, 2013, http://www.teenink .com/opinion/spirituality_religion/article/158476/I-am-Atheist.

5. Joaquin Vasquez-Duran, "Ask an Atheist Day @ Larkin High School," Illini Secular Student Alliance website, April 20, 2011, http://www.illinissa.com/2011/04/ask-atheist-day-larkin -high-school.html.

6. Evan Strozniak, "From Fearfull [*sic*] Catholic to Skeptical Atheist," *The Coming Out Godless Project* (forum), September 12, 2012, http://comingoutgodless.com/2012/09/12/from-fearfull -catholic-to-skeptical-atheist.

7. Mary Phan, email interview with author, April 14, 2010.

8. Leena Hölttä, email interview with author, April 16, 2010.

9. Barry, under "Letter[s] from Atheist Kids to American Atheist," "Humanism for Kids" page, Witty Humanist Youth website, accessed August 11, 2014, https://sites.google.com/a /wittyhumanistyouth.org/why/kids-page.

10. The Ginger Atheist, "Surviving High School as an Atheist," *Two Godless Teens* (blog), July 4, 2013, http://twogodlessteens.weebly.com/5/post/2013/07/surviving-high-school-as-an -atheist.html (site discontinued).

11. Brandon Paugh, email interview with author, April 13, 2010.

12. flamingbananas [Samantha], "My 'Friend' Dumped Me Because I'm an Atheist," *The Straight Dope* (forum), June 14, 2004, http://boards.straightdope.com/sdmb/showthread .php?p=4966260#post4966260.

13. Ibid.

14. Luke, "Ask Teen Atheist, #1," *Diary of a Teenage Atheist* (blog), April 13, 2008, http:// teenatheist.wordpress.com/2008/04/13/ask-teen-atheist-1.

15. Michelle Dubert-Bellrichard, "Why Atheists Deserve Scholarships Too: Standing Up for One's Beliefs Amid Adversity Takes a Lot of Courage and Determination," *Telegraph Herald* (Dubuque, IA), December 31, 2007, http://www.thonline.com/article.cfm?id=185592 (page discontinued).

16. Maggie H., "I Am Moral without a God," *Teen Ink* website, accessed July 1, 2013, http:// www.teenink.com/opinion/discrimination/article/558102/I-am-moral-without-a-God.

17. Teen Atheist, "Ask Teen Atheist, #1," *Diary of a Teenage Atheist* (blog), April 13, 2008, http://teenatheist.wordpress.com/2008/04/13/ask-teen-atheist-1.

18. Luke, "Ask Teen Atheist."

19. Teen Atheist, "Ask Teen Atheist."

20. flamingbananas, "My 'Friend' Dumped Me."

21. Jezabel, "I Am Atheist."

22. David Blauvelt, email interview with author, April 2010.

23. Bathija, "Commencement Controversy."

24. Vasquez-Duran, "Ask an Atheist Day."

25. Dan Carsen, "The Genesis of Alabama's Only HS 'Freethinkers' Club," Southern Education Desk website, October 23, 2012, http://www.southerneddesk.org/?p=6320.

26. Michael Allen, "Student Duncan Henderson Fights for Two Years to Start Atheist Club at Alabama High School," Opposing Views, November 1, 2012, http://www.opposingviews.com/i/religion/christianity/student-duncan-henderson-fights-two-years-start-atheist-club-alabama-high.

27. Jezabel, "I Am Atheist."

28. Darrel Ray, "How Should I Respond to Religious Harassment at School?," Kids without God website, accessed June 6, 2013, http://kidswithoutgod.com/teens/ask/how-should-i-respond-to-religious-harassment-at-school.

29. Blauvelt, email interview.

30. Ian Buckley, email interview with author, April 25, 2010.

31. Vasquez-Duran, "Ask an Atheist Day."

32. Kay Miller, email interview with author, April 26, 2010.

33. Christine Smith, email interview with author, April 17, 2010.

34. Emily Wappes, email interview with author, April 13, 2010.

35. Mark Turner, email interview with author, April 26, 2010.

36. Emily C., email interview with author, April 18, 2010.

37. Matt Cicero, email interview with author, April 13, 2010.

38. Mickey Roundtree, "Face to Faith: Befriending an Atheist in Mormon Country," *Huffington Post* blog, May 6, 2013, http://www.huffingtonpost.com/mickey-roundtree/face-to-faith-befriending-an-atheist-in-mormon-country_b_3188381.html.

39. Vasquez-Duran, "Ask an Atheist Day."

40. Wappes, email interview.

41. Emily C., email interview.

42. Djabarov, email interview.

43. Liz, email interview with author, April 14, 2010.

44. Djabarov, email interview.

45. Heather L. Downs, "The Deconversion Experience: A Qualitative Study of Students' Experiences with Leaving a Belief in the Christian God and Identifying with Nonbelief" (doctoral thesis, Center for Human Enrichment, University of Northern Colorado, 2002), 16, http://visibleatheist.files.wordpress.com/2010/01/deconarticle.pdf.

46. Alexander W. Astin and Helen S. Astin, *The Spiritual Life of College Students: A National Study of College Students' Search for Meaning and Purpose* (Los Angeles: Higher Education Research Institute at UCLA, 2005), 7, http://spirituality.ucla.edu/docs/reports/Spiritual_Life_College_Students_Full_Report.pdf.

47. Ibid.

48. Liz, email interview.

49. Paul V. Sorrentino, "What Do College Students Want? A Student-Centered Approach to Multifaith Involvement," *Journal of Ecumenical Studies* 45, no. 1 (Winter, 2010), TheFreeLibrary.com, under "The comments of an atheist student from my study illustrate this same point," http://www.thefreelibrary.com/What+do+college+students+want%3F+a+student-centered+approach+-to...-a0224100537.

50. Wappes, email interview.

12. How Do Unbelievers Handle Hostile Teachers, Principals, and Classmates?

1. Alex Haley, "*Playboy* Interview: Martin Luther King," *Playboy*, January 1965, 77.

2. Billy Hallowell, "Teen Atheist Behind Prayer Mural Ban Threatened with Rape: 'We Will Get You—Look Out!,'" TheBlaze website, April 12, 2012, http://www.theblaze.com/stories

/2012/04/12/teen-atheist-behind-prayer-mural-ban-threatened-with-rape-we-will-get
-you-look-out.

3. Mark Ahlquist v. City of Cranston, Robert F. Strom, and School Committee of the City of Cranston, C.A. No. 11-138-L (D.R.I April 4, 2011), 2–3, submitted by Lynette Labinger and Thomas R. Bender (ACLU of Rhode Island), http://www.riaclu.org/documents/Ahlquistv
.CranstonComplaint.pdf.

4. Jessica Ahlquist, "Student Activist Awards: Jessica Ahlquist, Thomas Jefferson Youth Activist Award—2011," Freedom from Religion Foundation website, 2011, accessed May 12, 2013, http://ffrf.org/outreach/awards/student-activist-awards/item/11995-jessica-ahlquist
-thomas-jefferson-youth-activist.

5. Jessica Ahlquist, "High Schoolers Need Help," *Evil Little Thing* (blog), July 23, 2011, http://www.jessicaahlquist.com/2011/07/high-schoolers-need-help.html (site discontinued).

6. Abby Goodnough, "Student Faces Town's Wrath in Protest against a Prayer," *New York Times*, January 26, 2012, http://www.nytimes.com/2012/01/27/us/rhode-island-city-enraged
-over-school-prayer-lawsuit.html.

7. "ACLU Files Suit over Cranston School Prayer Banner," ACLU of Rhode Island website, April 4, 2011, http://www.riaclu.org/news/post/aclu-files-suit-over-cranston-school-prayer
-banner.

8. Ahlquist, "Student Activist Awards."

9. Nina Golgowski, "Atheist Teen Still Getting Threats Over Campaign to Remove Prayer Banner While Vowing She Will Not Leave School," *Daily Mail*, January 28, 2012, http://www
.dailymail.co.uk/news/article-2093136/Atheist-teen-getting-threats-campaign-remove-prayer
-banner-vowing-leave-school.html.

10. Goodnough, "Student Faces Town's Wrath."

11. Lynn Arditi, "Jessica Ahlquist Wins Award from Foundation of *Playboy* Magazine Creator," *Providence Journal*, May 7, 2013, http://news.providencejournal.com/breaking-news/2013/05
/jessica-ahlquist-wins-award-from-foundation-of-playboy-magazine-creator.html (site discontinued).

12. Rene Lynch, "Prayer Banner: Atheist Teen Speaks Out, Lands $44,000 Scholarship," *Los Angeles Times*, February 22, 2012, http://articles.latimes.com/2012/feb/22/nation/la-nn-na
-jessica-ahlquist-atheist-teen-wins-40000-scholarship-20120222.

13. Caroline May, "ACLU, Atheist Teen Cheer Decision to Remove School Prayer Banner," *Daily Caller*, February 17, 2012, http://dailycaller.com/2012/02/17/aclu-atheist-teen-cheer
-decision-to-remove-school-prayer-banner.

14. Ahlquist, "High Schoolers Need Help."

15. SeriousMoad [Damon Fowler], "Threatened to Contact ACLU for Prayer at Graduation: They Seemingly Backed Down . . .," Reddit *r/atheism* (forum), accessed July 1, 2013, http://www.reddit.com/r/atheism/comments/hed7y/threatened_to_contact_aclu_for_prayer_at.

16. "Controversy over Prayer at Graduation in Bastrop, La.," Freedom from Religion Foundation website, May 19, 2011, http://ffrf.org/news/action/item/2120-controversy-over
-prayer-at-graduation-in-bastrop-la.

17. Quoted in Mark Rainwater, "Student Challenges Prayer at Bastrop Graduation," *Bastrop Daily Enterprise* website, May 18, 2011, http://www.bastropenterprise.com/article/20110518
/NEWS/305189997.

18. SeriousMoad, "Threatened to Contact."

19. Jlowe64 [Jerrett Fowler], comment on "Threatened to Contact ACLU for Prayer at Graduation," Reddit *r/atheism* (forum), accessed July 1, 2013, http://www.reddit.com/r
/atheism/comments/hed7y/threatened_to_contact_aclu_for_prayer_at/c1uut0n.

20. "Seniors Hold Prayer despite Atheist's Threats," Christian Broadcasting Network website,

May 24, 2011, http://www.cbn.com/cbnnews/us/2011/may/seniors-hold-prayer-despite
-atheists-threats.

21. Guest Contributor, "An Interview with Damon Fowler and his Brother Jerrett," *Friendly
Atheist* (blog), May 26, 2011, http://www.patheos.com/blogs/friendlyatheist/2011/05/26
/an-interview-with-damon-fowler-and-his-brother-jerrett.

22. Damon Fowler, "So If Anyone Remembers That Whole Thing with Damon Fowler's
Graduation Last Year, There's More," Reddit *r/atheism* (forum), accessed July 1, 2013, http://
www. reddit.com/r/atheism/comments/s88dy/so_if_anyone_remembers_that_whole_thing_with.

23. Quoted in Guest Contributor, "An Interview with Damon Fowler."

24. Emerson v. Board of Education of the Township of Ewing, 330 U.S. 1 (1947), Legal
Information Institute website, accessed March 21, 2014, http://www.law.cornell.edu
/supremecourt/text/330/1#writing-USSC_CR_0330_0001_ZO.

25. McCollum v. Board of Education, 333 U.S. 203 (1948), *Findlaw,* accessed July 25, 2013,
http://laws.findlaw.com/us/333/203.html.

26. *Engel v. Vitale*, 370 U.S. 421 (1962), FindLaw website, accessed July 25, 2013, http://laws
.findlaw.com/us/370/421.html.

27. Abington School District v. Schempp, 374 U.S. 203 (1963), FindLaw website, accessed July
25, 2013, http://laws.findlaw.com/us/374/203.html.

28. Lemon v. Kurtzman, 403 U.S. 602 (1971), FindLaw website, accessed July 27, 2013, http://
laws.findlaw.com/us/403/602.html.

29. Wallace v. Jaffree, 472 U.S. 38 (1985), FindLaw website, accessed July 25, 2013, http://
laws.findlaw.com/us/472/38.html.

30. Lee v. Weisman, 505 U.S. 577 (1992), FindLaw website, accessed July 25, 2013, http://
laws.findlaw.com/us/505/577.html.

31. Santa Fe Independent School District v. Doe, No. 99-62 (2000), FindLaw website, accessed
July 25, 2013, http://laws.findlaw.com/us/000/99-62.html.

32. Krystal Myers, "School Promotes Religion and Discrimination of Atheist Students,"
Knoxville News Sentinel, February 26, 2012, http://www.knoxnews.com/news/2012/feb/26
/krystal-myers-school-promotes-religion-and-of.

33. Hugh G. Willet, "Lenoir City High School Won't Publish Atheist Student's Editorial on
Religion in Schools," *Knoxville News Sentinel*, February 23, 2012, http://www.knoxnews.com
/news/2012/feb/23/lenoir-city-high-school-wont-publish-atheist-on.

34. Myers, "School Promotes Religion."

35. Willet, "Lenoir City High School."

36. Ibid.

37. Hugh G. Willet, "Lenoir City School System Curtailing Prayers at Public Meetings,"
Knoxville News Sentinel, March 21, 2012, http://www.knoxnews.com/news/2012/mar/21
/lenoir-city-school-system-curtailing-prayers-at.

38. Alex, email interview with author, April 23, 2010.

39. Matt, *The Catholic School Journals* (blog), April 25, 2012, http://atheistinsurgents.tumblr
.com/post/21818542371/i-am-sooo-sorry-that-you-have-to-go-to-a-catholic.

40. ANS, "Just an Introduction . . .", *An Atheist Student in a Christian School* (blog), July 28,
2013, http://damnitchristianity.blogspot.com/2013_07_01_archive.html.

41. Enri Galletti, "An Atheist in a Christian School . . .," deviantART website, December 15,
2011, http://enrii87.deviantart.com/journal/An-atheist-in-a-christian-school-274124613 (page
discontinued).

42. Ibid.

43. Matt, posting on *The Catholic School Journals* website, February 14, 2013, http://atheist
insurgents.tumblr.com/post/43098862773/i-got-into-an-argument-with-my-religion-teacher.

44. Micah White, "Student Battles for Secularism in Hostile High School," *Secular Humanist Bulletin* 15, no. 1 (Spring 1999), Council for Secular Humanism website, http://www.secularhumanism.org/library/shb/white_15_1.htm.

45. Ibid.

46. Micah White, "Atheist under Siege Starts Atheist Club" (speech, delivered to the 22nd Annual Convention of the Freedom From Religion Foundation, St. Anthony Hotel, San Antonio, November 6, 1999), http://ffrf.org/legacy/fttoday/2000/jan_feb2000/white.html.

47. Micah White, "New President Elected to the Campus Freethought Alliance," *The Cowtown Humanist* 2, no. 4 (July 2000), http://www.hofw.org/news/news2-4.htm.

48. "Student Activist Awards: Micah White—1999," Freedom from Religion Foundation website, accessed 2010, http://ffrf.org/outreach/awards/student-activist-awards/item/11970-micah-white.

49. White, "Atheist under Siege."

50. Kevin Allman, "Evolution vs. Creation," Gambit (BestofNewOrleans.com), March 8, 2011, http://www.bestofneworleans.com/gambit/weird-science/Content?oid=1608979.

51. Ibid.

52. Louisiana Science Education Act, S. 733 (2008), 1–2, National Center for Science Education website, accessed July 30, 2013, http://ncse.com/files/pub/legal/aflegislation/08_la_sb733-amend.pdf.

53. Sylvia Schon, "Bill Allows Teaching Creationism as Science," *Daily Star* (Hammond, LA), April 6, 2008, http://www.hammondstar.com/local_news/news/article_95832759-1abf-54c0-b67a-d2dbb99a570f.html.

54. "About," Louisiana Family Forum website, accessed July 29, 2013, http://www.lafamilyforum.org/about.

55. "Nobel Laureates Push Repeal of Louisiana Science Education Law," The Associated Press, April 21, 2011, *The Times-Picayune* website, http://www.nola.com/politics/index.ssf/2011/04/nobel_laureates_push_repeal_of.html.

56. "Repeal Effort Fails in Committee," National Center for Science Education website, May 26, 2011, http://ncse.com/news/2011/05/repeal-effort-fails-committee-006685.

57. "Endorsements and Letters" RepealCreationism, accessed July 29, 2013, http://www.repealcreationism.com/endorsements; Zack Kopplin, "77 Nobel Laureates Call for a Repeal of the LSEA," RepealCreationism.com, April 19, 2011, http://www.repealcreationism.com/397/nobellaureateletter.

58. Zack Kopplin, "Tell Louisiana to Teach Real Science in Public Schools, Not Creationism and Climate Change Denial," Change.org, accessed July 29, 2013, http://www.change.org/petitions/tell-louisiana-to-teach-real-science-in-public-schools-not-creationism-and-climate-change-denial.

59. Lawrence S. Lerner, Ursula Goodenough, John Lynch, Martha Schwartz, and Richard Schwartz, "Louisiana," *The State of State Science Standards 2012* (Washington, DC: Thomas B. Fordham Foundation + Institute), 2012, 82, http://www.edexcellencemedia.net/publications/2012/2012-State-of-State-Science-Standards/2012-State-of-State-Science-Standards-FINAL.pdf.

60. Flora Lichtman, "The Teenaged 'Troublemaker' Fighting for Science," *Talk of the Nation*, National Public Radio, April 12, 2013, http://www.npr.org/2013/04/12/177029255/the-teenaged-troublemaker-fighting-for-science.

61. Ken Thorbourne, "Kearny School Says Action was Taken against Teacher Who Preached Religion," *The Star-Ledger* (Newark, NJ), November 16, 2006, 54.

62. Tina Kelley, "Talk in Class Turns to God, Setting Off Public Debate on Rights," *New York Times*, December 18, 2006, http://www.nytimes.com/2006/12/18/nyregion/18kearny.html

?pagewanted=all&_r=0.

63. Matthew LaClair, "Saved by the Bell," *Harper's Magazine*, July 2007, 27.

64. Kelley, "Talk in Class."

65. Ken Thorbourne, "'You Belong—in Hell': Kearny High Preacher Teacher Uses Classroom to Condemn Non-Christians," *The Jersey Journal*, November 15, 2006, A5.

66. Ibid.; Ken Thorboune, "Student Tapes Teacher Proselytizing in Class: Accept Jesus or 'You Belong in Hell,' He Said," *The Star-Ledger* (Newark, NJ), November 15, 2006, 15.

67. Kelley, "Talk in Class."

68. Ibid.

69. Kelly Heyboer, "Kearny Student Moves to Sue District: He Cites Harassment after Challenging Teacher's Preaching," *The Star-Ledger* (Newark, NJ), February 20, 2007, 12.

70. "New Jersey District Will Train Teachers on Separation of Church and State," American School & University website, May 10, 2005, http://asumag.com/dailynews/kearnynj.

71. Kevin Canessa Jr., "Castelli Breaks Ranks, Makes Statements," *Hudson-Bergen-Essex Line Blog*, May 16, 2007, http://hudsonbergenessex.wordpress.com/2007/05/16/castelli-breaks -ranks-makes-statements.

72. August, "2010 Secular Student of Alliance Board of Directors Election Results," Secular Student Alliance website, May 10, 2010, http://www.secularstudents.org/node/3129.

73. Barry F. Seidman and Arnell Dowret, "Equal Time for Freethought," WBAI Radio website, accessed July 31, 2013, http://wbai.org/program.php?program=138.

74. Ashley Strain, "'In God We Teach' Revisits Student and Teacher Clash: Documentary Shows Faith Dispute from Both Sides," *The Jersey Journal*, April 9, 2011, A10.

13. Can You Celebrate Christmas? And Other Holiday FAQs

1. Meaghan Manders, email interview with author, 2010.

2. Luis Ruuska, "Merry Christmas from Your Friendly Neighborhood Atheist," *HuffPost Teen* (blog), December 23, 2012, http://www.huffingtonpost.com/luis-ruuska/merry-christmas -from-your_b_2348272.html.

3. Hazel [Hazel Cills], "Hazel Loves Christmas," *Rookie* website, December 8, 2011, http:// rookiemag.com/2011/12/jews-love-xmas.

4. Alex Charlton, "Atheist Christmas," *Young Freethought* (blog), December 13, 2009, http:// www.youngfreethought.net/2009/12/atheist-christmas.html.

5. Tovia Smith, "Removing Religion from Holidays a Tall Order," *Weekend Edition*, National Public Radio, December 23, 2007, http://m.npr.org/story/17558400.

6. Ruuska, "Merry Christmas."

7. Hemant Mehta, "An Atheist at the Thanksgiving Table," *The Washington Post* blog, November 24, 2011, accessed August 11, 2013 (page discontinued, URL unavailable).

8. Austin Cline, "Forum Discussion: Atheist Etiquette Advice," About.com (Agnosticism/ Atheism), accessed August 9, 2013, http://atheism.about.com/b/2012/12/05/forum-discussion -atheist-etiquette-advice.htm.

9. Bill Logan, "Bill Logan: Counsellor and Celebrant," Bill Logan website, accessed March 16, 2014, http://www.bl.co.nz.

10. Bill Logan, "A Secular Grace," Bill Logan website, accessed March 16, 2014, http://www .bl.co.nz/Prayers/Secular_Grace.htm.

11. "Earth's Seasons: Equinoxes, Solstices, Perihelion, and Aphelion, 2000–2020," Naval Oceanography Portal, accessed August 9, 2013, http://www.usno.navy.mil/USNO /astronomical-applications/data-services/earth-seasons.

12. "History," HumanLight website, accessed August 8, 2013, http://humanlight.org /wordpress/about/history (site discontinued); Patrick Colucci, "An Introduction to HumanLight," HumanLight website, December 20, 2008, http://humanlight.org/wordpress /about/introduction-to-humanlight (site discontinued).

13. Kimberly Winston, "Secularists See 'HumanLight' as New December Holiday," Religion News Service website, December 20, 2012, http://www.religionnews.com/2012/12/20 /secularists-see-humanlight-as-new-december-holiday; "Winter Solstice," Secular Seasons website, accessed August 10, 2013, http://www.secularseasons.org/december/winter _solstice.html.

14. "About," National Day of Prayer Task Force website, accessed August 9, 2013, http:// nationaldayofprayer.org/about/; 36 U.S.C. § 119 : US Code—Section 119: National Day of Prayer, FindLaw website, accessed August 9, 2013, http://codes.lp.findlaw.com/uscode/36 /I/A/1/119.

15. "About Us," National Day of Reason website, accessed August 9, 2013, http:// nationaldayofreason.org/about-the-national-day-of-reason.

16. Ibid.

17. "Events for Thursday, May 2nd, 2013," *Skepchick* (blog), accessed August 9, 2013, http:// events.skepchick.org/calendar/2013-05-02 (page discontinued).

18. "A Global Celebration," International Darwin Day Foundation website, accessed August 8, 2013, http://darwinday.org/about.

19. "Darwin Day Resources Page," Center for Inquiry website, accessed August 9, 2013, http:// www.centerforinquiry.net/oncampus/darwin_day; "Darwin Day Events," International Darwin Day Foundation website, accessed August 9, 2013, http://darwinday.org/events.

20. "Earth's Seasons Naval Oceanography Portal."

21. "About," Banned Books Week website, accessed August 9, 2013, http://www.bannedbooks week.org/about.

22. Brandon Paugh, email interview with author, April 13, 2010.

14. How Can You Handle Arguments against Your Being an Atheist?

1. Brandon Paugh, email interview with author, April 13, 2010.

2. Luke Muehlhauser, "How to Debate William Lane Craig," April 22, 2009, *Common Sense Atheism* (blog), http://commonsenseatheism.com/?p=1437.

3. Wendyloh [Wendy], comment on "Ask Richard: Teen Atheist Suffers Her Parents' Fear and Prejudice," *Friendly Atheist* (blog), January 8, 2010, http://www.patheos.com/blogs /friendlyatheist/2010/01/08/ask-richard-teen-atheist-suffers-her-parents%E2%80%99-fear -and-prejudice.

4. Angus Bohanon, email interview with author, April 17, 2010.

5. Mark, under "Letter[s] from Atheist Kids to American Atheist," "Humanism for Kids" page, Witty Humanist Youth website, accessed August 11, 2014, https://sites.google.com/a /wittyhumanistyouth.org/why/kids-page.

6. Kevin B, "5 Tips for Debating with Theists about Your Beliefs (or Lack Thereof)," Think Atheist blog, March 2, 2011, http://www.thinkatheist.com/profiles/blogs/5-tips-for-debating -with?xg_source=activity.

7. Ibid.

8. Austin Cline, "How to Talk to, Debate Theists: Ways Atheists Can Avoid Common Errors," About.com (Agnosticism/Atheism), accessed August 14, 2013, http://atheism.about.com/od /atheismatheiststheism/p/DebateTheists.htm.

9. Bryan Bailey, "What Should Atheists Avoid when Debating Christians?," *Secular Student* (blog), January 20, 2011, http://secularstudent.blogspot.com/2011/01/what-should-atheists-avoid-when.html.

10. David Smalley, "Top 10 Reasons I'm Atheist," Dogma Debate website, January 11, 2009, http://www.dogmadebate.com/2009/01/top-10-reasons-im-atheist.html (page discontinued).

11. Andrew, "More Advice on Atheist-Theist Debates," *Evaluating Christianity* (blog), April 30, 2009, http://evaluatingchristianity.wordpress.com/2009/04/30/more-advice-on-atheist-theist-debates.

12. Emily Jacob, email interview with author, April 26, 2010.

13. Meaghen Manders, email interview with author, 2010.

14. Nathonamore, comment on "Every Time I Tell My Parents I'm an Atheist," Reddit *r/atheism* (forum), June 24, 2013, http://www.reddit.com/r/atheism/comments/v53x5/every_time_i_tell_my_parents_im_an_atheist/c51i03s.

15. Aubriel_J, "Atheist Teen," Richard Dawkins Foundation website, May 20, 2013, http://www.richarddawkins.net/discussions/2013/5/19/atheist-teen.

16. Kyle Barton, "The Ramblings of a 17-Year-Old Atheist," Think Atheist website, April 4, 2013, http://www.thinkatheist.com/profiles/blogs/the-ramblings-of-a-17-year-old-atheist.

17. Joshua Otaku Reyes, "I'm Not Just Rebelling, I'm Also Disbelieving," Think Atheist *Godless Teens* (forum), June 11, 2013, http://www.thinkatheist.com/group/godlessteens/forum/topics/i-m-not-just-rebelling-i-m-also-disbelieving-p?xg_source=activity.

18. Greta Christina, "Godless is the New Black: Is Atheism Just a Trend?," *Greta Christina's Blog*, November 12, 2007, http://freethoughtblogs.com/greta/2007/11/12/godless-is-the/.

19. Sharad, "Just a Phase," *CollegeNET Science* (forum), April 5, 2013, http://www.collegenet.com/elect/app/app?service=external/Forum&sp=51088.

20. Wendyloh, comment, "Ask Richard: Teen Atheist."

15. How Can You Handle Arguments against Atheism in General?

1. *Urban Dictionary*, s.v. "atheist," March 1, 2005, http://www.urbandictionary.com/define.php?term=Atheist&defid=1093596.

2. Beatusum, "This Holy Week, Pray for the Teenage Atheist," *Working on Faith* (blog), March 14, 2008, http://faithiswork.blogspot.com/2008/03/this-holy-week-pray-for-teenage-atheist.html (site discontinued).

3. Klimberly, comment on "This Holy Week, Pray for the Teenage Atheist," *Working on Faith* (blog), April 3, 2008, http://faithiswork.blogspot.com/2008/03/this-holy-week-pray-for-teenage-atheist.html?showComment=1207267114000#c3105294309695772396 (site discontinued).

4. Frank Turek and Christopher Hitchens, "Hitchens vs. Turek, Virginia Commonwealth University," Hitchens Debates Transcripts website, September 8, 2008, http://hitchensdebates.blogspot.com/2010/11/hitchens-vs-turek-vcu.html.

5. Luke Muehlhauser, "Many Atheists Are Hypocrites about Morality," *Common Sense Atheism* (blog), May 9, 2010, http://commonsenseatheism.com/?p=8859.

6. Douglas Wilson and Farrell Till, "Justifying Non-Christian Objections," *Credenda/Agenda* 7, no. 1, accessed August 30, 2013, The Secular Web website, http://www.infidels.org/library/modern/farrell_till/wilson-till.html.

7. Albert Einstein, "Religion and Science," *New York Times*, November 9, 1930, SM1.

8. Richard Dawkins, *The God Delusion* (London: Bantam Press, 2006), 309.

9. Conversational Atheist, "Response to: 'Hitler Was an Atheist! . . . ,'" *Conversational Atheist*

(blog), accessed August 24, 2013, http://conversationalatheist.com/challenges/the-most
-effective-response-to-hitler-was-an-atheist.

10. Sam Harris, quoted in Jon Meacham, "The God Debate," *Newsweek*, April 9, 2007, 58,
http://www.newsweek.com/newsweek-poll-90-believe-god-97611.

11. Karen Loethen, "Your Life Has No Meaning," *My Own Mind* (formerly *Homeschool Atheist
Momma*) (blog), April 15, 2013, http://taytayhser.blogspot.com/2013/04/your-life-has-no
-meaning.html#.UiFEbzZQF6l.

12. Massimo Pigliucci, "On Being a Fulfilled Atheist," *Rationally Speaking* (blog), July 14,
2011, http://rationallyspeaking.blogspot.com/2011/07/on-being-fulfilled-atheist.html.

13. Ann Druyan, "A Voice for Science & Religion" (speech, the Twentieth Annual Convention
of the Freedom from Religion Foundation, Tampa, FL, December 6, 1997), http://webspace
.webring.com/people/nj/jwschmidt/books/druyan.html.

14. Dan Barker, "Godless—From Evangelical Preacher to Atheist," *Freethought Today* 26, no. 7
(September 2009), https://ffrf.org/publications/freethought-today/item/13453-godless-from
-evangelical-preacher-to-atheist, accessed August 30, 2013.

15. Case Drumheller, "Why Its Good to Be Atheist," *Spiritual Living 360* (blog), February 7,
2009, http://www.helium.com/items/1329879-why-its-good-to-be-atheist.

16. Nicole, email interview with author, April 14, 2010.

17. David G. McAfee, *Mom, Dad, I'm an Atheist: The Guide to Coming Out as an Unbeliever*
(London: Dangerous Little Books, 2012), 119.

18. Carl Sagan, *The Demon-Haunted World: Science as a Candle in the Dark* (New York:
Ballantine Books, 1997), 300.

19. Thomas May, "Interview with Sam Harris: The Mortal Dangers of Religious Faith,"
Amazon.com, accessed August 29, 2013, http://www.amazon.com/gp/feature.html?ie
=UTF8&docId=542154.

20. Keith M. Parsons, "Seven Common Misconceptions About Atheism" (speech, Houstonians
for Secular Humanism, October 18, 1998), The Secular Web website, http://www.infidels.org
/library/modern/keith_parsons/misconceptions.html#intolerant.

21. Penn Jillette, "Don't Replace Religion; End It," *New York Times*, January 22, 2013, http://
www.nytimes.com/roomfordebate/2013/01/22/is-atheism-a-religion/atheism-should-end
-religion-not-replace-it.

22. Barry A. Kosmin and Ariela Keysar, with Ryan Cragun and Juhem Navarro-Rivera,
American Nones: The Profile of the No Religion Population (Hartford, CT: Trinity College
Program on Public Values, 2009), 27, http://commons.trincoll.edu/aris/files/2011/08
/NONES_08.pdf.

23. Res Stecker, "Agnosticism Is Far Worse Than Atheism," *The Rocky Mountain Collegian*,
March 4, 2014, http://www.collegian.com/2014/03/agnosticism-is-far-worse-than-atheism
/68049.

24. Chris Stedman, *Faitheist: How an Atheist Found Common Ground with the Religious* (Boston:
Beacon Press, 2012), 146.

25. "About Us," Freethinkers Atheists & Agnostics for Religious Tolerance website, accessed
August 29, 2013, https://sites.google.com/a/isu.edu/freethinkers-atheists-agnostics-for
-religious-tolerance/about-us.

26. J. K. Rowling, *Harry Potter and the Deathly Hallows* (New York: Scholastic, 2007), 411–12 .

27. Princeling, "Happiness Beats God," *Teen Ink* website accessed March 24, 2014, http://
teenink.com/opinion/spirituality_religion/article/181475/Happiness-Beats-God/?page=5.

28. Bazzy, comment on "For All Atheists (Science Was Wrong) God Exist!! =D," *Battledawn*
(forum), January 12, 2010, http://www.battledawn.com/forum/viewtopic.php?f=112&t=5168.

29. Bertrand Russell, "Is There a God?," *The Collected Papers of Bertrand Russell, Volume 11: Last*

Philosophical Testament, 1943–68, ed. John G. Slater and Peter Köllner (London: Routledge, 1997), 543–48.

30. "Atheists in Foxholes, in Cockpits, and on Ships," Military Association of Atheists and Freethinkers website, accessed August 14, 2014, http://www.maaf.info/expaif.html.

31. "Personal Decorations: Bronze Star Medal," The Institute of Heraldry website, accessed June 19, 2014, http://www.tioh.hqda.pentagon.mil/Catalog/Heraldry.aspx?HeraldryId=15252 &CategoryId=3&grp=4&menu=Decorations%20and%20Medals&ps=24&p=0.

32. "Available Emblems of Belief for Placement on Government Headstones and Markers," United States Department of Veterans Affairs website, April 30, 2010, http://www.cem.va.gov /hm/hmemb.asp (page discontinued).

33. Kelly O'Connor, "RRS [Rational Response Squad] vs. Kirk Cameron / Ray Comfort," *Nightline Face-Off*, ABC TV, May 5, 2007, YouTube video, 1:18:58, uploaded by ChristopherHitchslap, October 24, 2011, http://www.youtube.com/watch?v=OPJ6ece-rII.

34. Blaise Pascal, *Pensées* ([Paris?]: Chez Guillaume Desprez, 1669), Gallica website, accessed March 20, 2014, http://gallica.bnf.fr/ark:/12148/btv1b8606964f.image.r=Pens %C3%A9es+de+M+Pascal.f9.langFR.

35. Brother P, "Owned by Pascal's Wager," Think Atheist website, August 3, 2011, http://www .thinkatheist.com/forum/topics/owned-by-pascal-s-wager.

36. Bob Robinson, " Musings on the Debate between Rick Warren and Sam Harris," *Vanguard Church* (blog), April 4, 2007, http://vanguardchurch.blogspot.com/2007/04/musings-on -debate-between-rick-warren.html.

37. Guy Raz, "A 'Collision' of Beliefs: Atheist vs. Theologian," *All Things Considered*, National Public Radio, October 25, 2009, http://m.npr.org/news/front/114115179?singlePage=true.

16. How Can You Handle Arguments for Religion?

1. Robert G. Ingersoll, "God in the Constitution," *The Arena, Volume 1* (No. 1–6), ed. B. O. Flower (Boston: Arena Publishing Co., 1890), 128, https://archive.org/stream /ArenaMagazine-Volume01/188912-arena-volume01#page/n135/mode/2up.

2. Godless Teen, "Top Ten Myths about Belief in God," *Godless Teen* (blog), accessed September 11, 2013, http://www.godlessteens.com/top-ten-myths-about-belief-in-god.

3. Godless Teen, "Top Ten Myths."

4. Nick Watt, "Stephen Hawking: 'Science Makes God Unnecessary,'" ABC News website, September 7, 2010, http://abcnews.go.com/GM A/stephen-hawking-science-makes-god -unnecessary/story?id=11571150 (page discontinued).

5. Bazzy, comment on "For All Atheists (Science Was Wrong) God Exist!! = D," *Battledawn* (forum), January 12, 2010, http://www.battledawn.com/forum/viewtopic.php?f=112&t=5168.

6. "If God Created the Universe, What Created God?," BioLogos Foundation website, accessed September 13, 2013, http://biologos.org/questions/what-created-god#.

7. Lawrence Krauss, "Science Refutes God" (Intelligence Squared U.S. debate; Kaufman Center, New York; December 5, 2012), 8–9, http://intelligencesquaredus.org/images/debates /past/transcripts/120512%20science%20god.pdf.

8. Steven Pinker, quoted in David Van Biema, "Can You Believe in God and Evolution? Four Experts with Very Different Views Weigh in on the Underlying Question," *Time*, August 7, 2005, StevenPinker.com, http://pinker.wjh.harvard.edu/articles/media/2005_08_07_time.html.

9. George Jean Nathan and H. L. Mencken, "Clinical Notes," *The American Mercury*, January 1924, 75, http://www.unz.org/Pub/AmMercury-1924jan-00075.

10. Don Hirschberg, quoted in "'Fascinating Facts' Conceal Facts, Prompt Atheist Responses,"

AA News (Nightowl Edition), November 15, 1996, The Skeptic Tank Text Archive file, http://www.skepticfiles.org/american/aane1200.htm.

11. Woody Allen, "My Philosophy," *The New Yorker*, December 27, 1969, 25, http://www.newyorker.com/magazine/1969/12/27/my-philosophy.

12. David Powers, "Quotes," *Believers vs. Nonbelievers* (blog), accessed August 14, 2014, http://believervsnonbelievers.wordpress.com/quotes/.

13. Dennis Miller, "Religious Quotes and Sayings," NutQuote.com, accessed August 14, 2014, http://www.nutquote.com/topic0/religion.

14. Penn Jillette, "Penn Jillette Quotes," TV.com , accessed August 28, 2014, http://www.tv.com/shows/penn-teller-bullshit/the-bible-fact-or-fiction-322029/trivia/.

15. Kathy Griffin, *Official Book Club Selection: A Memoir According to Kathy Griffin* (New York: Ballantine Books, 2010), 7.

16. Mark Twain, *Mark Twain's Notebook* ed. Albert Bigelow Paine (New York: Harper & Brothers, 1935), 379.

17. Richard Jeni, "Brought Up Catholic," *Comedy Central Presents*, season 6, episode 3 (2002), http://comedians.jokes.com/richard-jeni/videos/richard-jeni---brought-up-catholic.

18. Lenny Bruce, "Famous Quotes," The Lenny Bruce Official Website, accessed August 14, 2014, http://www.lennybruceofficial.com/famous-quotes/.

19. Bill Maher, Victory Begins at Home, 2003, available at I Am an Atheist website, accessed September 18, 2013, http://iamchristianiamanatheist.blogspot.com/2013/07/list-of-funny-atheistcomdeians-strong.html.

20. George Carlin, Atheism Quotes website, accessed 2010, http://www.atheismquotes.com/quotelist.php?pageNum_rs_Quote=1&totalRows_rs_Quote=60&person_name=&qtext=&subject=11 (site discontinued).

21. Dave Barry, *Dave Barry Turns 50* (New York: Ballantine Books, 1998), 183.

22. Butch Hancock, Atheism Quotes website, undated, http://www.atheismquotes.com/quotelist.php?pageNum_rs_Quote=2&totalRows_rs_Quote=60&person_name=&qtext=&subject=11 (site discontinued).

23. Gordon Stein, "The Great Debate: Does God Exist? Dr. Greg Bahnsen vs. Dr. Gordon Stein," (University of California, Irvine, 1985), 10, Bellevue Christian School website, accessed September 24, 2013, http://www.bellevuechristian.org/faculty/dribera/htdocs/PDFs/Apol_Bahnsen_Stein_Debate_Transcript.pdf.

24. Ibid.

25. Oliver Sacks, "Seeing God in the Third Millennium," *The Atlantic*, December 12, 2012, http://www.theatlantic.com/health/archive/2012/12/seeing-god-in-the-third-millennium/266134/; Bonnie Dlott, "The God Spot: Spirituality and the Brain" (sermon at Unitarian Universalist Society Sacramento), May 12, 2013, http://uuss.org/Sermons/The%20God%20Spot%202013.pdf; Michael Shermer, "Why a Near-Death Experience Isn't Proof of Heaven," *Scientific American* website, March 19, 2013, http://www.scientificamerican.com/article.cfm?id=why-near-death-experience-isnt-proof-heaven; Lorenzo Lazzerini Ospri, "Sacred Disease: A Neuroscience of God," *The Restriction Digest* (blog), accessed September 24, 2013, http://restrictiondigest.weebly.com/sacred-disease-a-neuroscience-of-god.html; Todd Murphy, "Epilepsy and Near-Death Experiences," Spirituality & The Brain website, 2012, http://www.shaktitechnology.com/epilepsy_NDEs.htm; Andrew Newberg, "Religious Experiences Shrink Part of the Brain," *Scientific American* website, May 31, 2011, http://www.scientificamerican.com/article.cfm?id=religious-experiences-shrink-part-of-brain.

26. Michael Inzlicht and Alexa M. Tullett, "Reflecting on God: Religious Primes Can Reduce Neurophysiological Response to Errors" (abstract), *Psychological Science* 21, no. 8 (December 28, 209), 1184–190, http://www.michaelinzlicht.com/research/publications/Inzlicht%20&%20

Tullett,%202010.pdf; "Belief in a Caring God Improves Response to Medical Treatment for Depression," Rush University Medical Center news release, February 23, 2010, http://www .rush.edu/webapps/MEDREL/servlet/NewsRelease?id=1353; Julie O'Connor, "Religion Benefits Traumatic Brain Injury Victims, Wayne State University Research Finds," Wayne State University news release, June 27, 2011, http://media.wayne.edu/2011/06/27/religion -benefits-traumatic-brain-injury-victims-wayne; "Most Physicians Believe that Religion Influences Patients' Health," ScienceDaily website, April 10, 2007, http://www.sciencedaily .com/releases/2007/04/070409164931.htm; J. Maselko, S. E. Gilman, and S. Buka, "Religious Service Attendance and Spiritual Well-Being Are Differentially Associated with Risk of Major Depression" (abstract), *Psychological Medicine* 39, 6 (June 2009): 1009–1017, http://journals. cambridge.org/action/displayAbstract?fromPage=online&aid=5556364; Richard Besser, "Is Religion Good for Your Health?," ABC News blog, March 25, 2013, http://abcnews.go.com /blogs/health/2013/03/25/is-religion-good-for-your-health; Jean L. Kristeller, Virgil Sheets, Tom Johnson, and Betsy Frank, "Understanding Religious and Spiritual Influences on Adjustment to Cancer: Individual Patterns and Differences" (abstract), *Journal of Behavioral Medicine,* 34, 6 (December 2011): 550–561, http://link.springer.com/article/10.1007 %2Fs10865-011-9335-7.

27. Frank Newport, Dan Witters, and Sangeeta Agrawal, "In U.S., Very Religious Have Higher Wellbeing Across All Faiths," Gallup Well-Being poll, February 16, 2012 http://www .gallup.com/poll/152732/Religious-Higher-Wellbeing-Across-Faiths.aspx#2.

28. Ibid.

29. David G. McAfee, *Mom, Dad, I'm an Atheist: The Guide to Coming Out as an Unbeliever* (London: Dangerous Little Books, 2012), 113.

30. Katy O'Donnell, "Nelson Recounts Religious Upbringing," *The Dartmouth* (Hanover, NH), February 21, 2007, http://thedartmouth.com/2007/02/21/news/nelson-recounts-religious -upbringing.

31. Richard Dawkins, "A Scientist's Case Against God," *The Independent* (London), April 20, 1992, 17.

32. Mark, under "Letter[s] from Atheist Kids to American Atheist," "Humanism for Kids" page, Witty Humanist Youth website, accessed August 11, 2014, https://sites.google.com/a /wittyhumanistyouth.org/why/kids-page.

17. How Can You Make Arguments for Atheism?

1. GurlGoddess [Lynn], "I Am an Atheist Because . . .," Gurl.com *Spirituality, Religion, Faith & Beliefs* (forum), July 20, 2007, http://my.gurl.com/forums/read/573.701564-I-am-an-atheist -because#18707927.

2. Katherine Rose Dautrich, comment on "The Atheist Challenge," *The BitterSweet End*, May 28, 2012, http://bittersweetend.wordpress.com/2012/05/28/the-atheist-challenge.

3. Michael Tooley, "The Problem of Evil," *The Stanford Encyclopedia of Philosophy* (Summer 2013 Edition), ed. Edward N. Zalta, http://plato.stanford.edu/archives/sum2013/entries/evil.

4. Wayne Blank, "Why Does God Allow Suffering?," Daily Bible Study website, accessed October 10, 2013, http://www.keyway.ca/htm2002/whysufer.htm.

5. John Hick, "Evil and Soul-Making," in *Evil and the Hiddenness of God*, ed. Michael Rea (Stanford, CT: Cengage Learning, 2014), 92–96.

6. Randy Alcorn, *90 Days of God's Goodness: Daily Reflections that Shine Light on God's Goodness* (Colorado Springs: Multnomah Books), 129.

7. "The Argument from Unbelief," Philosophy of Religion website, accessed October 7, 2013,

http://www.philosophyofreligion.info/arguments-for-atheism/the-problem-of-evil/the
-argument-from-unbelief; Daubmir Nadir, "3.2.7: The Argument from Unbelief," *KinkOsho*
(blog), July 2006, http://kinkazzosho.blogspot.com/2006/07/39-argument-from-unbelief
.html; "Arguments for Atheism," The Freethought Zone website, accessed October 7, 2013,
http://drprometheus.tripod.com/reason/rationalview.html; *Iron Chariots*, s.v. "argument
from nonbelief," last modified July 19, 2012, http://wiki.ironchariots.org/index.php?title
=Argument_from_nonbelief; "Arguments for and against God's Existence (from AU-LA),"
Backyard Skeptics website, February 2012, http://backyardskeptics.com/wordpress/arguments
-for-and-against-gods-existence; "Reason 85. Arguments against the Existence of God," God
Does Not Exist website, accessed October 7, 2013, http://www.god-does-not-exist.org/reasons
/reason-84-arguments-against-the-existence-of-god; *Academic Kids Encyclopedia*, s.v. "argument
from nonbelief," last modified June 10, 2005, http://www.academickids.com/encyclopedia
/index.php/Argument_from_nonbelief; *Kids.net.au*, s.v. "argument from nonbelief," accessed
October 7, 2013, http://encyclopedia.kids.net.au/page/ar/Argument_from_nonbelief.
8. Kyle, "The Argument from Nonbelief," The Skeptical Christian website, February 27, 2006,
http://www.skepticalchristian.com/nonbelief.htm.
9. Ibid.; William Kesatie, "A Bit of Undigested Beef: Does the Existence of Non-Belief Prove
God's Non-Existence?," Christian CADRE website, 2004, accessed October 9, 2013, http://
www.christiancadre.org/member_contrib/bk_anb.html.
10. Jeffrey Jay Lowder, "The Evidential Argument from Divine Hiddenness: The General Fact
and 10 More Specific Facts," *The Secular Outpost* (blog), January 12, 2013, http://www.patheos
.com/blogs/secularoutpost/2013/01/12/the-evidential-argument-from-divine-hiddenness
-the-general-fact-and-10-more-specific-facts; Matt McCormick, "Drange — Argument from
Nonbelief," McCormick Philosophy website, accessed October 9, 2013, https://sites.google
.com/site/mccormickphilosophy/home/philosophy-of-religion-syllabus/philosophy-of-religion
-schedule/drange-argument-from-nonbelief; John Schellenberg, "What Divine Hiddenness
Reveals, or How Weak Theistic Evidence is Strong Atheistic Proof," The Secular Web website,
2008, http://www.infidels.org/library/modern/john_schellenberg/hidden.html; Adam Lee,
"One More Burning Bush," *Daylight Atheism* (blog), accessed October 9, 2013, http://www
.patheos.com/blogs/daylightatheism/essays/one-more-burning-bush; Tristan D. Vick, "The
Argument from Divine Hiddenness: Why It's a Knock Down Argument Against the Existence
of the Theistic God," *Philosophies of Men Mingled with Scripture* (blog), April 1, 2013, http://
philosophiesofmen.blogspot.com/2013/04/the-argument-from-divine-hiddenness-why.html;
Ted Poston and Trent Dougherty, "Divine Hiddenness and the Nature of Belief," *Religious
Studies* 43, no. 2 (June 2007): 183–198, doi:10.1017/S003441250700894; Justin P. McBrayer
and Philip Swenson, "Scepticism about the Argument from Divine Hiddenness," *Religious
Studies* 48, no. 2 (June 2012): 129–150, doi:10.1017/S003441251100014X.
11. McBrayer and Swenson, "Scepticism about the Argument."
12. Daubmir Nadir, "3.3: Problems with Divine Omnipotence," *KinkOsho* (blog), July 2006,
http://kinkazzosho.blogspot.com/2006/07/33-problems-with-divine-omnipotence.html;
Rational Wiki, s.v. "omnipotence paradox," last modified April 8, 2014, http://rationalwiki.org
/wiki/Omnipotence_paradox.
13. "The Paradox of the Stone," *Existence of God* (blog), 2004, accessed October 9, 2013, http://
www.existence-of-god.com/paradox-of-the-stone.html.
14. *Rational Wiki*, s.v. "omnipotence paradox."
15. Ernest Hemingway, *A Farewell to Arms* (New York: Simon & Schuster, 1929), 7.
16. Annie Laurie Gaylor, ed., *Women without Superstition: No Gods—No Masters* (Madison, WI:
Freedom from Religion Foundation, 1997), 469–85.
17. Jean-Paul Sartre, *The Flies*, Act 2, from *No Exit and Three Other Plays* (New York: Vintage

International, 1989), 103.

18. Sigmund Freud, *New Introductory Lectures on Psycho-Analysis,* trans. and ed. James Strachey (New York: W. W. Norton, 1989), 216.

19. George Bernard Shaw, "Preface on the Prospects of Christianity," *Androcles and the Lion* (1912), Project Gutenberg website, last updated December 10, 2012, http://www.gutenberg .org/files/4004/4004-h/4004-h.htm.

20. Myrna Blyth, "Kate Talks Straight", *Ladies' Home Journal,* October 1991, 215.

21. Thomas Paine, under "Part First, Section 1, *The Age of Reason* (1794), Independence Hall Association website, accessed March 21, 2014, http://www.ushistory.org/paine/reason /singlehtml.htm.

22. Richard Carrier, "Why I Am Not a Christian," The Secular Web website, 2006, accessed October 9, 2013, http://www.infidels.org/library/modern/richard_carrier/whynotchristian .html#brain.

23. Glenn G. Dudley, "Atheists Are in Big Doo-Doo," *God and Brain* (blog), April 28, 2012, http://www.godandbrain.com/atheists-are-in-big-doo-doo/; Carl Weiland, "Brain Split between Atheism and Theism," Creation Ministries International website, June 15, 2013, http://creation.com/atheism-theism-brain-split.

24. Dan, comment on "Please Lock the Homosexuality Thread," *Dyspraxic Teens Forum,* October 27, 2009, http://www.dyspraxicteens.org.uk/forum/viewtopic.php?f=24&t=5422#p79883.

25. "Arguments for and against God's Existence"; John O'Leary-Hawthorn, "Arguments for Atheism," from *Reason for the Hope Within,* ed. Michael J. Murray, 117–20, http://www .colorado.edu/philosophy/heathwood/pdf/hawthorn.pdf; Theodore M. Drange, "Nonbelief vs. Lack of Evidence: Two Atheological Arguments," The Secular Web website, 1998, http://www .infidels.org/library/modern/theodore_drange/anbvslea.html; Austin Cline, "Scientifically, God Does Not Exist: Science Allows Us to Say God Does Not Exist," About.com (Agnosticism/Atheism), accessed October 8, 2013, http://atheism.about.com/od/arguments againstgod/a/GodScience.htm.

26. Dylan Jackson, "About Me," *TESOF* (forum), accessed October 7, 2013, http://www.tesof .com/user-sir-dj-fails-alot.

18. What If You Turn from Atheist to Believer?

1. Isaac Asimov, *I.Asimov: A Memoir* (New York: Bantam, 1995), 338.

2. The Pew, *U.S. Religious Landscape Survey* (Washington, DC: Pew Forum on Religion & Public Life, 2008), 22–26, http://religions.pewforum.org/pdf/report-religious-landscape -study-full.pdf.

3. Amy M, "Me and My Shadow," *Sporadic Maunderings* (blog), October 1, 2005, http:// qalmlea.blogspot.com/2005/10/me-and-my-shadow.html.

4. Marc Hessel, "Searching for the Needle in the Haystack," Web Pages for Jesus website, 2001, http://wpfj.org/hessel (site discontinued).

5. "Biography," Lacey Mosley website, accessed October 21, 2013, http://laceymosley.com.

6. Shaun, "Life After Death," Fish the Net website, accessed October 21, 2013, http://www .fishthe.net/testimony.htm#LIFE.

7. Rick Bartlett, "Belonging and Believing," *Direction Journal* 29, no. 2 (Fall 2000): 185–90, http://www.directionjournal.org/article/?1057.

8. Lissa, "Convert from Atheism," Mormon Apologetics website, accessed August 17, 2008, http://www.mormonapologetics.org/index.php?showtopic=5796&pid=144213&mode=threaded &start= (site discontinued).

9. Hessel, "Searching for the Needle."

10. "Chi Alpha Campus Ministries," Chi Alpha website, accessed October 22, 2013, http://www.chialpha.com (site discontinued).

11. Chris Bergman, email to author, June 10, 2008.

12. Neil McKenzie, "Goodbye Atheism," Cornerstone Church website, accessed August 12, 2008, http://cornerstoneuk.org.uk/investigate/changedlives/neil (page discontinued).

13. Jennifer Fulwiler, "The Chemicals and Me," *Conversion Diary* (blog), July 2, 2008, http://www.conversiondiary.com/2008/07/the-chemicals-and-me.html.

14. Ibid.

15. Roger Edwards, "On Religion, Atheism, Science and Logic," *Weather or Not* (blog), May 26, 2005, http://stormeyes.org/wp/2005/05/on-religion-atheism-science-and-logic .

16. John N. Clayton, "Why I Left Atheism," Does God Exist? website, last modified 2006, accessed October 22, 2013, http://www.doesgodexist.org/AboutClayton/PastLife.html.

17. A. S. A. Jones, "From Skepticism to Worship," Evidence Press website, September 1, 2002, http://evidencepress.com/articles/from-skepticism-to-worship/.

18. Mushfiqur Rahman, "Dr. Jeffrey Lang (b. 1954)," Welcome Back to Islam website, January 2001, accessed October 23, 2013, http://www.welcome-back.org/profile/jeffrey_lang.shtml (site discontinued).

19. John Daquila, email to author, August 13, 2008.

20. Will Shetterly, "Speculation and Revelation," *UU World: The Magazine of the Unitarian Universalist Association* 19, no. 2 (March/April 2005): 54–56, UU World, http://www.uuworld .org/2005/02/bookshelf.html.

21. Maz, "Teenage Convert from Atheism," About.com (Islam), accessed March 21, 2014, http://islam.about.com/u/sty/converts/converts_st/Teenage-Convert-From-Atheism.htm.

22. Anita Mathias, "I Was a Teenage Atheist: Memoirs of a Naughty Catholic Girlhood," *Commonweal*, October 8, 1999, 13.

23. Dan Ewald, "The Rebirth of Kirk Cameron," *Christian Reader* (March–April 2003): 20, Pentecostal Evangel website, accessed October 22, 2013, http://www.pe.ag.org/Articles2004 /4706_cameron.cfm.

24. Tony Woodlief, "Smugness as Theology," *World* magazine website, October 26, 2007, http://www.worldmag.com/2007/10/smugness_as_theology.

25. Bergman, email to author.

26. Ibid.

27. Daquila, email to author.

28. Lissa, "Convert from Atheism."

29. Daquila, email to author.

30. Fulwiler, "The Chemicals and Me"; "Suppressing the Soul," Jennifer Fulwiler, *Conversion Diary* (blog), April 12, 2007, http://www.conversiondiary.com/2007/04/suppressing-soul .html; Jennifer Fulwiler, "The Viewing," *Conversion Diary* (blog), April 4, 2008, http://www .conversiondiary.com/2008/04/the-viewing.html.

31. Amy M, "Me and My Shadow."

32. Edwards, "On Religion, Atheism, Science."

33. Clayton, "Why I Left Atheism."

34. John Samuel Jeremiah, "My Journey out of Mental Egypt," Rational Christianity website, accessed August 16, 2008, http://www.rationalchristianity.net/testimonies/jjeremiah.html (page discontinued).

35. Daquila, email to author.

36. Torah Love Outreach, http://www.tloutreach.org and http://www.facebook.com/pages /Torah-Love-Outreach/7642535549, both accessed August 19, 2008 (both sites discontinued);

Marc Hessel, email to author, August 14, 2008.

37. Devin Rose, "Atheism to Christ," *St. Joseph's Vanguard* (blog), accessed August 17, 2008, http://www.devinrose.heroicvirtuecreations.com/blog/my-conversion-from-atheism-to-christianity/; Devin Rose, "Why Catholic?," *St. Joseph's Vanguard* (blog), accessed August 17, 2008, http://www.devinrose.heroicvirtuecreations.com/blog/why-i-became-catholic/.

38. Clayton, "Why I Left Atheism."

39. C. S. Lewis, *Mere Christianity* (New York: HarperOne, 2001; originally published in 1952 by Geoffrey Bles), 140.

19. What's Your Future Going to Look Like?

1. Peter L. Berger, "A Bleak Outlook Is Seen for Religion," *New York Times*, February 25, 1968, 3.

2. Daniel M. Abrams, Haley A. Yaple, and Richard J. Wiener, "Dynamics of Social Group Competition: Modeling the Decline of Religious Affiliation," *Physical Review Letters*, August 19, 2011, 107, 8, DOI:10.1103/PhysRevLett.107.088701.

3. Nigel Barber, "Atheism to Defeat Religion by 2038," *HuffPost Science* (blog), June 5, 2012, http://www.huffingtonpost.com/nigel-barber/atheism-to-defeat-religion-by-2038_b_1565108.html.

4. "Least Religious Students," The Princeton Review website, accessed October 18, 2013, http://www.princetonreview.com/schoollist.aspx?type=r&id=749.

5. "Most Religious Students," The Princeton Review website, accessed October 18, 2013, http://www.princetonreview.com/schoolList.aspx?id=753.

6. Jamila Bey, "Secular Student Alliance Discusses Future of Atheism at Annual Conference," Voice of Russia website, August 2, 2012, http://voiceofrussia.com/us/radio_broadcast/72286564/83815905 (page discontinued).

7. Vlad Chituc, "So I'm Probably Not Quitting Atheism," *NonProphet Status* (blog), August 8, 2013, http://nonprophetstatus.com/2013/08/08/so-im-probably-not-quitting-atheism.

8. Bey, "Secular Student Alliance."

9. Chituc, "So I'm Probably Not."

10. Elaine Howard Ecklund and Christopher P. Scheitle, "Religion among Academic Scientists: Distinctions, Disciplines, and Demographics," *Social Problems* 54, no. 2 (2007): 289–307, DOI:10.1525/sp.2007.54.2.289.

11. Farr A. Curlin, Shaun V. Odell, Ryan E. Lawrence, Marshall H. Chin, John D. Lantos, Keith G. Meador, and Harold G. Koenig, "The Relationship between Psychiatry and Religion among U.S. Physicians," *Psychiatric Services* 58, no. 9 (September 2007): 1193–98, http://psychiatryonline.org/data/Journals/PSS/3816/07ps1193.pdf.

12. Will M. Gervais, Azim F. Shariff, and Ara Norenzayan, "Do You Believe in Atheists? Distrust Is Central to Anti-Atheist Prejudice," *Journal of Personality and Social Psychology* 101, no 6, (2011): 1189–206, DOI:10.1037/a0025882.

13. Joseph H. Hammer, Ryan T. Cragun, Karen Hwang, and Jesse M. Smith, "Forms, Frequency, and Correlates of Perceived Anti-Atheist Discrimination," *Secularism & Nonreligion* 1 (2012): 43–67, www.secularismandnonreligion.org/article/download/snr.ad/4.

14. Greta Christina, "Why Atheism Plus Is Good for Atheism," *Greta Christina's Blog*, August 21, 2012, http://freethoughtblogs.com/greta/2012/08/21/why-atheism-plus-is-good-for-atheism.

15. "Jen McCreight," Secular Student Alliance website, accessed October 21, 2013, https://www.secularstudents.org/speakers/JenMcCreight; Jennifer McCreight's Facebook page, accessed October 21, 2013, https://www.facebook.com/jennifurret?fref=ts

16. Jen McCreight, "How I Unwittingly Infiltrated the Boy's Club & Why It's Time for a New Wave of Atheism," *Blag Hag* (blog), August 18, 2012, http://freethoughtblogs.com/blaghag /2012/08/how-i-unwittingly-infiltrated-the-boys-club-why-its-time-for-a-new-wave-of -atheism.

17. Ibid.

18. Ibid.

19. Jen McCreight, "Atheism+," *Blag Hag* (blog), August 19, 2012, http://freethoughtblogs .com/blaghag/2012/08/atheism.

20. *Urban Dictionary*, s.v. "Atheism Plus," accessed October 21, 2013, http://www .urbandictionary.com/define.php?term=Atheism%20Plus.

21. Christina, "Why Atheism Plus."

22. *Daily Mail* Reporter, "'There's Probably No God . . . Now Stop Worrying and Enjoy Your Life': Atheist Group Launches Billboard Campaign," *Daily Mail* website, January 7, 2009, http://www.dailymail.co.uk/news/article-1106924/Theres-probably-God--stop-worrying -enjoy-life-Atheist-group-launches-billboard-campaign.html.

Glossary

agnostic. A person who doesn't know whether or not God exists.

argument from divine hiddenness. The argument that the all-wise, all-powerful, all-loving god of Judaism, Christianity, and Islam doesn't exist, because no entity who's all-wise, all-powerful, and all-loving would let people seek him out but would hide himself from them.

argument from evil. The argument that the all-wise, all-powerful, all-loving god of Judaism, Christianity, and Islam doesn't exist, because no entity who's all-wise, all-powerful, and all-loving would allow evil to make people suffer as they do.

argument from lack of evidence. The argument that there's not enough proof to justify belief in God.

argument from unbelief. The argument that the god of Judaism, Christianity, and Islam doesn't exist, because unbelievers do exist—and no entity who's all-powerful and wants everyone to worship him would allow unbelievers to exist.

Atheism Plus. A new trend in unbelief saying that unbelief alone isn't enough and that unbelievers must also believe in social justice.

atheist. A person who doesn't believe in God.

bright. A recently coined synonym for **unbeliever**.

deconversion. The process of turning from religion to unbelief.

Flying Spaghetti Monster. A parody of God that's often used to tease theists.

freethinker. A person who doesn't accept old ways of thought, particularly religious ways.

hard atheism. A form of unbelief holding that religion is intolerable and that there is proof that God does not exist. Also known as **positive atheism** or **strong atheism**.

humanist. A person who believes that people should focus on humanity's needs rather than on God's commands. See also secular humanist.

materialist. A person who believes that the only reality is that of physical matter.

naturalist. A person who believes that natural forces explain the universe.

negative atheism. A form of unbelief holding that religion is tolerable and that there is no proof that God exists. Also known as **soft atheism** or **weak atheism**.

objectivist. A follower of the philosophy of atheist writer Ayn Rand.

paradox of the stone. The argument that the god of Judaism, Christianity, and Islam doesn't exist, because he's supposed to be all-powerful, but he isn't powerful enough to create a stone so heavy that he can't lift it.

Pascal's wager. An argument for theism, holding that believing in God can save people from God's punishments while not believing can hurt them.

positive atheism. A form of unbelief holding that religion is intolerable and that there is proof that God does not exist. Also known as **hard atheism** or **strong atheism**.

rationalist. A person who believes in reason rather than faith.

Russell's Teapot. Author Bertrand Russell's answer to "you can't prove God doesn't exist," which uses a teapot instead of God.

secular humanist. A humanist who is atheist, agnostic, or otherwise unreligious.

soft atheism. A form of unbelief holding that religion is tolerable and that there is no proof that God exists. Also known as **negative atheism** or **weak atheism**.

strong atheism. A form of unbelief holding that religion is intolerable and that there is proof that God does not exist. Also known as **hard atheism** or **positive atheism**.

theist. A person who believes in God.

unbeliever. An atheist or agnostic. See also **argument from unbelief**.

weak atheism. A form of unbelief holding that religion is tolerable and that there is no proof that God exists. Also known as **negative atheism** or **soft atheism**.

About the Author

David Seidman has written dozens of books by and for young people—everything from *Teens in Iran* to *Fantastic Four: The Photo Novel*—not to mention books for adults such as *The Longevity Sourcebook* and *All Gone: Things That Aren't There Anymore*. He has been an editor at the *Los Angeles Times*'s newspaper syndicate, a magazine journalist, a biographer, a novelist, and a comedy writer.

He lives in southern California with his beloved, Lea Hernandez, and Lea's daughter, Summer, plus a dog, a cat, and heaps of reference material.